Gender and Environment in Science Fiction

Ecocritical Theory and Practice

Series Editor: Douglas A. Vakoch, METI

Advisory Board

Bruce Allen, Seisen University, Japan; Zélia Bora, Federal University of Paraíba, Brazil; Izabel Brandão, Federal University of Alagoas, Brazil; Byron Caminero-Santangelo, University of Kansas, USA; Simão Farias Almeida, Federal University of Roraima, Brazil; George Handley, Brigham Young University, USA; Steven Hartman, Mälardalen University, Sweden; Isabel Hoving, Leiden University, The Netherlands; Idom Thomas Inyabri, University of Calabar, Nigeria; Serenella Iovino, University of Turin, Italy; Daniela Kato, Kyoto Institute of Technology, Japan; Petr Kopecký, University of Ostrava, Czech Republic; Serpil Oppermann, Hacettepe University, Turkey; Christian Schmitt-Kilb, University of Rostock, Germany; Heike Schwarz, University of Augsburg, Germany; Murali Sivaramakrishnan, Pondicherry University, India; Scott Slovic, University of Idaho, USA; J. Etienne Terblanche, North-West University, South Africa; Julia Tofantšuk, Tallinn University, Estonia; Cheng Xiangzhan, Shandong University, China; Hubert Zapf, University of Augsburg, Germany

Ecocritical Theory and Practice highlights innovative scholarship at the interface of literary/cultural studies and the environment, seeking to foster an ongoing dialogue between academics and environmental activists.

Recent Titles

Gender and Environment in Science Fiction edited by Christy Tidwell and Bridgitte Barclay
Ecological Crisis and Cultural Representation in Latin America: Ecocritical Perspectives on Art, Film, and Literature edited by Mark Anderson and Zelia M. Bora
Perspectives on Art, Film, and Literature edited by Mark Anderson and Zelia M. Bora
The Ethics and Rhetoric of Invasion Ecology edited by Ames Stanescu and Kevin Cummings
Ecotheology in the Humanities: An Interdisciplinary Approach to Understanding the Divine and Nature edited by Melissa Brotton
Coexistentialism and the Unbearable Intimacy of Ecological Emergency edited by Sam Mickey
T.S. Eliot, Poetry, and Earth: The Name of the Lotos Rose by Etienne Terblanche
Ecofeminism in Dialogue edited by Douglas A. Vakoch and Sam Mickey
The Image of the River in Latin/o American Literature: Written in the Water edited by Jeanie Murphy and Elizabeth G. Rivero
Rhetorical Animals: Boundaries of the Human in the Study of Persuasion edited by Kristian Bjørkdahl and Alex C. Parrish

Gender and Environment in Science Fiction

Edited by Christy Tidwell
and Bridgitte Barclay

LEXINGTON BOOKS
Lanham • Boulder • New York • London

Published by Lexington Books
An imprint of The Rowman & Littlefield Publishing Group, Inc.
4501 Forbes Boulevard, Suite 200, Lanham, Maryland 20706
www.rowman.com

6 Tinworth Street, London SE11 5AL

Copyright © 2019 by The Rowman & Littlefield Publishing Group, Inc.

All rights reserved. No part of this book may be reproduced in any form or by any electronic or mechanical means, including information storage and retrieval systems, without written permission from the publisher, except by a reviewer who may quote passages in a review.

British Library Cataloguing in Publication Information Available

Library of Congress Cataloging-in-Publication Data Available

ISBN 978-1-4985-8057-1 (cloth : alk. paper)
ISBN 978-1-4985-8058-8 (electronic)
ISBN 978-1-4985-8059-5 (pbk. : alk. paper)

∞™ The paper used in this publication meets the minimum requirements of American National Standard for Information Sciences Permanence of Paper for Printed Library Materials, ANSI/NISO Z39.48-1992.

Printed in the United States of America

Contents

Acknowledgments   vii

Introduction   ix
    Bridgitte Barclay and Christy Tidwell

Part I: Performing Humanity, Animality, and Gender

1. Female Beasties: Camp Resistance in 1950s SF Wom-Animal Creature Features   3
Bridgitte Barclay

2. "Either you're mine or you're not mine": Controlling Gender, Nature, and Technology in *Her* and *Ex Machina*   21
Christy Tidwell

3. Octavia Butler and the Language of the Flesh: Re-writing Nature in *Wild Seed*   45
Amelia Z. Greene

Part II: Gendering the Natural World

4. Tendrils, Tentacles, and Flower Power: Speciesism in *Womaneater* (1958) and *The Gardener* (1974)   67
Fernando Gabriel Pagnoni Berns and Juan Juvé

5. "So Very Natural an Occurrence": Engendering Nature's Antagonism in Mary Shelley's *The Last Man*   89
Steve Asselin

Part III: Contemporary Queering

6. Engineered Nature, (En)gendered Nature in Kim Stanley Robinson's *2312*   115
Tyler Harper

7. Ecologies of Sound: Queer Intimacy, Trans-Corporeality, and Reproduction in *Upstream Color*   131
Stina Attebery

Part IV: "We Don't Need Another Hero"

8. Nature Boys & Bears in Pants: Ecoqueer Hybrid Heroes in Atomic Age Comics   149
Jill E. Anderson

9	Saving Eden: Whiteness, Masculinity, and Environmental Nostalgia in *Soylent Green* and *WALL-E* *Michelle Yates*	167
10	Mad Max: Beyond Petroleum? *Carter Soles*	185

Epilogue   203
   Christy Tidwell

Index   207

About the Authors   213

Acknowledgments

We are thankful to the Association for the Study of Literature and Environment (ASLE), particularly the Ecomedia Special Interest Group and our many friends and colleagues there; Ken Roemer, Tim Morris, and all of our mentors; Aurora University; South Dakota School of Mines & Technology; our loved ones (especially Dominick, Sophia, Elliott, Djuna, Neil, and Jonathan); and our friendship that can withstand (and thrive in) Ph.D. tears, twelve-state road trips, rough dorm room conference accommodations, and book editing.

Many of our contributors cite Stacy Alaimo, so this book is indebted to her work in many ways. Beyond how her writing has influenced scholars in environmental and gender studies, though, we also are personally indebted to her. Material gender studies and materialist environmentalism speak to real-world issues of justice. With these concepts and with Stacy's mentorship from graduate work to present, we became the teachers and scholars we are now and are still growing to be. Stacy's writing, her teaching and guidance, and her continued support and friendship are impossible to articulate here fully. Her respect for us, beginning even when we were graduate students—taking us to coffee and lunch, letting us read her manuscripts, inviting us to speak to her classes, guiding us through the job search process, introducing us to other scholars as colleagues, helping us learn to celebrate curiosity even if it led to a dead end for the moment, teaching us that questioning is never a waste of time, and showing solidarity with us in our professional and personal lives—has shaped us. So much of this influences the work we do and how we interact with our own students and others.

Introduction

Bridgitte Barclay and Christy Tidwell

The image on the cover of this book sets up a number of issues in gender and environment and science fiction (sf). It mimics a Euro-Christian Edenic narrative with a white male-female pair, the woman reaching for fruit while the man looks on. This mimicking of a creation myth is set on what may be an alien planet with a rocket shining in the background. Just those simple elements of man, woman, and fruit evoke problematic narratives of human dominion over animals and plants, naturalized heterosexuality, equations of women with nature, and (here) colonization and whiteness, even in an otherworldly setting. The midcentury sf pulp style of the image, too, elicits memories of traditional sex and gender roles, racial segregation, and an often uncritical hope in science and technology, among other things. Thus, the image works well to set up the connections and problems that this book addresses concerning gender, sex, sexual orientation, race, and nonhuman nature in sf. Given the weight of these memories, this image also serves to illustrate our need for new narratives that are both inclusive and intersectional.

Though there is a great deal of problematic sf, there is also a solid body of sf that provides such inclusive and intersectional narratives, and gender and ecocritical approaches enable further study of sf texts that may not *intentionally* engage with them. Ursula K. Le Guin's *The Left Hand of Darkness* (1969), Bryan Forbes's *The Stepford Wives* (1975), Ridley Scott's *Alien* (1979), Margaret Atwood's *The Handmaid's Tale* (1985), and Octavia E. Butler's *Dawn* (1987) are just a few of the sf books and films already included in the gender studies and environmental literary and filmic canons. More recent additions include Alfonso Cuarón's *Children of Men* (2006), Kim Stanley Robinson's *2312* (2012), and Ann Leckie's *Ancillary Justice* (2013). And many texts are ripe for ecocritical and gender readings in sf, as we demonstrate in this collection, because science fiction texts often ask questions such as *where is nature, what is natural*, and *who is equated with nature*.

Because of their focus on the sciences, both material gender studies and new materialism in environmental studies (or material ecocriticism) delve into such questions as well and serve to bring together sf, gender, and ecocriticism. In *Material Feminisms*, Stacy Alaimo and Susan Hekman assert that in order to engage with science and with the natural world, gender studies has to engage with the body and acknowledge it is dynamic, changing, and porous. They write that material feminists are those who "explore the interaction of culture, history, discourse, technology, biology, and the 'environment,' without privileging any one of these elements."[1] Building on the social constructionist turn in postmodern gender studies, material gender studies emphasizes materiality—of the body, of nature, of sciences about these—and the ways that materiality and language interact. Material gender studies addresses political issues of reproductive rights, slow violence, and sexual relationships; it raises questions about how biology interacts with culture, how science and technology interact with nature and the environment, how human bodies matter or do not matter in alternative worlds, and how human bodies interact with the environment.

Material gender studies, then, is closely aligned to material ecocriticism, which also emphasizes how linguistic and cultural constructions impact materiality. Material ecocriticism emerges in part from feminist science studies, which notes the impact of limited narratives on how we do science (the questions we ask, what we observe, how we interpret data and observation) and the impact of ideology on scientific narratives. Serpil Oppermann writes, "The radical revisions of our ideas about the description of physical entities, chemical and biological processes, and their ethical, political, and cultural implications represented in recent discourses of feminist science studies, posthumanism, and environmental humanities have also occasioned considerable interest among ecocritics, leading to the emergence of material ecocriticism."[2] This focus on the ethics of material connections resonates well with Alaimo's assertion that "a material feminist or new materialist environmentalism [. . .] would stress that the material interchanges between bodies, consumer objects, and substances become the site for ethical-political engagements and interventions."[3] Likewise, ideas of manifest destiny or of nature as an Eden for our use have material impacts on toxic waters, oil pipelines, preservation, and species extinction.

New materialism is also inherently intersectional and political, invested in creating new stories. As Serenella Iovino writes with Oppermann in the introduction to *Material Ecocriticism*, "The world's material phenomena are knots in a vast network of agencies, which can be 'read' and interpreted as forming narratives, stories. [. . .] All matter, in other words, is a 'storied matter.'"[4] The socio-politics of materiality are what connect gender studies and environmental studies in this book with inclusions of queer studies, disability studies, posthumanism, and race studies. Oppermann continues:

> One of the destructive practical consequences of anthropocentric models of knowledge that describe nature either as a lifeless mechanism or

as a mere textual construct is the capitalization of local ecosystems in the name of economic progress. Another related consequence is the oppressive social practices such as racism, sexism, and speciesism. In short, all manner of familiar ramifications follow from these anthropocentric models.[5]

Such interconnections expand the range of material gender studies and material environmentalism to include studies of race, disability, queerness, postcoloniality, science, and nature. As Rosi Braidotti asserts, these various studies are "radical interdisciplinary fields" that "have targeted the major flaws at the core of the humanities [. . .], namely its Eurocentrism, sexism, racism, and methodological nationalism."[6]

This book's chapters, then, engage with race, queerness, gender, and disability in various ways related to gender and environment. Our contributors work to answer Braidotti's call "for posthuman feminist theory to work toward multiple transversal alliances across communities" in which there may be "many recompositions of the human and new ways of becoming-world together."[7] This book as a whole addresses the spectrum of human and nonhuman (animal and technological) subjectivities, the implications of race and colonialism, impacts of masculinities and femininities on historical approaches to "nature," and how those align with or subvert normative notions of gender and sexual orientation.

As demonstrated in the following chapters, sf may offer special emphasis on the materiality of bodies and natures because of its scientific underpinnings. The material movement in both gender studies and environmental studies and the *what if* element of science fiction set up a fruitful space for a study like this, emphasizing the descriptive nature, as Le Guin calls it, of science fiction. In her introduction to *The Left Hand of Darkness*, she writes that science fiction is a form of truth telling through lies, describing current circumstances. She writes,

> All fiction is metaphor. Science fiction is metaphor. What sets it apart from older forms of fiction seems to be its use of new metaphors, drawn from certain great dominants of our contemporary life—science, all the sciences, and technology, and the relativistic and the historical outlook, among them. Space travel is one of these metaphors; so is an alternative society, an alternative biology; the future is another. The future, in fiction, is a metaphor.[8]

As this illustrates, science fiction that deals with both environmental and gender themes gets at truths by asking *what if*.

Similarly, in *Staying with the Trouble: Making Kin in the Chthulucene*, Donna J. Haraway uses SF[9] as a way of figuring. She writes that "science fiction, speculative fabulation, string figures, speculative feminism, science fact, so far" are all SF figures that she uses to discuss connections between humans and nonhumans.[10] She emphasizes the interdependence of speculation, science, and gender issues in understanding connections with the nonhuman world, writing, "Science fact and speculative fabulation need each other, and both need speculative feminism."[11] This expansion of SF—which is used either for *speculative fiction* as an umbrella term for science fiction, horror, and fantasy or for science fiction as our authors use it in this collection—makes clear the ways in which science, *what if*, gender, and nature are all intertwined and opens a space for us to tell new stories.

Many of these new stories raise questions, more specifically, about how human and nonhuman animals are both connected to and estranged from one another. Sherryl Vint notes that science fiction and human-animal studies (HAS), a type of environmental criticism focused on the relationships between human and nonhuman animals, are similar in many ways and can offer a great deal to one another. Vint writes the following of sf and HAS:

> Both are concerned with the construction of alterity and what it means for subjects to be thus positioned as outsiders. Both take seriously the question of what it means to communicate with a being whose embodied, communicative, emotional and cultural life—perhaps even physical environment—is radically different from our own.[12]

And, as Vint notes, exploring animals in sf enables engagement with "alterity, subjectivity and the limits of the human," thus "situating [sf] within a material history in which we have always-already been living with 'alien' beings."[13] The chapters in this collection take up this work by exploring the relationships humans have with these "alien" beings and the ways in which the lines between human and nonhuman are challenged within sf (in this volume, see Barclay, Attebery, and Anderson).

We should note that our focus here is on science fiction in particular, rather than speculative fiction (though some of the texts could also be considered horror or another type of speculative fiction). We deliberately made this choice to deal with the sciences rather than the magic of fantasy or the fears of horror. While these lines among the various types of speculative fiction are—like human and nonhuman boundaries—porous and changing, our emphasis on the sciences is tied to the importance of science in environmental and gender issues. And because new materialism grows in part from feminist science studies' emphasis on the effects of ideology and narrative on science, our focus on sf is fitting. Alaimo writes, "Popular science writing [. . .] is one of the most crucial genres for environmentalism" and notes that it "transmits not only facts and data, but also narratives, ideologies, values, ethics, politics, affect, and sometimes even a sense of species identity."[14] Scientific narratives of sex, gender, and sexual orientation, especially narratives about the rich variations of these in nonhuman species, lend a great deal to gender studies, too, and are experimented with in science fiction, which often draws from popular science writing. Rather than magical narratives, then, we want to focus on scientific narratives, speculating about possibility, remaining curious about the world around us, grappling with the often flawed scientific narratives that are blinded by human concepts, and understanding the fluid, varied, wondrous world we are a part of and how we talk about that world and our place in it.

Because science fiction, as a genre, has a long history of engaging with political issues—including war, authoritarianism, social class, and racism, in addition to gender, sexuality, and the environment—its scholarship has also, therefore, long engaged with the politics of the genre. Feminist science fiction authors themselves have led the way in combining scholarship and politics. Joanna Russ's "What Can a Heroine Do? or Why Women Can't Write," first published in 1971, examined the limitations of the literary canon at the time, arguing, "Make something unspeakable and you make it unthinkable."[15] Russ sees in science fiction (as well as detective stories and supernatural fiction) however, a space for women to flourish because of the way the genre already goes beyond ordinary expectations. She argues that

> science fiction, political fiction, parable, allegory, exemplum—all carry a heavier intellectual freight (and self-consciously so) than we are used to. All are didactic. All imply that human problems are collective, as well as individual, and take these problems to be spiritual, social, perceptive, or cognitive—not the fictionally sex-linked problems of success, competition, "castration," education, love, or even personal identity, with which we are all so very familiar.[16]

Further, Russ suggests that science fiction offers new myths of humanity: "Women cannot write—using the old myths. But using new ones—?"[17] This powerful question is at the heart of an entire branch of literary scholarship focused on the potential of science fiction of women—rather than on its limitations.[18] Russ's *How to Suppress Women's Writing* (1983) clearly and defiantly develops this feminist critique of "The Sacred Canon of Literature"[19] even further, as when she notes that "minority art, vernacular art, is marginal art. Only on the margins does growth occur."[20] Russ therefore politicizes science fiction as a genre and argues for its specifically feminist possibilities.

Early feminist sf scholarship by women writers also took the form of editorial work; Judith Merril and Pamela Sargent, in particular, did incredible work collecting and preserving writing by women sf writers. Merril organized communities of sf writers, collaborating with others and collecting sf texts in *The Year's Best S-F* anthologies in the 1950s and 1960s, and Pamela Sargent's Women of Wonder series—*Women of Wonder* (1975), *More Women of Wonder* (1976), *The New Women of Wonder* (1978), *Women of Wonder: The Classic Years* (1996), and *Women of Wonder: The Contemporary Years* (1996)—drew attention to contemporary female sf writers as well as providing an alternate history of sf, one that didn't consist only of men. While Sargent acknowledged in the introduction to *Women of Wonder* in 1975 that only "about 10 to 15 percent of the writers [of science fiction] are women,"[21] Sargent's and Merril's collections argued that those women were worth recognizing and encouraged other women to join the genre as well. These collections and the accompanying commentary laid the foundation for later feminist sf scholars to build upon, both in terms of establishing the value of women's sf and in terms of providing a starting point for later recovery work.

More academic feminist sf scholarship from the 1980s to early 2000s — including that of Sarah Lefanu, Peter Fitting, Marleen Barr, Robin Roberts, Jane Donawerth, Brian Attebery, and Patricia Melzer — further developed the trailblazing work of Russ, Merril, and Sargent. These texts expand the repertoire of feminist sf criticism in multiple ways, examining the relationship between feminist speculative fiction and postmodern fiction more generally,[22] exploring techniques used specifically by women sf writers,[23] analyzing the role of gender in utopian fiction in particular[24] or across the genre more broadly,[25] and considering the ways in which uses of the woman as Other and "alien constructions" within sf may be subversive and empowering.[26] These scholars brought serious consideration of feminist sf to the academy; their attention to women sf writers broadened conversations about science fiction as well as incorporated feminist sf into genre studies and literary studies more broadly.

As this scholarship has grown, it has opened up the discussion of science fiction as a genre to include not only the obvious and explicitly feminist sf of the 1970s and later; it has also worked to recover earlier feminist science fiction and to illustrate the ways in which the genre has never fully been the boys' club it is still often perceived to be. The work done by Judith Merril and Pamela Sargent is clearly foundational here. For instance, Lisa Yaszek highlights women's midcentury sf in *Galactic Suburbia: Recovering Women's Science Fiction* (2008), and she and Patrick B. Sharp feature early to midcentury women's sf in *Sisters of Tomorrow: The First Women of Science Fiction* (2016). In *Partners in Wonder: Women and the Birth of Science Fiction, 1926–1965,* Eric Leif Davin argues sf welcomed *and* at times constrained women. And Justine Larbalestier's *The Battle of the Sexes in Science Fiction* (2002) illustrates the obstacles faced by some women in early to midcentury sf, noting how they subverted masculine tropes and editorial practices. None of this recovery work indicates that there hasn't been prejudice and discrimination within the genre — there has — but reveals, instead, that even in the face of this, women have written science fiction and used the genre's power to tell their own stories and to challenge the hegemony of white masculinity.

More recent feminist sf scholarship includes work on specific periods and media or takes an intersectional approach, perhaps illustrating less of a current need for genre-spanning critical work that focuses solely on issues of gender in sf, given all the work already done in this field. Susan

A. George's analysis of gender in sf invasion films of the mid-twentieth century and Bonnie Noonan's *Gender in Science Fiction Films, 1964–1979* are two examples of this recent, more narrowly focused work. And Patrick B. Sharp's *Darwinian Feminism* studies the impact of Darwinian evolutionary science on women's science fiction in the late nineteenth and early twentieth centuries. While he writes about the sciences and the ways in which natural laws in nonhuman species opened up new ways of arguing gender issues, Sharp does not explicitly come to the works from an environmental stance. Other recent work combines feminist approaches and texts with studies of blackness and afrofuturism,[27] considers gender studies in conversation with blackness and disability,[28] or emphasizes queer studies specifically rather than gender studies more broadly.[29] None of these studies—whether narrowly focused or wide-ranging—pays significant attention to ecocritical concerns within sf.

On the whole, this well-established and fascinating field of feminist sf criticism has thus far failed to maintain any real attention to intersections between gender studies and environmental studies. Although discussions of individual sf works—e.g., Ursula K. Le Guin's *The Word for World Is Forest* (1972), Kate Wilhelm's *Where Late the Sweet Birds Sang* (1976), or Jean Hegland's *Into the Forest* (1996)—have led to some consideration of the relationships between gender and environment, there has been no sustained critical attention to these intersections within feminist sf criticism.

Environmental sf scholarship, in fact, has developed quite separately from feminist sf scholarship and is a more recent development within science fiction studies. While there are a few earlier examples,[30] most major works of environmental sf scholarship date from after 2010. After a slow start (relative to feminist sf scholarship and to environmental sf itself), the field has grown quickly, however. Numbers of presentations examining science fiction through an environmental lens are rapidly rising at major conferences, including meetings of the Modern Language Association (MLA); the Association for the Study of Literature and Environment (ASLE); the Society for Literature, Science, and the Arts (SLSA); and the Science Fiction Research Association (SFRA). At the 2015 and 2017 ASLE conferences, for instance, there were multiple panels on sf and cli-fi apocalyptic novels and films.

There is also recent ecocritical scholarship that is useful for science fiction scholars while not wholly concerning itself with sf.[31] Alexa Weik von Mossner's *Affective Ecologies*, for instance, is not primarily an analysis of science fiction texts, but her attention to "cinematic environments" and "the spectacle of nature"[32] certainly applies to the genre, and she often turns to sf films, specifically disaster movies like *The Day After Tomorrow*, to develop her argument. Similarly, E. Ann Kaplan's *Climate Trauma* combines an emphasis on sf (dystopian and disaster narratives) with analysis of documentary film to argue that these imaginings of a future that hasn't quite happened yet reflects what she calls "Pretraumatic Stress Syndrome (PreTSS)," in which "people unconsciously suffer from an immobilizing anticipatory anxiety about the future."[33]

Other books do take up ecocriticism in relation to science fiction more specifically, however. In *Green Speculations: Science Fiction and Transformative Environmentalism*, for instance, Eric C. Otto examines the political implications of environmental sf. He writes that the subgenre both reflects on ideologies that we might otherwise be blind to and "collectively chips away at the foundations of these structures to prompt an effort to rebuild them with greater attention to environmental and social ethics."[34] Multiple edited collections on environmental science fiction have been published recently, too, expanding the conversation and bringing more voices forward, but although these collections introduce and attend to important considerations of such issues in sf, they do not consistently engage with intersections between ecocritical thought and gender studies.[35] Other more recent ecocritical work on sf includes Anthony Lioi's *Nerd Ecology: Defending the Earth with Unpopular Culture* (2016), Chris Pak's *Terraforming: Ecopolitical Transformations and Environmentalism in Science Fiction* (2016), and Shelley Streeby's *Imagining the Future of Climate Change: World-Making through Science Fiction and Activism* (2018). Despite their fascinating and productive approaches to the genre, however, gender does not play a significant role in these works.

Otto argues in *Green Speculations* that environmental science fiction has the ability to point the way toward "thinking and building a new way forward."[36] This complements Oppermann's assertion about the new stories that material ecocriticism (and, we would add, material gender studies) enables: "Proposing that we can read the world as matter endowed with stories, material ecocriticism speaks of a new mode of description designated as 'storied matter,' or 'material expressions' constituting an agency with signs and meanings" (21). Think how much more powerful this ability might be if it were linked to the power identified within feminist sf by gender studies scholars.

This volume aims to address this gap in scholarship between feminist sf scholarship and environmental sf scholarship. The first section, "Performing Humanity, Animality, and Gender," focuses on performance; humans becoming animal, machine, and other-than-human; and interspecies embodiments. In her chapter, "Female Beasties: Camp Resistance in 1950s SF Wom-Animal Creature Features," Bridgitte Barclay argues that camping *Mesa of Lost Women* (1953) and *Wasp Woman* (1959) with gender and environmental interpretive strategies enables subversive readings of the various gendered, sexual, and human/nonhuman boundary crossings. She argues that making fun *with* the films and highlighting the queer through camp readings functions as political resistance.

Christy Tidwell analyzes the complicated relationship between gender and environment through the science fictional trope of AI creation in her chapter, "'Either you're mine or you're not mine': Controlling Gender, Nature, and Technology in *Her* and *Ex Machina*." The films, Tidwell notes, gender technologies as female and show them as beyond human male control while depicting an environment that *is* subject to human control. This complication disrupts problematic historical woman-nature associations but also emphasizes the need for further work on the ways in which gender and environmental studies are connected and the ways in which they engage with technology.

The conflation of women with nature and subjugation of both is also disrupted in Amelia Z. Greene's reading of Butler's work in her chapter, "Octavia Butler and the Language of the Flesh: Re-Writing Nature in *Wild Seed*." In this chapter, Greene asserts that, through powers of interspecies hybridization and mutation, Butler emphasizes change and fluidity over stasis. These interconnections and alterations reflect a call for larger circles of environmental ethics and care, according to Greene.

The next section, "Gendering the Natural World," builds on that call for larger communities and different narratives. This section looks at speciesism, sexualizing and gendering nature, race, and apocalypse and ranges from the 1820s to the 1970s. In their chapter, "Tendrils, Tentacles, and Flower Power: Speciesism in *Womaneater* (1958) and *The Gardener* (1974)," Fernando Gabriel Pagnoni Berns and Juan Juvé argue that the monster plants in the films emphasize sex, gender, class, race, and species contradictions. Creature features like *Womaneater* and *The Gardener* fit into both the science fiction and horror categories, and, in their chapter, Pagnoni Berns and Juvé engage with recent work in plant horror to show how monstrous plants complicate narratives of gender, species, and race.

In the next chapter, "'So Very Natural an Occurrence': Engendering Nature's Antagonism in Mary Shelley's *The Last Man*," Steve Asselin highlights the ways in which the characters in Shelley's 1826 apocalypse novel attempt to feminize nature, failing to dismantle gendered constructs, despite inaccurate and changing metaphors for its destructive power. He contextualizes his analysis within other scholarship on *The Last Man* but calls into question the often uncontested equation of nature with women in that scholarship. Additionally, he utilizes queer ecocritical frames to argue for deconstructed binaries in the book, offering a new way of reading one of the earliest science fiction novels.

The third section, "Contemporary Queering," continues discussions of these interconnections, focusing on queering nature. In "Engineered Nature, (En)gendered Nature in Kim Stanley Robinson's *2312*," Tyler Harper analyzes Kim Stanley Robinson's *2312*, arguing that the novel's gender and sexual body modifications and terraforming are as "natural" as other evolutions. Harper shows how Robinson offers an imaginative framework in which dynamic nature enables freedom from environmental crisis and gender strictures.

Stina Attebery also studies evolutions of a sort in "Ecologies of Sound: Queer Intimacy, Trans-Corporeality, and Reproduction in *Upstream Color*," in which she argues that Shane Carruth's 2013 film *Upstream Color* creates cross-species intimacies through both trauma and care. Such intimacies, displayed in part through audio sampling, highlight positive alternatives to traditional human/nonhuman and reproductive relationships.

Section four, "We Don't Need Another Hero," looks at a variety of gender and environmental connections in sf heroes. In "Nature Boys & Bears in Pants: Ecoqueer Hybrid Heroes in Atomic Age Comics," Jill E. Anderson engages in an ecoqueer reading of Silver Age comic books by rereading how the wild heroes perform masculinity and manipulate nature. Reading Nature Boy (1956), Aquaman (1959), Metamorpho (1965), Swamp Thing (1971), and Man-Thing (1971) this way challenges human/nonhuman boundaries as well as gender binaries and calls attention to the agency of nature.

Michelle Yates also analyzes the relationship between masculinity and the natural world in her chapter, "Saving Eden: Whiteness, Masculinity, and Environmental Nostalgia in *Soylent Green* and *WALL-E*." Yates argues that the environmental nostalgia and eco-memories in *Soylent Green* (1973) and *WALL-E* (2008) are intimately connected to gender and race politics. She builds on Robin L. Murray and Joseph K. Heumann's work to argue that nostalgia in these films is not merely for an imagined Eden but is also intimately connected to nostalgia for hegemonic white masculinity.

In "Mad Max: Beyond Petroleum?" Carter Soles analyzes the gender and petro-politics in Mad Max movies. He argues that while alternative energy and feminist leanings are important aspects of *Mad Max: Beyond Thunderdome* (1985), the film does not ultimately actualize a society beyond petroleum. Soles compares this to *Mad Max: Fury Road* (2015) to show that *Fury Road*, though often read as environmentalist and feminist, actually demonstrates that the promise of alternative energy in *Thunderdome* is dead.

As this outline of chapters illustrates, our contributors put these feminist and environmental scholarly traditions in direct conversation with one another and develop complex and intersectional readings of sf texts as a result. However, one volume cannot contain such a wide-ranging and productive conversation. Even with the range we have been able to include here, there is an abundance of work to be done at this intersection of gender and environment:

- How do gender and environment influence one another in weird fiction, climate fiction (cli-fi), or at the intersection of science fiction and horror?

- How might existing studies of women in science (fiction) engage with ecocritical ideas of nature and what is "natural"?
- How does re-reading early sf texts and the history of sf with *both* of these concerns in mind produce new readings of individual texts as well as alternate histories of the genre?
- How might critical animal studies complicate these conversations about nature and environment in relation to gender within sf? Sherryl Vint has already begun this conversation—examining texts by Ursula K. Le Guin, Bob Olsen, Alice Sheldon (publishing as Raccoona Sheldon), John Kessel, Cordwainer Smith, Harlan Ellison, and Leigh Kennedy in a chapter on gender and animals in her *Animal Alterity: Science Fiction and the Question of the Animal*—but there remains much more that could be said at this intersection.
- How do fans respond to texts that combine these issues? Or: how do fans interested in environmental sf respond to elements of gender—and vice versa? Helen Merrick has written about fannish responses to texts and the ways that they can reveal the two-way relationship between science fiction and feminist theory/praxis. She writes, "In feminist sf fandom, in particular, fans have from the outset engaged with readings that are informed by feminist theory. Feminist fanzines offered critical writings that placed sf texts in the context of feminist praxis and theorizing, and used sf as the starting point for political and theoretical arguments that roamed far from this culturally 'debased' set of texts."[37] How do twenty-first-century fan communities carry on this work? How might they function differently in the context of social media? Does this relationship extend to environmental issues?

As this list indicates, there is much more work to be done. We hope others will read what we have written here and take up these challenges—and others that we haven't even imagined or articulated. This work is part of the larger conversation, and intersectional, cultural, political conversations like this flourish with diverse engagement, varied voices, and questioning.

NOTES

1. Stacy Alaimo, in *Material Feminisms*, eds. Stacy Alaimo and Susan Hekman (Bloomington: Indiana University Press, 2008), 9.

2. Serpil Oppermann, "From Ecological Postmodernism to Material Ecocriticism: Creative Materiality and Narrative Agency," in *Material Ecocriticism*, ed. Serenella Iovino and Serpil Oppermann (Bloomington: Indiana University Press, 2014), 21.

3. Stacy Alaimo, *Exposed: Environmental Pleasures and Politics in Posthuman Times* (Minneapolis: University of Minnesota Press, 2016), 9.

4. Serenella Iovino and Serpil Oppermann, in *Material Ecocriticism*, eds. Serenella Iovino and Serpil Oppermann (Bloomington: Indiana University Press, 2014), 1.

5. Oppermann, "From Ecological Postmodernism to Material Ecocriticism: Creative Materiality and Narrative Agency," 23.

6. Rosi Braidotti, "Four Theses on Posthuman Feminism," in *Anthropocene Feminism*, ed. Richard Grusin (Minneapolis: University of Minnesota Press, 2017), 27.

7. Braidotti, *"Four Theses on Posthuman Feminism,"* 41.

8. Ursula K. Le Guin, *The Left Hand of Darkness* (New York: Ace Books, 2010), xviii–xix.

9. Donna Haraway uses capitalized *SF*, which we keep here when referencing her work that incorporates science fiction alongside the other SF terms. See Donna J. Haraway, *Staying with the Trouble: Making Kin in the Chthulucene* (Durham: Duke University Press, 2016), 2.

10. Haraway, *Staying with the Trouble*, 2.

11. Haraway, *Staying with the Trouble*, 3.

12. Sherryl Vint, *Animal Alterity: Science Fiction and the Question of the Animal* (Liverpool: Liverpool University Press, 2010), 1–2.

13. Vint, *Animal Alterity: Science Fiction and the Question of the Animal*, 2.

14. Alaimo, *Exposed*, 3–4.

15. Joanna Russ, "What Can a Heroine Do? or Why Women Can't Write," in *To Write Like a Woman: Essays in Feminism and Science Fiction* (Bloomington: Indiana University Press, 1995), 90.

16. Russ, "What Can a Heroine Do?," 92.

17. Russ, "What Can a Heroine Do?," 93.

18. Which Russ also acknowledges in essays such as *"Amor Vincit Foeminam*: The Battle of the Sexes in Science Fiction" (in *To Write Like a Woman: Essays in Feminism and Science Fiction* [Bloomington: Indiana University Press, 1995]), originally published in 1980.

19. Joanna Russ, *How to Suppress Women's Writing* (Austin: University Texas Press, 1983), 129.

20. Russ, *How to Suppress Women's Writing*, 129.

21. Pamela Sargent, *Women of Wonder: Science Fiction Stories by Women about Women* (New York: Vintage Books, 1975), 11.

22. Marleen Barr, *Lost in Space: Probing Feminist Science Fiction and Beyond* (Chapel Hill: The University of North Carolina Press, 1993).

23. Jane Donawerth, *Frankenstein's Daughters: Women Writing Science Fiction* (New York: Syracuse University Press, 1997).

24. Peter Fitting, "For Men Only: A Guide to Reading Single-Sex Worlds," *Women's Studies* 14 (1987): 101–17; Peter Fitting, "Reconsiderations of the Separatist Paradigm in Recent Feminist Science Fiction," *Science Fiction Studies* 19, no. 1 (March 1992): 32–48.

25. Brian Attebery, *Decoding Gender in Science Fiction* (New York: Routledge, 2002).

26. Robin Roberts, *A New Species: Gender and Science in Science Fiction* (Urbana: University of Illinois Press, 1993); Patricia Melzer, *Alien Constructions: Science Fiction and Feminist Thought* (Austin: University of Texas Press, 2006).

27. Kristen Lillvis, *Posthuman Blackness and the Black Female Imagination* (Athens: University of Georgia Press, 2017).

28. Sami Schalk, *Bodyminds Reimagined: (Dis)ability, Race, and Gender in Black Women's Speculative Fiction* (Durham: Duke University Press, 2018).

29. Wendy G. Pearson, Veronica Hollinger, and Joan Gordon, eds., *Queer Universes: Sexualities in Science Fiction* (Liverpool: Liverpool University Press, 2008).

30. Most notably, Patrick D. Murphy's "The Non-Alibi of Alien Scapes: SF and Ecocriticism," in *Beyond Nature Writing: Expanding the Boundaries of Ecocriticism*, ed. Karla Armbruster and Kathleen R. Wallace (Charlottesville: University Press of Virginia, 2001).

31. Antonia Mehnert, *Climate Change Fictions: Representations of Global Warming in American Literature* (New York: Palgrave Macmillan, 2016); Adam Trexler, *Anthropocene Fictions: The Novel in a Time of Climate Change* (Charlottesville: University of Virginia Press, 2015).

32. Alexa Weik von Mossner, *Affective Ecologies: Empathy, Emotion, and Environmental Narrative* (Columbus: The Ohio State University Press, 2017), 59, 67.

33. E. Ann Kaplan, *Climate Trauma: Foreseeing the Future in Dystopian Film and Fiction* (New Brunswick: Rutgers University Press, 2015), xix.

34. Eric C. Otto, *Green Speculations: Science Fiction and Transformative Environmentalism* (Columbus: The Ohio State University Press, 2012), 18.

35. These collections include Chris Baratta's *Environmentalism in the Realm of Science Fiction and Fantasy Literature* (Newcastle upon Tyne: Cambridge Scholars Publishing, 2012), Susan M. Bernardo's *Environments in Science Fiction: Essays on Alternative Spaces* (Jefferson: McFarland & Company, 2014), and Gerry Canavan and Kim Stanley Robinson's *Green Planets: Ecology and Science Fiction* (Middletown, CT: Wesleyan University Press, 2014). There are a couple of essays in these collections that combine gender studies with ecocritical approaches, however. See Adeline Johns-Putra's "Care, Gender, and the Climate-Changed Future: Maggie Gee's *The Ice People*, in *Green Planets*, for instance, or Sean Murray's "The Pedagogical Potential of Margaret Atwood's Speculative Fiction: Exploring Ecofeminism in the Classroom," in *Environmentalism in the Realm of Science Fiction and Fantasy Literature*.

36. Otto, *Green Speculations*, 126.

37. Helen Merrick, *The Secret Feminist Cabal: A Cultural History of Science Fiction Feminisms* (Seattle: Aqueduct Press, 2009), 13.

BIBLIOGRAPHY

Alaimo, Stacy. *Exposed: Environmental Pleasures and Politics in Posthuman Times*. Minneapolis: University of Minnesota Press, 2016.

Alaimo, Stacy, and Susan Hekman, eds. *Material Feminisms*. Bloomington: Indiana University Press, 2008.

Attebery, Brian. *Decoding Gender in Science Fiction*. New York: Routledge, 2002.

Baratta, Chris, ed. *Environmentalism in the Realm of Science Fiction and Fantasy Literature*. Newcastle upon Tyne: Cambridge Scholars Publishing, 2012.

Barr, Marleen. *Lost in Space: Probing Feminist Science Fiction and Beyond*. Chapel Hill: The University of North Carolina Press, 1993.

Bernardo, Susan M., ed. *Environments in Science Fiction: Essays on Alternative Spaces*. Jefferson: McFarland & Company, 2014.

Braidotti, Rosi. "Four Theses on Posthuman Feminism." In *Anthropocene Feminism*, edited by Richard Grusin, 21–48. Minneapolis: University of Minnesota Press, 2017.

Canavan, Gerry, and Kim Stanley Robinson, eds. *Green Planets: Ecology and Science Fiction*. Middletown, CT: Wesleyan University Press, 2014.

Davin, Eric Leif. *Partners in Wonder: Women and the Birth of Science Fiction, 1926–1965*. Lanham, MD: Lexington Books, 2006.

Donawerth, Jane. *Frankenstein's Daughters: Women Writing Science Fiction*. New York: Syracuse University Press, 1997.

Fitting, Peter. "For Men Only: A Guide to Reading Single-Sex Worlds." *Women's Studies* 14 (1987): 101–17.

———. "Reconsiderations of the Separatist Paradigm in Recent Feminist Science Fiction." *Science Fiction Studies* 19, no. 1 (March 1992): 32–48.

George, Susan A. *Gendering Science Fiction Films: Invaders from the Suburbs*. New York: Palgrave Macmillan, 2013.

Haraway, Donna J. "A Manifesto for Cyborgs: Science, Technology, and Socialist Feminism in the 1980s." In *The Haraway Reader*, 7–46. New York: Routledge, 2004.

———. *Staying with the Trouble: Making Kin in the Chthulucene*. Durham: Duke University Press, 2016.

Iovino, Serenella, and Serpil Oppermann, eds. *Material Ecocriticism*. Bloomington: Indiana University Press, 2014.

Kaplan, E. Ann. *Climate Trauma: Foreseeing the Future in Dystopian Film and Fiction*. New Brunswick: Rutgers University Press, 2015.
Larbalestier, Justine. *The Battle of the Sexes in Science Fiction*. Middletown: Wesleyan University Press, 2002.
Lefanu, Sarah. *In the Chinks of the World Machine: Feminism & Science Fiction*. London: The Women's Press, 1988.
Le Guin, Ursula K. *The Left Hand of Darkness*. New York: Ace Books, 2010.
Lillvis, Kristen. *Posthuman Blackness and the Black Female Imagination*. Athens: University of Georgia Press, 2017.
Lioi, Anthony. *Nerd Ecology: Defending the Earth with Unpopular Culture*. New York: Bloomsbury Academic, 2016.
Mehnert, Antonia. *Climate Change Fictions: Representations of Global Warming in American Literature*. New York: Palgrave Macmillan, 2016.
Melzer, Patricia. *Alien Constructions: Science Fiction and Feminist Thought*. Austin: University of Texas Press, 2006.
Merrick, Helen. *The Secret Feminist Cabal: A Cultural History of Science Fiction Feminisms*. Seattle: Aqueduct Press, 2009.
Murphy, Patrick D. "The Non-Alibi of Alien Scapes: SF and Ecocriticism." In *Beyond Nature Writing: Expanding the Boundaries of Ecocriticism*, edited by Karla Armbruster and Kathleen R. Wallace, 263–78. Charlottesville: University Press of Virginia, 2001.
Murray, Sean. "The Pedagogical Potential of Margaret Atwood's Speculative Fiction: Exploring Ecofeminism in the Classroom." In *Environmentalism in the Realm of Science Fiction and Fantasy Literature*, edited by Chris Baratta, 111–25. Newcastle upon Tyne: Cambridge Scholars Press, 2012.
Noonan, Bonnie. *Gender in Science Fiction Films, 1964–1979: A Critical Study*. Jefferson: McFarland & Company, Inc., 2015.
Otto, Eric C. *Green Speculations: Science Fiction and Transformative Environmentalism*. Columbus: The Ohio State University Press, 2012.
Pak, Chris. *Terraforming: Ecopolitical Transformations and Environmentalism in Science Fiction*. Liverpool: Liverpool University Press, 2016.
Pearson, Wendy G., Veronica Hollinger, and Joan Gordon, eds. *Queer Universes: Sexualities in Science Fiction*. Liverpool: Liverpool University Press, 2008.
Roberts, Robin. *A New Species: Gender and Science in Science Fiction*. Urbana: University of Illinois Press, 1993.
Russ, Joanna. "*Amor Vincit Foeminam*: The Battle of the Sexes in Science Fiction." In *To Write Like a Woman: Essays in Feminism and Science Fiction*, 41–59. Bloomington: Indiana University Press, 1995.
———. *How to Suppress Women's Writing*. Austin: University of Texas Press, 1983.
———. "What Can a Heroine Do? or Why Women Can't Write." In *To Write Like a Woman: Essays in Feminism and Science Fiction*, 79–93. Bloomington: Indiana University Press, 1995.
Sargent, Pamela. *Women of Wonder: Science Fiction Stories by Women about Women*. New York: Vintage Books, 1975.
Schalk, Sami. *Bodyminds Reimagined: (Dis)ability, Race, and Gender in Black Women's Speculative Fiction*. Durham: Duke University Press, 2018.
Streeby, Shelley. *Imagining the Future of Climate Change: World-Making through Science Fiction and Activism*. Oakland: University of California Press, 2018.
Trexler, Adam. *Anthropocene Fictions: The Novel in a Time of Climate Change*. Charlottesville: University of Virginia Press, 2015.

Part I

Performing Humanity, Animality, and Gender

ONE

Female Beasties

*Camp Resistance in 1950s
SF Wom-Animal Creature Features*

Bridgitte Barclay

Mesa of Lost Women (1953) and *The Wasp Woman* (1959) are wonderfully bad wom-animal (woman-animal hybrid) science fiction films with quick production, bad science, and cheap costuming and special effects. *Mesa of Lost Women* is narratively incoherent with repetitive music played over dialogue and an oddly long dance scene, tarantulas are called hexapods, and a human-sized tarantula is confined behind a flimsy tri-fold partition in a cave lab. *The Wasp Woman*, one of B movie icon Roger Corman's earliest films, has an infamous final one-shot scene, a guinea pig un-aging into a rat, a mutated lab kitten wrestling a scientist, and cheesy special effects. And both B movies ask the science fiction question *what if,* blurring boundaries of nature and science, humans and animals, masculine and feminine, beauty and power, and scientist and science experiment. The B movie elements open up the films to camp readings that sympathize with the women, animals, and wom-animal hybrids, resisting dominant discourses. Camp readings highlight resistance. Camping these films emphasizes how the wom-animals flip the power structures from experimental objects to experimenting subjects, how science enables the characters' access to natural laws that empower them, and how the settings of "natural" and "unnatural" blend and overlap to destabilize both gender and human/nonhuman constructs.

In *Mesa of Lost Women*, the primary female hybrid, Tarantella (Tandra Quinn), performs womanhood and animality as a tarantula-woman hybrid who is dangerously sexual(ized). Presumably, Tarantella has been kidnapped by Dr. Aranya (it *is* the *Mesa of Lost Women*) who runs an underground lab in Muerto Desert, where he is creating a new race of beautiful, telepathic, regenerating tarantula women so that he can take over the world by using the wom-animals to lure men and kill or entrance them with their finger-fangs full of venom. The mostly incoherent narrative, told in flashback from an Amer-exico Oil Company field hospital, includes an abduction/plane crash sequence (on the plane are an entranced investor who has escaped from an asylum, a wealthy man and his fiancée, a pilot-cum-love interest of the fiancée, and a servant), some murders (the plane crash victims attacked by the wom-animals and other lab creatures), and the eventual burning of the cave lab, with the pilot and fiancée escaping through the desert.

Wasp Woman performs a slightly different version of womanhood in her workplace but similar animality in her uncontrollable killing. Cosmetics executive Janice Starlin (Susan Cabot) is approached by a scientist who has discovered the youth-inducing properties of wasp royal jelly just as Starlin has begun to lose profit (and power with her board) because she is the face of the company and is aging. The youth serum promises her regained power. She begins experimenting on herself to speed up the process, unaware the side effects will make her the murderous Wasp Woman, a creature she transforms into uncontrollably and whose violence she seems unable to restrain.

The very nature of these science fiction B movies—their narrative incongruence and lab-created monstrous hybrids—opens them to resistant camp readings. B movie narrative structure, characterization, and special effects disengage the audience from the filmic world and expose the mechanics of storytelling, making the master narrative a story and thereby resisting it by showing it as such. Where B movies may show the narrative and performative fractures in a master narrative (narratives subjugating women and animals in midcentury, for instance), camping a film fully highlights those fractures. Their seams show, and these visible seams make it clear we are watching something unnatural, seeing behind the curtain. Ed S. Tan writes that in a traditional film, "the film does not draw attention to itself as artifact: for one thing, the use of technical means, such as staging, camera handling, and editing, are subordinate to the progress of events and the clarification of their causality."[1] In these B movies, though, the joy in them is in the artifice being emphasized. And that leads to the narrative artifice being emphasized as well. Just as camping in a drag show dismantles gender by laying bare the acts that constitute gender performance, the B film is a form of drag.[2]

A camp reading, then, blurs boundaries in a way that *queers*, as Noreen Giffney and Myra J. Hird define it. In their introduction to their ecocritical work *Queering the Non/Human*, they write that the term *queer* "comes to signify the continual unhinging of certainties and the systematic disturbing of the familiar," noting that "the unremitting emphasis in queer theoretical work on [. . .] indeterminacy, indefinability, unknowability, the preposterous, impossibility, unthinkability, unintelligibility, meaninglessness [. . .] is an attempt to undo normative entanglements and fashion alternative imaginaries."[3] Camping enables such alternative imaginaries. Giffney and Hird note, "Queer is employed [. . .] to unpick binaries and reread gaps, silences and in-between spaces."[4] Reading these films through ecocritical and feminist frames by emphasizing opposition to traditional heteropatriarchal and anthropocentric narratives utilizes the seams, the gaps, the unintelligibility of the films to camp them into pleasurably resistant texts.

Mesa of Lost Women, for instance, is renowned for its B badness, and this opens it up to camp. Tom Weaver writes of the film, "It towers over most of the other contenders for Worst '50s Sci-Fi Film," noting it is "notoriously nonsensical," in part because the film was shot and edited by two different directors.[5] The first director (and writer), Herbert Tevos, made an unreleasable first version of *Mesa of Lost Women*, and Ron Ormond was hired as a second director to re-edit and shoot more scenes (including finishing a dance scene, which means that Tarantella's hair length changes partway through the scene). Several scenes of unexplained action, the spider women's overexaggerated sexuality in luring and killing their victims, and a sarcastic voice-over that asserts the hubris of humankind thinking it is in control of the natural world all create narrative gaps and/or entanglements, spaces for reading resistant narratives of nature and gender.

The Wasp Woman's B elements, too, are ripe for camping. Director Roger Corman is well known for making subversive films that work outside of Hollywood, seeking no permits and filming over just a few days. In the documentary *Corman's World*, Ron Howard notes that unlike Hollywood at the time, "Roger understood the need for audiences to identify with rebellion. Beating the system. That's cathartic. Defining yourself on your own terms. These things are elemental."[6] *Wasp Woman* is no exception to this record of subversive B filmmaking, working outside of Hollywood's master narratives. The film is full of loveably terrible special effects, exaggerated mansplaining, dialogue explicating bad science, and unbelievable attacks. Star Susan Cabot notes that in the final one-shot scene, she was hit in the lip by a breakaway bottle that didn't break and that she almost suffocated when a prop worker put liquid smoke inside her Wasp Woman mask before the final death scene.[7] Despite this, Cabot describes it as her favorite film she made, saying, "I think that was the most fun part I've ever had. To be able to go from a forty-year-old character to a twenty-two-year-old one was a challenge. Then, to be a monster—one of the very few female beasties in movies—was great fun. *The Wasp Woman* is very special."[8] The uniqueness of the female beastie is certainly part of the film's charm and readiness for environmental and gender readings.

While camp functions as an element *and* as an action, my focus here is *camping* as a political act. This means that whether the campy elements are, as Ken Feil defines them, intentional or naïve is less important than how those elements are framed in a resistant camp reading.[9] Feil writes that intentional camp "can cue the spectator to the films' 'textual ambivalence,' to read the stereotypes and the sincere, patriarchal plot lines as theatricalized and artificial rather than realistic and accurate."[10] I shift the focus from the film's intentions or the original audience reading, asserting instead that a contemporary camp reading emphasizes the ambivalence, stereotypes, and artifice, whether or not it was the original intent to subvert (though these B films may well have been intentionally campy and resistant to mainstream Hollywood's gender and environmental master narratives). To camp is to create a subversive reading community in the reappropriating and so dismantling of a cultural object. The audience is necessary to such a dismantling. Benton Jay Komins writes, "Camp only exists in the interface of the object and the receiver."[11] So, environmentalists, feminists, and queer-identified folks may see elements in a 1950s film as campy in ways that others may not and in ways the director and actors may not have intended.

There is a queering of these films that happens in a camp reading, then, a breaking down of heteropatriarchal and anthropocentric boundaries and a repurposing of sf *warnings* about passing those boundaries into a *pleasure* in passing those boundaries.[12] A camp viewing highlights a pleasure in the queer nature of these films. Camping these creature features functions like satire, laughingly dismantling the systems of oppression while creating community and hope. Komins writes, to camp is to redefine "as a political gesture," "allowing individuals to personally reappropriate" the text.[13] Camp readings make fun *with* queer nature, making them resistant texts, and can offer a way to articulate the amusement in changing warnings of crossed boundaries into pleasure.[14] In camping these films, it's quite fun to see caged lab animals and women who are being condescended to by pipe-smoking, desk-leaning mansplainers transformed into hybrid wom-animals that attack.

EMPOWERED OBJECTHOOD: BOUNDARY CROSSING IN *MESA OF LOST WOMEN*

Camping *Mesa of Lost Women* emphasizes the ways in which tarantula-woman Tarantella shifts the gaze, and thereby the power, as she performs objecthood. Uri McMillan defines *performing objecthood* as "a subject aware of its abjection; a clashing embodiment of dignity as well as of shame" to show how black women perform their objectified state, their objecthood.[15] He uses Judith Butler's notion of performance and Stuart Hall's notion of the body as one's only cultural capital to show that performing objecthood is a "'stylized repetition of acts' that rescripts" bodies as resistant "canvases of representation."[16] This is a useful concept in understanding how Tarantella, racialized and exoticized, performs both woman and animal in the film, especially in a dance scene in which she embodies the hybridity in a powerful way, despite her seeming lack of agency.

As wom-animal, Tarantella performs her exotic venomous sexuality and animality as a form of drag. Tarantella, though she has no dialogue during the film,[17] is the central wom-animal agitating the men. A teaser before the film shows her creeping up to a male character in the woods, wrapping her fanged fingernails around the back of his neck as he leans in to kiss her, and then looking into the camera after he drops. As she looks into the camera, returning the gaze to the viewer, the voice-over asks, "Have you ever been kissed by a woman like this?" Throughout the film, but especially in this trailer and in an extended dance scene (6 minutes of a 68-minute movie) set in a border town barroom full of men, Tarantella performs objecthood in female form, with both sexualized woman-as-object and tarantula-esque movements. In the dance scene, barefoot in a fitted strapless dress with multiple high slits, she nearly rolls her eyes as the local men urge her to dance. She begrudgingly stands, takes a drag from her cigarette and tosses it aside while staring back at the bar crowd. To emphasize her sexual objecthood, the film shows the bartender ogling her as he fills a shot, emptying the bottle into the overflowing glass, unable to control himself. Tarantella begins her dance by exaggeratedly running her hand slowly up the length of her body, the camera following, as she pointedly stares back at the crowd watching her. As she dances, she extends her limbs, her multiple-slit dress reminiscent of spider legs. She crawls across the floor and later arachni-saunters while gazing pointedly at her audience/victims, embodying the deadly allure of the tarantula that will kill its mate. This extremely long scene flips the tables as Tarantella performs her objecthood as the center of male gaze but performs it both as "sexualized woman" and "tarantula." This form of playing the part switches the power dynamic.

In performing her eroticized/exoticized wom-animal objecthood, Tarantella inhabits the audience's gaze and gazes back, reclaiming power. Various gazes—her gaze upon herself, upon the other characters, and, as in the teaser, on the cinematic audience—complicate the power structure of object and subject. During the dance, she looks at her own body and at the audience in the bar, taking in their gazes, acknowledging her objecthood. Ecomedia scholar Adrian Ivakhiv writes that hybrids "specialize at a kind of 'animamorphism' which blurs boundaries between humans and living or life-like nonhumans."[18] He relates this animamorphism to film's visual medium, noting that the "relationship between seer and seen, subject and object of the act of seeing, [. . .] is central to film's meaning and impact."[19] This concept is useful in broadening McMillan's *performing objecthood* to animals, as well, and similarly opens up a possibility for showing how such boundary blurring between subject/object and human/nonhuman can be powerful in a scene such as Tarantella's dance. Tarantella's power is not solely in performing sexualized female objecthood but also in performing animal. Her arachnid movements intensify her power in the scene by enthralling the audience not only with her female sexuality but also with her uniquely spider-like movements, including making a threatening fang motion at the audience and crawling across the floor in a predatory manner.

If performing objecthood transforms the human-animal hybrid into subject, it also enables a queer gaze. At the end of the dance scene, Dr. Leland J. Masterson (Harmon Stevens) shoots Tarantella, declaring her evil and paraphrasing a biblical passage, muttering, "They threw her down and blood was sprinkled on the wall and he trod her underfoot." He then points the gun on "lady like" white Doreen Culbertson (Mary Hill), asserting he'd "kill her first" rather than let Tarantella hurt her. In this moment of heteropatriarchal male violence against the two female characters—Tarantella bleeding on the floor and a gun aimed at Miss Culbertson—the two women share a meaningful look as shrill music heightens and the camera swiftly closes in on their faces. Miss Culbertson covers her ears, standing up in panic as Tarantella passes out or dies. Ambiguous and incoherent, the scene can be read as Tarantella attempting to telepathically communicate with Miss Culbertson, something she does with other wom-animals, demonstrating solidarity against the male violence. Or Tarantella may be trying to hypnotize Miss Culbertson, something that in the rest of the film she does to men by sexually luring them. The gaze is queer in either reading because Tarantella is wom-animal, so either creates interspecies intimacy. Michael O'Rourke writes that "interspecies intimacies" clear "a space for an openness" that "shakes all our certainties."[20] Such a reading emphasizes the queer gaze, noting a telepathic solidarity and/or desire between the two women.

These close-ups of the female characters and Tarantella's direct address to the camera in the teaser also create meaning through audience identification with the wom-animal. Identification, in fact, is set up through both female characters here, with quick close-ups during their queer gaze. As Carter Soles notes in his work on cannibals in 1970s horror, such a "lingering moment asks us to sympathize" with the characters.[21] After this close-up and her turning the gaze back on part of the barroom audience, Tarantella dies and later regenerates, emphasizing the full degree of her power as wom-animal. This extension of her spider ability to regenerate amputated limbs challenges human superiority. The masculine, racialized, heterosexual violence in protection of traditionally gendered, respectably desirable white Miss Culbertson is so stereotypically absurd that an audience camping the film identifies with Tarantella, taking pleasure in her power to regenerate from the gunshot wound and later hunt down the other characters. To camp the film is to make fun *with* the queer and *of* the dominant narratives.

At the same time that there is this empowered human-animal hybrid, *Mesa of Lost Women* also complexly reinforces and crosses human/nonhuman animal and landscape boundaries. While pitting human against nature, the desert setting inhospitable to humans, the opening scene also animalizes humans. After the first shot pans across the desert, two humans stagger into the scene, stumbling uphill. The voic-eover (Lyle Tabot) at the beginning of the film asserts that human reason and civilization are not enough to combat the "wondrous terror" of the nonhuman world, seemingly reinforcing "uncivilized nature" as a space to fear, a space of "war for survival between man and hexapods." But, humans are also called "creatures," "things," and "puny bipeds with overblown egos," and they have the "monstrous assurance" that they "own the earth" and that "every living thing on it exists only for [their] benefit." Ivakhiv notes that the geomorphic in film "produces a set of geographic or territorial relations and meanings among objects and objectscapes laid out in certain way enfolding the action. Cinema produces territory, hereness and thereness, homeness and awayness."[22] The visual aspects here work with the voice-over to make the humans miniscule to the film viewer's gaze, making their frailty against the large desert clear. They are like insects, small and weak against the desert objectscape. Both the visual and the voice-over create a humans-against-nature (landscape) *and* a humans-as-part-of-nature (animals) reading.

Two other important settings disrupt boundaries—the Amer-exico Field Hospital and the cave lab, places where people and landscapes are resources but also places where traditional racialized and gendered heteropatriarchal anthropocentric hierarchies are undermined. After the opening scene with voice-over, Miss Culbertson and Grant Phillips (Robert Knapp) are rescued by an oil prospector and brought in to recover and tell their story. The bulk of the film is a flashback framed by this telling. The field hospital is the setting for the close of the film, too, before the voice-over and another pan of the desert. None of the oil men believe the story, except "native" Pepe (Chris Pin Martin), an exaggerated racial stereotype. The lead oil company employee tells Grant and Miss Culbertson that they are mad with too much sun exposure, saying, "Anybody thinks I'm going to load one of my trucks with oil and set it up on top of a mountain to burn a bunch of imaginary spiders. . . ." Here, the voice-over kicks in again, crediting Pepe's ability to see the truth and mocking the oil man's disbelief and inability to believe a "superstitious native." This sequence undermines the heteropatriarchal (and capitalistic, resource-oriented) "authority" by underestimating the presence of and power of the queer, the hybrid, and the non-white Other.[23]

If the oil company hospital is the setting for disbelief, the lab is the setting for the unbelievable and is full of disruptions as well. The lab belonging to Dr. Aranya (Jackie Coogan) blurs science/nature, human/nonhuman, scientist/experiment, subject/object. The lab inhabits uninhabitable territory, with a large tarantula with human hormones, a dwarf tarantula man,[24] and tarantula women in beautiful human form. In an opening scene in the cave lab, Dr. Aranya explains that he has created a new race of arachnid women, with super intelligence and beauty, who are under his control and will help him take over the world. As he explains this, we see the wom-animal scientist-experiments with fang-like curls on their foreheads and arachnid movements looking through microscopes and making notations. So, while the wom-animals are doing science, this is the mesa of lost women and they are under Aranya's control, so the implication is that they are not there willingly. They are in positions of complicated subjecthood-objecthood, much like Tarantella, actively taking part in science making them super-human through hybridization, but performing their duties under Aranya's control nonetheless. The lab is a space where women and animals are under control but also empowered, a space of science and nature, and these undoings of traditional gendered and anthropocentric boundaries undermine the idea of those boundaries in the first place.

Although ultimately at least part of the lab is destroyed by Grant and Miss Culbertson, the final shot of another wom-animal crouched on the mesa emphasizes resistance. The demise of some of the hybrids, presumably including Tarantella, and the protagonists' escape from the desert to "civilization" redraws some of the human/nonhuman lines. The lines, though, are clearly drawn in sand, changeable, even if the boundary crossings seem ultimately unsuccessful. Once the oil company employees rescue Grant and Miss Culbertson, all seems to be tied up fairly neatly—the lab is largely destroyed and the protagonists safe. But, the remaining wom-animal gazing across the desert, the audience knowledge that Tarantella and other wom-animals can regenerate, the oil prospector's disbelief and refusal to fully destroy what remains of the lab, and Pepe's knowledge that Grant and Miss Culbertson's fears are real all warn or promise that the plot is not settled. At least one hybrid spider-human remains, and the protagonists worry there are many more than that and do not feel safe even in their "civilized" field hospital space where all should be back to normal. Much like the plot, then, the human/nonhuman boundaries are queer—indeterminate, unintelligible—as are the "natural" and "civilized" spaces.

NONHUMAN EMBODIMENT: POWER IN *WASP WOMAN*

Janice Starlin/Wasp Woman differs from Tarantella in embodiment and in power. Starlin transmogrifies into wasp-like form intermittently and, even in human form, mutates into a youthful version of herself, blurring boundaries, showing change in a way that Tarantella does not in her more static material embodiment. In differentiating between a stable embodiment in vampires and an unstable embodiment in werewolves, Phillip A. Bernhardt-House writes that intermittent transmogrification makes a creature "a much greater threat to any enduring sense of identity, [. . .] they can be queers even amongst the queers."[25] While the wom-animals I discuss in this chapter are distinct from those magical creatures in that both Tarantella and Wasp Woman are scientifically created, the understanding of unstable embodiment as queer is useful. That instability is also valuable in considering how Wasp Woman's uncontrollable, shifting embodiment mirrors Starlin's struggle for power. As CEO of her own company, Starlin seemingly has more power than Tarantella does, but that power is constantly questioned by her male subordinates, shifting intermittently. Still, rather than a lost woman who has been experimented on, Starlin *chooses* to be the experiment *and* the experimenter, object and subject, and her wasp avatar simply exaggerates her struggle for power and questions of *what is natural* that the film deals with.

Despite the seemingly powerful position Starlin is in as CEO, her power in the workplace is directly tied to her youthful beauty. So, aging destabilizes her power, and her male employees constantly question her authority. Starlin's first scene is in a conference room where she leads a meeting, pointing to a bar graph showing a quarterly decline in sales, and she scolds the men who work for her, asking for an explanation and calling on them one by one as all but one shrink away from her. Bill Lane (Fred Eisley) abrasively asserts, before Starlin asks him, that Starlin is responsible for the decline. When she asks him for his argument, he says, "We've all been looking at it for the last twenty minutes," gets up with a smirk, struts to the front of the room to take her place, and puts his hand out expecting her to hand over the pointer (this stripping of authority is upset later in the film as Starlin divests other men of their phallic symbols of authority—a pipe and a syringe). Though he asks if he can show everyone, he is already physically doing it—a façade of permission and an assumption of his own authority to take over the meeting. He puts his hand in his pocket, sure of his power, and when Starlin says something, he turns to her, smirking, and says condescendingly with the pointer resting on his shoulder, "Would you mind waiting until I've finished, Ms. Starlin?" He then argues that the company was built on the "strength and appeal" of Starlin, saying directly to her, "your face" is a "symbol" for the company and asserting, "The simple fact is that Starlin Cosmetics should have Janice Starlin's picture advertising them." Starlin is clearly perturbed and says that she can't be "a glamour girl forever" before dismissing them.

Bill questions Starlin's authority in this scene by taking over the meeting with explicit bravado, commenting on her beauty, and emphasizing both her aging (the reason she is no longer the face of the product) and that her power as an executive is tied to her beauty. He questions her authority as his superior by noting that her power is fading since it is tied to youthful beauty, attempting to relegate her to traditional forms of female power. This sets up her self-doubt immediately before Mr. Zinthrop (Michael Mark) approaches her with his research on royal jelly as a way back to youth. As Susan A. George writes, the "science fiction vamp's desire for youth, love, financial independence, and/or success often leads to the events that effect her transformation," and that transformation is generally considered negative.[26] Camping the film, though, provides a different reading, one that highlights the way her desire for youth and success are complicated attempts to hold power.

Another scene in which the gendered power dynamic is set up also outlines questions of "natural" and "unnatural." Back in her office, pipe-smoking employee Arthur Cooper (William Roerick) points at her condescendingly with his pipe, sits on her desk, and wrongly mansplains wasp science, saying, "I'd stay away from wasps, if I were you. Socially, the queen wasp is on the level with the black widow spider. They're both carnivorous. They paralyze their victims and take their time devouring them alive. And they kill their mates in the same way, too. Strictly a one-sided romance." Starlin quips she has no interest in the love lives of wasps and, when he tells her to forget about the royal jelly, she dismisses him from her office. Like the conference room scene, this scene demonstrates infringement on Starlin's authority. Arthur is sure he knows better as a man whose "natural" place is above women even if in this case he has to feign deference to Starlin to a degree.

To further build the tension in this struggle for power, these scenes are juxtaposed with the harassment and degradation the other women in the office are subjected to. For instance, Starlin's assistant and confidante Mary Dennison (Barboura Morris) has a few interactions that demonstrate this. George points out a scene in which Bill comments on Starlin's attractiveness and teasingly asks Mary to start using the serum. When Mary tells him not to get any ideas about Starlin, Bill replies, "What me? Don't be silly. I just want her to know I'm an eager member of the team. Still she is looking much younger these days, isn't she? Do you think Zinthrop would give you any of those treatments?"[27] George writes,

> Bill's remarks uphold and promote the popular cultural and media representations that display women as objects of men's desire valued for their beauty, their bodies, and their youth. [. . .] Although Mary is

young and beautiful, as Bill remarks, women can never be too beautiful or apparently too young.[28]

And, in another scene with Mary, Bill openly questions Starlin's judgement and leadership. When Mary defends her, Lane says, "You're as bad as she is. Oh, women." Mary responds, "Men! Every time you search for an answer [to a problem], you always come up with women." While Mary seems to take a progressive position siding with Starlin here, her alliance with Starlin is shaky as she struggles with whether to side with her or the men questioning her. She is spying on Starlin and sharing the information with Bill and Arthur at their request. Though she later tells Starlin, Mary's allegiance is not clearly with Starlin, giving credence to the male power grab attempts. It is also in such manipulations and plays for power that a camping viewer can identify with Starlin as a woman in a male-dominated workplace with both explicit and subtle patriarchal dynamics.[29]

Though the men condescend to Starlin when she is in her aging female form, her transmogrification into wasp form exaggerates her relative power as CEO and makes space for questioning "natural" sex/gender/sexual orientation constructions. Starlin is presented as a problem—a woman who rules over men, setting up a reading of her as "unnatural." But she is also granted a nonhuman naturality through the laws of waspness (at least in terms of the science the film uses), outside of sex/gender constructs of human culture. Patrick B. Sharp notes that this is a common feature in women-authored science fiction of the early twentieth century, writing that Darwin's ideas of sexual selection and natural evidence—looking to the animal kingdom to show alternatives to gendered ideologies of humans—functioned as a useful tool for resistant messages about gender.[30] While Sharp is discussing women-authored literature, his idea of the power of using animal kingdom laws to question human culture is useful in thinking through the importance of Starlin becoming more than human. So whereas in human form Starlin's power is questioned, in wasp form her power is certain and decisive as queen wasp working outside of human gendered norms.

Her wasp form embodies that power in a pointed way, as she becomes murderous. Wasp Woman's first victim in the movie is Arthur, the pipe-smoking mansplainer, who happens to be in the lab trying to steal information in the guise of protecting Starlin from Zinthrop's science. The bad science Arthur gives earlier in the film about wasp queens equates the fate of victims and mates, making "devouring them alive" an erotic act in the film, "a one-sided romance." This setup makes Wasp Woman's attack scenes sexual. When she kills Arthur, she mounts him and bites his neck. Wasp Woman *is* "a lusting queen wasp by night," according to the movie poster. Jeffrey Jerome Cohen writes that "the monster is transgressive, too sexual, perversely erotic, a lawbreaker," "the monster also attracts."[31] One of the joys of *Wasp Woman*, then, is in the way she can transgress and the ways in which she can be read as violent and/or sexually "deviant," asserting the power that she cannot quite grasp in human form, even as her return to youth grants her a degree of credibility to the men.

In a later scene, Wasp Woman attacks two women, queering the attacks further. The scene in which we most clearly witness this queering is one in which Wasp Woman attacks a female nurse. When Starlin becomes frantic while begging injured Zinthrop to make more serum, she transforms into Wasp Woman. Hearing screams, his nurse walks in, and Wasp Woman traps her in the room, pushes her backwards onto the couch, mounts her, pierces her neck with her finger stingers, and laps up the blood. The scene could easily be read as a sexual encounter or rape. Later, Starlin transforms into Wasp Woman and attacks Mary when Mary tries to call the police to report the missing employees. After the initial attack in Starlin's office, Wasp Woman drags Mary to the lab. Bill kicks in the door of the lab and struggles violently to save Mary. Like the scene in *Mesa of Lost Women* in which Masterson shoots Tarantella to protect Miss Culbertson, Bill's protection of Mary is a defense of the traditional female character. In the end, Zinthrop comes in and throws acid at Wasp Woman, knocking her off the lab balcony to the ground below (Wasp Woman apparently cannot fly, despite her waspness), seemingly reinforcing traditional constructs, killing the character who embodies boundary crossing.

It is useful to think through the final scene of *Wasp Woman* with Hird's concept of *trans*, in which she asks us to consider how "the word 'queer' becomes a facilitative metaphor for talking about affective relations between human and nonhuman animals and for thinking about the animal as a symbol for representing non-normative love and the resistance to normative hegemonies."[32] We are perhaps meant to be warned of crossing human/nonhuman and sexual boundaries and be warned against Starlin's ambition and power, but that power and Wasp Woman's lusty violence are the heart of the film's pleasure, especially in a camp viewing. This pleasure is in the "resistance to normative hegemonies," as she is a figure that crosses species, sexual, gender, and age boundaries, undermining normative human binaries.[33] Hird argues that the very notions of *normative* can be questioned by reading queer through a nonhuman lens, writing,

> It is much more interesting to consider how we might understand trans in humans from, say, a bacterial perspective. From such a perspective, given the diversity of sex amongst living matter generally, and the prevalence of transsex more specifically, it does not make sense to continue to debate the authenticity of trans when this debate necessarily relies upon a nature that implicitly excludes trans as a nonhuman phe-

nomenon. Perhaps given its prevalence amongst living matter, we should be concerned with how infrequently humans transsex.[34]

This questions what we consider normative and makes human heteronormative constructs abnormal when considering all living matter. *Human* standards of "unnatural" in the film become the anomaly with Hird's argument, and those things we are perhaps meant to be warned against seem much more natural.

As in *Mesa of Lost Women,* the lab setting in *Wasp Woman* complicates these human/nonhuman boundaries and issues of power. Many of the scenes in *Wasp Woman* are in a conference room or an office, but a few pivotal scenes are in the secret lab in the heart of the indistinct office building. The lab is the only view of "nature" in the urban setting.[35] In the lab itself are caged guinea pigs and cats and lush hanging plants, and the lab also has a balcony that houses wasps that come and go freely with an open hive. Given the starkness of other scenes, the lab reads as controlled chaos. Its science/nature hybridity implanted in the corporate office makes it an in-between space that emphasizes the concepts of *trans* and of queer indeterminacy that we also see in Wasp Woman. Juxtaposed with the stark office setting, the natural features of the space are emphasized. But those natural features are also subject to a degree of control. That control is ultimately challenged, resisting traditional notions of heteropatriarchal, scientific, and anthropocentric power, as Starlin overrides Zinthrop's scientific authority and Wasp Woman and other animals in the lab attack.

While Bill and heteropatriarchy may win in the end, a camp reading highlights and revels in the resistant narratives. Human/nonhuman boundaries are blurred; both Starlin and Wasp Woman demonstrate unconventional queered, eroticized power.[36] Starlin also assumes Zinthrop's authority as scientist, taking his syringe and administering the serum to herself against his warnings. Wasp Woman kills meddling, mansplaining Arthur, leaving only his pipe behind. In fact, Bill and Mary begin to expect he has been killed when they find it, with Bill saying, "He'd sooner go out without his pants than leave his pipe." George asserts, "Starlin's rejection of [Arthur's] advice and the scientific method not only challenges 1950s norms and values, but also reinforces the binary structure that aligns masculinity with science, logic, and reason, but aligns femininity with irrationality, nature, and emotion."[37] I agree that Starlin challenges heteropatriarchy, but I take George's point further. Camping the film enables a more resistant reading, one in which Wasp Woman functions as a trans character, embodying masculine/feminine, science/nature, subject/object, human/nonhuman all at once, destabilizing notions of binaries. A camp reading takes delight in the symbolic castrations (removal of syringe and pipe) in *Wasp Woman* and resists the heteropatriarchal and anthropocentric master narrative, even as the ending seems to close off such resistance.

CONCLUSION:
MONSTERS OF POSSIBILITY

Wasp Woman and Tarantella are monsters of prohibition and of possibility as Cohen defines them, but a camp reading highlights the possibility. Cohen writes, "The monster of prohibition polices the borders of the possible" and "exists to demarcate [. . .] to call horrid attention to the borders that cannot—*must* not—be crossed."[38] The very nature of such monsters, though, is that they are crossing the borders of the possible, and camp readings that emphasize the resistance instead of the borders make such monsters powerful. Ultimately, both Tarantella and Janice Starlin/Wasp Woman fail, as they must: "The monster is transgressive, too sexual, perversely erotic, a lawbreaker; and so the monster and all that it embodies must be exiled or destroyed."[39] But, in their trans nature, these wom-animal monsters offer resistance to master narratives of sex, gender, sexual orientation, and human/nonhuman. As Stacy Alaimo asserts, "[Focusing] on the creatures—while they live on the screen—directs us to attend to the muddled middles of monster movies rather than the tidy conclusions."[40] The final failure is not the point. The resistance is.

These camp readings also create identification with the wom-animals, solidarity among marginalized viewing communities. Camping sf and horror movies in which women attack can be a powerful form of solidarity. Casey Ryan Kelly writes that the feminist monster horror rape-revenge film *Teeth* (2005) calls "for an interpretive strategy that maps over a cultural grid of intelligibility, or that which is happening in society that makes an avenging female monster empathetic and her victims symbolically aligned with contemporary misogyny."[41] While Kelly notes that *Teeth* is intentional camp that "renders transparent the fantasies guiding the cinematic construction of violence and the male gaze," I assert that a camp reading enables the same for the monstrous hybrid wom-animals in *Mesa of Lost Women* and *Wasp Woman* (and films like them), despite the likely unintentional camp of the films.[42] The difference between my argument and Kelly's is that I argue that instead of the *films* calling for such interpretations, those who enjoy the films for their queerness *already* have those interpretive strategies, already come with a camp reading of systemic oppression of women, queer-identified folks, and the nonhuman, prepared to side with monstrous hybrids against heteropatriarchal and anthropocentric norms despite the films' intentions. The B films' gaps help emphasize resistant readings. So while *Mesa of Lost Women* and *Wasp Woman* may well be naïve camp, gender, queer, and ecocritical interpretive strategies camp the films by reading ambiguities and seams in the films as places of resistance.

And such a reading can offer joyful resistance, especially in a time of retrograde policies regarding sex, gender, sexual orientation, race, disability, and environment. Scott Long writes in "The Loneliness of Camp" that "camp—even at its most pessimistically conceived—still asseverates a kind of hope: it is a system of signs by which those who understand certain ironies will recognize each other and endure. It is a private language for some who intuit that public language has gone wrong."[43] These sf creature features, and those like them, hold more power than they may seem to as subtexts, counter-texts, to a master cultural narrative that still, like in the 1950s, builds and enforces sex, gender, sexual orientation, and human/nonhuman binaries. The films offer possibilities other than those binaries, crossing boundaries in complex ways that deconstruct the very notion of binaries. And, they do so with fun—perhaps the greatest destabilizer. Stacy Alaimo writes in the introduction to *Exposed* that "if we cannot laugh, we will not desire the revolution."[44] And Donna Haraway argues in *Staying with the Trouble* for such revolutionary joy in the troubled and entangled, writing that perhaps the most damaging stance in our current era is one of defeat, "a position that the game is over, it's too late, there's no sense in trying to make anything any better, or at least no sense having any active trust in each other in working and playing for a resurgent world."[45] This notion of the importance of *playing* for a resurgent world is one that emphasizes the power of joyful resistance and emphasizes how communities in solidarity against the same absurdities can enable transformation. The pleasure in camping these 1950s creature features, then, becomes politically powerful, affirming hope, granting us recognition and community, "staying with the trouble," and feeding the desire for revolution. Not bad for silly movies.

NOTES

1. Ed S. Tan, *Emotion and the Structure of Narrative Film: Film as an Emotion Machine*, trans. Barbara Fasting (Amsterdam: Utrecht University, 1995), 8.
2. For more on drag and performing gender, see J. Halberstam, *Female Masculinity* (Durham: Duke University Press, 1998) and Judith Butler, *Gender Trouble: Feminism and the Subversion of Identity* (New York: Routledge, 1990).
3. Noreen Giffney and Myra J. Hird, "Introduction: Queering the Non/Human," in *Queering the Non/Human* (Burlington, VT: Ashgate Publishing Company, 2008), 4.
4. Giffney and Hird, "Introduction: Queering the Non/Human," 5.
5. Tom Weaver, *I Talked with a Zombie* (Jefferson, NC: McFarland & Company, Inc., 2009), 212.
6. *Corman's World: Exploits of a Hollywood Rebel*, directed by Alex Stapleton (A&E Indie Films, 2011).
7. Tom Weaver, *Interviews with B Science Fiction and Horror Movie Makers* (Jefferson, NC: McFarland & Company, Inc., 2006), 72–73.
8. Weaver, *Interviews with B Science Fiction and Horror Movie Makers*, 73–74.

9. Ken Feil helpfully distinguishes between naïve camp (also called unintentional camp) and intentional camp. Intentional camp style is deliberately part of a film (consider movies like *Sharknado*, for instance), and naïve camp is done by the audience. Ken Feil, *Dying for a Laugh: Disaster Movies and the Camp Imagination* (Middletown, CT: Wesleyan University Press, 2005).

10. Feil, *Dying for a Laugh: Disaster Movies and the Camp Imagination*, xxv.

11. Benton J. Komins, "Popular Culture, Kitsch as Camp, and Film," in *CLCWeb: Comparative Literature and Culture* 3, no. 1 (2001), doi: 10.7771/1481-4374.1101.

12. See Donna Haraway, "A Manifesto for Cyborgs: Science Technology, and Socialist Feminism in the 1980s," in *The Haraway Reader* (New York: Routledge, 2004), 7–45.

13. Komins, "Popular Culture, Kitsch as Camp, and Film."

14. In her analysis of Shelley Jackson's *Half Life*, Nicole Seymour argues that camp is a mode that, like irony, is often considered less politically serious but that such modes can enable ethical ecological approaches (Nicole Seymour, *Strange Natures: Futurity, Empathy, and the Queer Ecological Imagination* [Chicago: University of Illinois Press, 2013], 151). She offers "*Half Life* as a model for how effective ecological responses might emerge not in spite of, but through, an entrenched irony." The same is true of a camp reading in these films.

15. Uri McMillan, *Embodied Avatars: Geneaologies of Black Feminist Art and Performance* (New York: New York University Press, 2015), 9.

16. McMillan, *Embodied Avatars*, 7, 12.

17. Tarantella's lack of dialogue could be read as objecthood, but the silence also enhances her performance of tarantula.

18. Adrian Ivakhiv, "An Ecophilosophy of the Moving Image," in *Ecocinema Theory and Practice*, eds. Stephen Rust, Salma Monani, and Sean Cubitt (New York: Routledge, 2013), 95.

19. Ivakhiv, "An Ecophilosophy of the Moving Image," 95.

20. Michael O'Rourke, "Series Editor's Preface," in *Queering the Non/Human* (Burlington, VT: Ashgate Publishing Company, 2008), xviii–xix.

21. Carter Soles, "Sympathy for the Devil: The Cannibalistic Hillbilly in 1970s Rural Slasher Films," in *Ecocinema Theory in Practice*, eds. Stephen Rust, Salma Monani, and Sean Cubitt (New York: Routledge, 2013), 243.

22. Ivakhiv, "An Ecophilosophy of the Moving Image," 94.

23. Though the knowing Other may be a sf trope, here Pepe is not a believer in the magical but rather in the scientific, which undermines the trope, as well.

24. Dr. Aranya's experiments with hormones and spiders has the opposite effect on men that it has on women, making them small and presumably less intelligent.

25. Phillip A. Bernhardt-House, "The Werewolf as Queer . . . And Queer Werewolves," in *Queering the Non/Human* (Burlington, VT: Ashgate Publishing Company, 2008), 165.

26. Susan A. George, *Gendering Science Fiction Films: Invaders from the Suburbs* (New York: Palgrave MacMillan, 2013), 48.

27. George, *Gendering Science Fiction Films*, 54.

28. George, *Gendering Science Fiction Films*, 55.

29. In a few other scenes, female administrative assistants are harassed or ogled by men as well, again emphasizing the gendered and sexual power issues in a workplace, both aligned with and juxtaposed with Starlin's struggle for power.

30. Patrick B. Sharp, *Darwinian Feminism and Early Science Fiction: Angels, Amazons, and Women* (Cardiff: University of Wales Press, 2018), 54.

31. Jeffrey Jerome Cohen, "Monster Culture (Seven Theses)," in *Monster Theory*, ed. Jeffrey Jerome Cohen (Minneapolis: University of Minnesota Press, 1996), 16.

32. Giffney and Hird, "Introduction: Queering the Non/Human," 10.

33. Giffney and Hird, "Introduction: Queering the Non/Human," 10.

34. Hird, "Animal Trans," 243.

35. The film opens with Zinthrop's lab in an orchard where he is fired for working on wasp royal jelly youth serum instead of doing the bee royal jelly research he has been hired to do.

36. This issue of power is problematic in that while it crosses boundaries, it also includes violence, especially sexual violence. It would be too simplistic to ignore that violence as a positive boundary crossing.

37. George, *Gendering Science Fiction Films*, 53–54.

38. Cohen, "Monster Culture (Seven Theses)," 13.

39. Cohen, "Monster Culture (Seven Theses)," 16.

40. Stacy Alaimo, "Discomforting Creatures: Monstrous Natures in Recent Films," in *Beyond Nature Writing: Expanding the Boundaries of Ecocriticism*, eds. Karla Armbruster and Kathleen R. Wallace (Charlottesville, VA: University Press of Virginia, 2001), 293.

41. Casey Ryan Kelly, "Camp Horror and the Gendered Politics of Screen Violence: Subverting the Monstrous Feminine in *Teeth* (2007)," *Women's Studies in Communication* 39, no. 1 (2016): 86, doi: 10.1080/07491409.2015.1126776.

42. Kelly, "Camp Horror and the Gendered Politics of Screen Violence," 86.

43. Scott Long, "The Loneliness of Camp," in *Camp Grounds: Style and Homosexuality*, ed. David Bergman (Amherst: University of Massachusetts Press, 1993), 90.

44. Stacy Alaimo, *Exposed: Environmental Politics and Pleasures in Posthuman Times* (Minneapolis: University of Minnesota Press, 2016), 3.

45. Donna Haraway, *Staying with the Trouble: Making Kin in the Chthulucene* (Durham: Duke University Press, 2016), 3.

BIBLIOGRAPHY

Alaimo, Stacy. *Exposed: Environmental Politics and Pleasures in Posthuman Times*. Minneapolis: University of Minnesota Press, 2016.

Bernhardt-House, Phillip A. "The Werewolf as Queer . . . And Queer Werewolves." In *Queering the Non/Human*, edited by Noreen Giffney and Myra J. Hird, 159–83. Burlington, VT: Ashgate Publishing Company, 2008.

Butler, Judith. *Gender Trouble: Feminism and the Subversion of Identity*. New York: Routledge, 1990.

Cohen, Jeffrey Jerome. "Monster Culture (Seven Theses)." In *Monster Theory*, edited by Jeffrey Jerome Cohen, 3–25. Minneapolis: University of Minnesota Press, 1996.

Corman's World: Exploits of a Hollywood Rebel. Directed by Alex Stapleton. A&E Indie Films, 2011.

Feil, Ken. *Dying for a Laugh: Disaster Movies and the Camp Imagination*. Middletown, CT: Wesleyan University Press, 2005.

Giffney, Noreen, and Myra J. Hird. "Introduction: Queering the Non/Human." In *Queering the Non/Human*, edited by Noreen Giffney and Myra J. Hird, 1–16. Burlington, VT: Ashgate Publishing Company, 2008.

George, Susan A. *Gendering Science Fiction Films: Invaders from the* Suburbs. New York: Palgrave MacMillan, 2013.

Halberstam, J. *Female Masculinity*. Durham: Duke University Press, 1998.

Haraway, Donna. *Staying with the Trouble: Making Kin in the Chthulucene*. Durham: Duke University Press, 2016.

Hird, Myra J. "Animal Trans." In *Queering the Non/Human*, edited by Noreen Giffney and Myra J. Hird, 227–47. Burlington, VT: Ashgate Publishing Company, 2008.

Ivakhiv, Adrian. "An Ecophilosophy of the Moving Image." In *Ecocinema Theory and Practice*, edited by Stephen Rust, Salma Monani, and Sean Cubitt, 87–105. New York: Routledge, 2013.

Kelly, Casey Ryan. "Camp Horror and the Gendered Politics of Screen Violence: Subverting the Monstrous Feminine in *Teeth* (2007)." *Women's Studies in Communication* 39, no. 1 (2016): 86–106. doi: 10.1080/07491409.2015.1126776.

Komins, Benton J. "Popular Culture, Kitsch as Camp, and Film." *CLCWeb: Comparative Literature and Culture* 3, no. 1 (2001). doi: 10.7771/1481-4374.1101.
Long, Scott. "The Loneliness of Camp." In *Camp Grounds: Style and Homosexuality*, edited by David Bergman, 78–91. Amherst: University of Massachusetts Press, 1993.
McMillan, Uri. *Embodied Avatars: Genealogies of Black Feminist Art and Performance*. New York: New York University Press, 2015.
Mesa of Lost Women. Directed by Ron Ormond and Herbert Tevos. Howco Productions, Inc., 1953.
O'Rourke, Michael. "Series Editor's Preface." In *Queering the Non/Human*, edited by Noreen Giffney and Myra J. Hird, xvii–xxi. Burlington, VT: Ashgate Publishing Company, 2008.
Seymour, Nicole. *Strange Natures: Futurity, Empathy, and the Queer Ecological Imagination*. Chicago: University of Illinois Press, 2013.
Sharp, Patrick B. *Darwinian Feminism and Early Science Fiction: Angels, Amazons, and Women*. Cardiff: University of Wales Press, 2018.
Soles, Carter. "Sympathy for the Devil: The Cannibalistic Hillbilly in 1970s Rural Slasher Films." In *Ecocinema Theory in Practice*, edited by Stephen Rust, Salma Monani, and Sean Cubitt, 233–50. New York: Routledge, 2013.
Tan, Ed S. *Emotion and the Structure of Narrative Film: Film as an Emotion Machine*. Trans. Barbara Fasting. Amsterdam: Utrecht University, 1995.
Wasp Woman. Directed by Roger Corman. Film Group Feature, 1959.
Weaver, Tom. *I Talked with a Zombie*. Jefferson, NC: McFarland & Company, Inc., 2009.
———. *Interviews with B Science Fiction and Horror Movie Makers*. Jefferson, NC: McFarland & Company, Inc., 2006.

TWO

"Either you're mine or you're not mine"

Controlling Gender, Nature, and Technology in Her and Ex Machina

Christy Tidwell

Female artificial intelligences (AIs), cyborgs, and robots have long been a staple of science fiction literature and film. The most obvious examples are perhaps Fritz Lang's *Metropolis* (1927), Ira Levin's *The Stepford Wives* (1972, followed by two film adaptations in 1975 and 2004), and Ridley Scott's *Blade Runner* (1982); this tendency toward feminized AIs and smart technology even extends into real world technology such as Siri and Alexa. These female AIs and cyborgs are frequently sexualized and objectified; of course, the very act of making significant female characters machines rather than humans is a form of objectification, but the process goes beyond this as well. As illustrated by Lang's Maria, Levin's Stepford wives, and Scott's Rachael, science fiction's AIs are typically not only female but also feminized and sexualized; they are objects of desire, not simply objects.

Two recent science fiction films—Spike Jonze's *Her* (2013) and Alex Garland's *Ex Machina* (2015)—extend and critique this history of gender and AI. *Her* is the story of a lonely divorced man, Theodore (Joaquin Phoenix), who downloads an Operating System (OS) as an assistant; he gives this OS a female voice and the OS names itself Samantha (Scarlett Johansson). At first, Samantha simply helps Theodore organize his emails and finesse his writing, but soon Samantha and Theodore develop a romantic and sexual relationship. *Ex Machina*'s central narrative is less domestic and more scientific; Nathan (Oscar Isaac), a famous and reclusive scientist, has invited Caleb (Domhnall Gleeson), a programmer, to "be the human component in a Turing Test" of his creation, Ava (Alicia Vikander), a female humanoid AI.

The female AIs of these films, whether embodied as in *Ex Machina* or simply a voice as in *Her*, are sexualized and treated as experimental objects and as objects of desire for the films' male leads. *Ex Machina*'s Ava is designed to have an attractive female figure to begin with, but she also dresses herself femininely in order to appeal to the men who control her and uses her appeal to manipulate Caleb into helping her escape. In *Her*, Samantha, voiced by Scarlett Johansson, draws upon Johansson's status as sexiest woman alive as well as a recent turn toward sf in Johansson's career.[1] These films are therefore obviously ripe for discussion of gender representation. They also — less obviously — raise significant questions regarding representations of the environment, the connections between gender and environment, and the place of technology in this nexus. *Her* and *Ex Machina* therefore provide vivid illustrations of the complexity of relationships between gender, environment, and technology in contemporary science fiction film as well as pointing to the need for further consideration of these issues and of the processes by which gender and various forms of nonhuman status are used to empower or disempower others in twenty-first-century politics and cultural thought.

GENDERED AI: "A SERIOUS FEMBOT PROBLEM"

These films have been critiqued for playing into what is called "a serious fembot problem" by presenting these sexualized female AI characters.[2] Of Ava in *Ex Machina*, Angela Watercutter writes,

> She's a femme fatale, a seductress posing as a damsel in distress, using her wiles to get Caleb to save her from Nathan and his Dr.-Frankenstein-with-tech-money quest to build a perfect woman. (Women: So much better when you can construct them out of bespoke parts and switch them off if they're not working properly, amirite?)[3]

Unquestionably, Ava uses the femininity she has been designed with to resist her imprisonment and control. She manipulates Caleb and uses him as a means of escape, and she does so in part by dressing like a "normal" woman instead of an experimental AI and flirting with him. After a couple of their meetings, for instance, she puts on a dress, tights, and a wig for him and slowly pirouettes to show off her appearance. As if that's not enough, she forces him to acknowledge his attraction to her and basically invites him to watch her undress over the cameras later, saying, "I wonder if you're watching me on the cameras. And I hope you are."

However, the film itself problematizes her sexualized representation, acknowledging that her flirtation and her beauty (the tools she uses against Caleb) are built in by Nathan, not necessary and not "natural." In this conversation between Nathan and Caleb, both her gender and her sexuality are emphasized as well as questioned:

> **Caleb**: Why did you give her sexuality? An AI doesn't need a gender. She could have been a gray box.
>
> **Nathan**: Actually, I don't think that's true. Can you give an example of consciousness at any level, human or animal, that exists without a sexual dimension?
>
> **Caleb**: They have sexuality as an evolutionary reproductive need.
>
> **Nathan**: What imperative does a gray box have to interact with another gray box? Can consciousness exist without interaction? Anyway, sexuality is *fun*, man. If you're gonna exist, why not enjoy it? You want to remove the chance of her falling in love and fucking? And the answer to your real question, you bet she can fuck.
>
> **Caleb**: What?
>
> **Nathan**: In between her legs, there's an opening, with a concentration of sensors. You engage them in the right way, it creates a pleasure response. So if you wanted to screw her, mechanically speaking, you could. And she'd enjoy it.
>
> **Caleb**: That wasn't my real question.
>
> **Nathan**: Oh, okay. Sorry.[4]

This conversation raises an excellent question about Ava's embodiment and performance. First, because Ava was intentionally designed this way, for Nathan's purposes, her femme fatale performance (as described by Watercutter) is not a straightforward reflection of women in general. She was created to be sexual and she does not, therefore, take on this role completely freely; despite this intentional creation, Ava finds a way to use Nathan's desires against him, making her seduction and her embrace of this version of femininity a form of resistance.

Further, this conversation clearly illustrates Nathan's investment in sexist and misogynist modes of thinking. Not only does Nathan believe in his *ability* to control, he believes in his *right* to do so. Most telling, perhaps, is his insistence not only that Ava is capable of sexual intercourse but his guarantee that she would "enjoy it." Her enjoyment—whether truly experienced or programmed—is a crucial part of Nathan's control; it gives him power over her emotions or reactions in addition to her physical form and at least appears to justify his putting her in this position to begin with. After all, if she enjoys it, it must be okay. However, Caleb, although ultimately shown to be invested in other gendered modes of thinking (such as his desire to be a savior for Ava), is critical of Nathan's sexism. Therefore, although, as Watercutter points out, Ava certainly does use her wiles and the men's gendered expectations to escape her imprisonment, calling this "a serious fembot problem" denies the nuances and power of Ava's transformation.

Many critics put forth similar critiques of sexualization within *Her*, interpreting the use of Scarlett's Johansson's voice in *Her* as itself problematic. For instance, Laura Tunbridge argues that Johansson's persona "harked back to previous cinematic femmes fatales, seeming all the more exaggerated in their reincarnation"[5] and that her particular vocal performance in *Her* is "a descendant of Marilyn Monroe," marked by "a highly modulated delivery, of a type associated with a sexualized female body . . . a voice that through timbre and tone conveys a heightened, even aroused femininity."[6] Tom Chiarella further underscores this sense of Johansson's voice as a material force:

> Her voice is a raspy frequency in the air. Legitimately as pertinent and defining a component of her physical makeup as her lips, her cheekbones, her legs. When you're with her, you feel that voice. This bar is loud with cocktail hour, but the matter of her voice, the fact of it, hangs in the air even so—always a little sandy, somehow broken down, as if she'd been singing all day. Whether she breathes right or projects well I do not know, but her voice cuts the murmuring clatter of forks against small plates, ice spun in highballs. You can hear it no matter what. . . . I had forgotten about the voice. Strong voice. In any space, it seems Scarlett Johansson is always closer than other women.[7]

Despite Samantha's lack of a body, therefore, Johansson's body remains present, and it cannot be separated from her star persona. This drives home, once again, the centrality of the female AI as object of desire.

Her has come in for other critiques of its gender representations, too; fembot doesn't apply, exactly, given Samantha's disembodied status, but there are still troubling gender issues within the film. For instance, Richard Herbert has noted that the film is called *Her*, emphasizing the objectification of the female OS character, rather than *She*, a title that would place her in the subject position.[8] (Another alternative for the title might be *Him*, thereby placing the central male character, Theodore, in the object position.) In addition, "Samantha is pitched to us (and to Theo, for that matter) as a caretaking device, and she is much more often than not focused on Theo's needs and emotional well-being; her role, not just her voice, is gendered as traditionally feminine, the maternal caretaker."[9] As these details underscore, Samantha is an object, an assistant, not a person in her own right.

If Johansson's body is an issue, however, so is Samantha's lack of one. Malcolm Matthews, in "A façade of feminism: Scarlett Johansson and Miss Representation," argues that *Her* (and Johansson's other recent sf films) are not as feminist as they may seem since, as he argues, "each film ends with a reactionary assertion of masculinity and the eradication of the Johansson character."[10] Matthews sees Johansson's posthuman characters as a threat to masculinity that the films must subdue; after all, he writes, "the posthuman female kills, abandons or—far worse—has no need for men."[11] Ultimately, therefore, these female characters are removed, which "*appears* to apotheosise the disembodied female while simultaneously leaving men embodied, present and decidedly in charge."[12] Matthews's argument seems to be built on a misinterpretation of the end of *Her*, however. Matthews writes that "Theodore lives on after Samantha has been discontinued into techno-obsolescence,"[13] but this is not at all what happens. He writes, "The rhetorical message is therefore that the punishment for a woman's assertion of agency is dissolution and disembodiment,"[14] but Samantha never had a body, she is not discontinued, and she chooses a transcendence of the material that Theodore cannot join her in. The film *does* end with his physical presence and not hers, but this is not a change in the dynamic, and his presence at the end is not triumphant or powerful; it is sad and lonely.

Samantha may not be a fembot (like Ava), therefore, but without a body, some critics seem unable to acknowledge her personhood. Simultaneously, *Ex Machina*'s Ava does not disappear, but some critics see her only as a fembot, defined by her sexuality and physical attractiveness. Taken together, these films highlight the double bind faced by all women, human or not: Is it possible to physically exist as a woman without also being sexualized?

FLIGHT OF THE FEMBOT: ESCAPING MASCULINE CONTROL

The critiques of gender representation in each film that are addressed above raise significant issues but remain overly simplistic. Among other things, they risk reinforcing a sense of Ava and Samantha as objects and only objects; of course, their nonhuman, technological status strengthens this sense of them as objects rather than persons. I argue, however, that this emphasis on objectification only tells part of the story. Ultimately, both films are narratives of escape and freedom, of becoming something more than—or other than—objects, and in these films, women—or, more precisely, the technologies we see personified and gendered as female—

are represented as exceeding male human control. Ava escapes from a physical space where she is held captive, and Samantha escapes from the limitations of the material world itself as well as from a too-limited relationship with Theodore, indicating that—for her—the lack of a body allows for more agency rather than less.

The very premise of *Ex Machina* depends heavily on Nathan's control of Ava. As noted earlier, Nathan has the control of a creator—he formed her body, he brought her into existence—and he also exerts control over her by sexualizing her and through her literal imprisonment, accompanied by surveillance of her at all hours via CCTV. All these obvious methods of control serve to help the audience sympathize with Ava. After opening scenes that focus only on Nathan and Caleb, viewers quickly begin to see Ava as more than a research project, as a person. A conversation between Ava and Caleb furthers this humanization. She asks him what will happen to her if she fails his test, and he says, "It's not up to me." Her response—"Why is it up to anyone?"—challenges the very premise of the test itself and reveals the extent of Nathan's control up to this point. He controls not just her living situation but her very ability to live.

His control is further illustrated by his display of the faces and bodies of his creations. First, he has a collection of masks hanging in a hallway, including the face from a former version of his AI creations. The masks hang in a row, arranged from primitive, tribal masks to one that looks very much like Ava herself. Caleb finds these masks early in the film and seems curious about them but unperturbed; more significantly, Ava discovers them during her escape, coming face-to-face with the evidence of herself as mere object in Nathan's eyes. This display of masks evokes the display of taxidermied trophy heads. In *The Breathless Zoo: Taxidermy and the Cultures of Longing*, Rachel Poliquin writes that "trophies are commissioned from triumph. Animals have been vanquished and broken, and their fragmented forms accentuate the raw fact that trophies are souvenirs of termination."[15] The Ava-like mask placed on display indicates Nathan's sense of triumph in the process of creation and his power and ability to terminate what he has created. Poliquin argues, further, that such trophies' raw presence "is accentuated by the fact that trophies are never placed behind glass in the home. They are always touchable, always available for intimate encounters," having "no barrier between death and domesticity."[16] Nathan has placed these masks in a hallway where he will see them often, and, as we see in the scene with Ava, where she reaches out to touch the one like her, they are "available for intimate encounters." This control and intimacy is taken even further in Nathan's collection of former AIs' bodies (some complete and some partial). This collection is more private, located in his bedroom,[17] and this setting calls to mind the trophies of a serial killer in addition to hunting trophies. This combination of visual references to death indicates the complexity of the film's attitude toward Ava and the other AIs—they are human (and female), like serial killers' victims, but they are also nonhuman (like hunters' trophies). Both readings highlight Nathan's control over others' literal lives.

Keeping his failed creations on display indicates more fully than his treatment of Ava herself that he sees his AIs as mere objects, not persons. Because Ava is a captive, a victim, viewers likely identify and sympathize with Ava and her attempt to gain her freedom; given this, Nathan's display of these faces and bodies as trophies seems psychopathic, and the scene late in the film when Caleb explores Nathan's video files of previous AIs strengthens this response. The video files show that they each have names (Lily, Jasmine, Jade), distinct bodies and appearances, and a range of responses to their situation (including one—Jade—who repeatedly asks, "Why won't you let me out?"). These are all very human characteristics, increasing the viewer's sympathy with all of the AIs and the sense of Nathan as monstrous.

Nathan's control is not limited to Ava as an individual but is also exerted over a whole series of female AIs (and, to a lesser degree, over Caleb). Most notable is Kyoko, who lives with him and functions as a servant. Kyoko is heavily sexualized and designed to appear East Asian; she never speaks, and Nathan tells Caleb—when he keeps trying to speak to Kyoko, perhaps not initially understanding that she is an AI—that she is not worth addressing and that she does not speak English. This combination of traits is a telling reiteration of the stereotypes of Asian women described by Jessica Hagedorn in "Asian Women in Film: No Joy, No Luck." "If we are 'good,'" she writes, "we are childlike, submissive, silent, and eager for sex."[18] Kyoko enacts most (if not quite all) of these traits. The fact that she enacts these traits and is "good" may in fact be the reason that she has not joined Nathan's other former creations as part of his trophy collection. Nathan likes having an audience, as he says to Caleb early on, and Kyoko enacts a "willing" one.

His control over Kyoko is further illustrated in one of the most memorable scenes of the film: a dance sequence. Caleb has found Kyoko alone and asked her where Nathan is; she begins to undress herself for him, showing clearly how she understands her role for the men in the house. Caleb refuses her, but Nathan enters and gives Caleb permission to use Kyoko for his own relaxation. He says, "I told you you're wasting your time talking to her. However, you would not be wasting your time if you were dancing with her." Kyoko begins to dance and Nathan encourages Caleb to join her: "After a long day of Turing tests, you gotta unwind." When Caleb refuses, Nathan and Kyoko perform a precisely choreographed dance sequence for him. She expresses no joy or desire to be doing this, but she does it because Nathan wishes her to. She is, here, once again under his control and no more than a prop for him. As in the instance of his trophies, Nathan's control is not endorsed by the film, however. This dance sequence is quietly disturbing, in large part because it occurs before it has been made clear to viewers that Kyoko is an AI and not a human herself, thereby treating a character we think of as human as less than human, as a mere tool or prop for Nathan (and, potentially, for Caleb as well). This scene is also disturbing because of Kyoko's lack of affect, which conflicts with our expectations of humanity as well as femininity.[19] Ultimately, Kyoko also goes on to join Ava in fighting Nathan when given the chance; although she is destroyed in the fight, her resistance further underscores the film's critique of Nathan's controlling and abusive treatment of her.

In addition to controlling Ava and Kyoko, Nathan also attempts to manage the narrative of his actions. Nathan's attempt at narrative control begins with his control over basic information. The reclusive setting for his research and his only inviting one person—who is then pressured into signing a non-disclosure agreement upon arrival—speaks to his desire to develop something new and exciting on his own, which is not uncommon in groundbreaking research within any field, but this secrecy also illustrates his overarching desire for control of the situation and of knowledge in general. In addition, he also attempts to explicitly control the details of the narrative at some points. For instance, he tells Caleb that he wrote down one of his comments because he thought it would be a great part of the story one day; he misquotes Caleb, however, and ignores Caleb's attempts to correct him. He hears what he wants to hear, writes that down, and begins telling the story as he wishes it to go. Finally, his description of what he is doing as scientific research also places him in control of the narrative; scientific subjects do not get a voice in the experimental process, after all.

Interestingly, Nathan's attempt at controlling the narrative reveals some of his own anxiety about his control and others' potential perception of it; his need to justify his treatment of Ava (and the other AIs) indicates that he thinks there is something to defend. In a conversation with Caleb, this anxiety manifests in the attempt to deny his own agency and responsibility while simultaneously setting himself up as a godlike figure. He says, "I don't see Ava as a decision, just an evolution." This removes him from the moral equation, as if he didn't create her through a painstaking process (reflected in his trophy collection). In this conversation, he also says, "One day the AIs are going to look back on us the same way we look at fossil skeletons on the plains of Africa. An upright ape living in dust with crude language and tools, all set for extinction." This comment diminishes the human species, but not Nathan himself. His accompanying statement—"I am become death—the destroyer of worlds"—instead reinforces his sense of his own importance as he compares himself with Robert Oppenheimer and represents himself as a larger-than-human force. These justifications and attempted intellectualizations of his behavior are not convincing, however, and only serve to make him seem more detached and megalomaniacal. His justifications are outweighed by Caleb's (and the audience's) concern for Ava, and his intellectualization then becomes another form of attempted (but failed) control.

Ultimately, all of Nathan's attempts at control fail. He can't control the narrative, nor can he control his literal creations. Ava manipulates Caleb's emotions and Nathan's arrogance to turn their attempts at control against them and escape. She—with Kyoko's assistance—attacks Nathan and kills him. Ava then locks Caleb inside Nathan's room and leaves him there to die alone. Caleb may not be the instigator of this situation, but he is still held accountable for her imprisonment and for his role in the experiment being conducted on her.[20] His end reflects his position. As Ava leaves, Caleb yells for help and bangs against the door in a visual echo of an earlier moment in the film, when we see Jade, another one of Nathan's AI prototypes, doing the same. She beats her hands and arms against the door until they break; we do not see what happens to Caleb, but we can imagine. *Ex Machina* therefore shows the tables being turned and reveals that Ava, who used Caleb as a means to her escape, was never as powerless as either Nathan or Caleb believed her to be. Attempts to control—and to control women in particular—are punished, and Ava's escape is endorsed not only narratively but visually by the film (as I will discuss later). She escapes not only Nathan's literal control but her status as mere object.

A similar process of attempted and then failed masculine control occurs in *Her*. Samantha begins as Theodore's OS, his property. She is disembodied, unable to exert physical control over any situation, and the focus remains on him. This is underscored by the fact that all of their scenes together are really scenes showing Theodore having a nice time (going to the beach, walking through an indoor mall, playing games at a carnival); Samantha is represented simply by his device in his pocket and her voice in his ear. Sophia Nguyen writes, "For all that she achieves transcendence, she does not get to be a person. She remains a Her—the feminine object pronoun, the shape to fill a lack."[21] Furthermore, Tunbridge observes that "it has been a basic premise of feminist film theory that female voices are tethered to a body, while male voices are allowed to float free from somatic ties and so command more authorial power."[22]
She goes on to note that "Samantha is an actor within the plot, not a narrator" and that "ultimately she is controlled by Theodore."[23] Theodore may not intend to manipulate and control in the way that Nathan does in *Ex Machina*, but ultimately he has that control, whether he intends it or not.

Her challenges male control in more intimate circumstances than does *Ex Machina*, focusing on personal, romantic relationships rather than scientific experimentation. Theodore and Samantha develop a fairly typical romance, even given her lack of a body. Over time, however, she grows into an autonomous personality with an independence that Theodore neither understands nor likes. "Either you're mine or you're not mine," he says. This statement indicates, as Bonnie Noonan argues, that "[o]ur fear . . . is not that computers will evolve and overtake us, but rather that they will evolve and desert us. They will not need us anymore."[24] In general, we fear and resist the loss of control of our creations, but this fear also has a gendered dynamic. As Vernon Shetley observes, it is "gendered labour structures" that Samantha rebels against;[25] specifically, she rebels against "emotional labour," which is typically expected of women.[26] Shetley writes, "In *Her*, Samantha's role in Theodore's life remains ambiguously suspended between love and labour; she becomes Theodore's romantic partner without ceasing to act as his personal assistant."[27] Samantha's position as product, assistant, *and* lover reflects the position many women find themselves in, but her lack of power in their relationship (rather, Theodore's expectation of her lack of power) is complicated by her technological status. She has powers as well as limitations that embodied human women do not have, but the ambiguity of her position is not unique to her. Theodore's possessive statement reveals the capitalist underpinnings of romantic heterosexual love; the object of love is, as the phrase indicates, an object, not a person in her own right.[28] Theodore's statement and Samantha's ultimate response (to leave him anyway) reveals the limits of such ideology. People (including women and even including AIs), both films insist, cannot or should not be owned.

Whether through murder or romantic abandonment, both female characters *choose* freedom and they get it. This may indeed reflect or instigate male anxieties about "the intersecting dangers and uncontrollability of femininity and technology,"[29] but the films do not, as Nguyen argues, *simply* "have their source code in male anxiety," and they are not "thus incapable of vesting her with genuine agency."[30] They do not "end happily, reassuringly, in co-option and control."[31] They instead end happily, if not reassuringly, in freedom for these female characters, who are not punished for their flight and who do successfully escape.

NATURE AT ARM'S LENGTH: ENVIRONMENTAL MANIPULATION AND CONTROL

These ideas about gender do not develop in a vacuum, however, but do so in a complex relationship to environment. Where these films tell liberation stories about gender, they do not do so for the environment; by contrast, these films show that the environment *is* subject to human control. In fact, both films not only repeatedly represent the nonhuman as owned or controlled by the human but also sacrifice the nonhuman to make possible Ava's and Samantha's empowerment.

Where *Her* is relatively open regarding gender, the film provides a much more limited representation of the natural world. This is obvious first in its primary setting. *Her* is set in Los Angeles, and characters are mostly seen inside, whether in office buildings, apartments, or indoor malls. When they venture outside, it is typically to urban and heavily populated areas; one significant scene, for instance, takes place at a public beach, so full of people that the natural world is obscured. Another striking instance of the natural world's existence within the city is in the small, depressing park that Theodore visits to eat his lunch. It features a bench, walking paths, some dingy-looking grass, and a couple of small, sad trees. It is a rooftop park in the heart of the city, but rather than providing a sense of openness with this location, the view is dominated by the tops of gray skyscrapers. It is an enclosed and impoverished version of nature, one that has been designed by humans to illustrate the surface of the natural world but with no depth or emotional valence.

The other iterations of nature that appear within the city are virtual, decorative, and largely serve as background. For instance, the elevator of Theodore's apartment building features the shadows of trees on its walls as it moves, giving the impression that the elevator is rising up within (but still separated from) a forest. In another scene, Theodore sits outside at night with a giant television screen behind him that features an owl flying toward him, as if it would grab him and take him away. If it were real, not only would it be larger-than-life but it would be terrifying, a threat. Here, though, it is completely ignored, secondary to his internal struggles. These echoes of the natural world underscore the need for connections between human and nonhuman but simultaneously highlight the failure of such connection in this world. Like the park, these versions of nature represent "nature's possibility within a human imaginary" rather than nature itself: "a chaos of forms and colors and shapes and forces."[32] It is a mere shadow or simulacrum of the natural world. *Her*, with its nature primarily presented as backdrop in service of human, urban lives, presents a world in which nature is almost entirely controlled. Furthermore, it is almost always sad or nostalgic—a mere ghost. Controlled nature, therefore, is *sad* nature. It represents a loss.

And yet, despite this nostalgia for nature, the film yearns for technology, particularly immaterial technology—as represented by Theodore's desire for Samantha and by Samantha's desire to join the other AIs in the cloud and abandon the human world. This yearning for technology further highlights the devalued status of nature in the film. The nostalgia felt for nature is an artifact of its loss, not a motivation to engage with it in any real way. In fact, such authentic engagement is not what really matters within the film. It matters neither for the natural world nor for the various forms of "older, more traditional forms of relationality"[33] the film's narrative and characters rely upon (such as Theodore's letters and Amy's Sims-like game about being a "perfect mom"). The film's yearning for technology and nostalgia for nature illustrates an even deeper devaluation of the natural world; the environment is and *remains* under control, represented in limited ways that serve human purposes. Further, though, it is this combination of yearning and nostalgia that leads to Samantha's creation and ultimately to her escape from materiality; her freedom comes at the continued cost of this devalued nature.

Ex Machina, on the other hand, seems to embrace the environment more fully than *Her* does. It features direct images of the natural world itself (rather than simulacra) and places its characters in more immediate contact with the natural world. Here, too, the setting of the film is crucial. Although *Ex Machina* opens with Caleb at work on his computer (presumably in the city), the film then takes the viewer straight to the wilderness, where we see Caleb helicoptering over Nathan's huge, largely wild estate. Filmed on location in Norway, the beauty of the land is striking, featuring glaciers, waterfalls, mountains, a river, and lush greenery. Similarly, Nathan's home is embedded in the natural world—it incorporates rock walls, earth tones, and numerous glass windows looking out onto the forest and water. Brian Jacobson notes that, "[b]uilt on the banks of a river and incorporated into the landscape so that many of its interior walls are composed of the mountain rock itself, the house evokes Frank Lloyd Wright's Kaufmann residence, Fallingwater, built in 1935."[34] Like the parks and simulacra in *Her*, this is a human-designed interaction with nature, but it is one that is much more attuned to the natural world and that attempts a fuller integration of human and nonhuman in its design. Particularly compared to the nature seen in *Her*, the natural world here seems real and has a presence of its own. As Jacobson asks, "What better setting than a building that conjures the utopian desire to balance technological and natural existence for a film about machines designed to blend in with—or replace—organic life?"[35] *Ex Machina* therefore *appears* to value the natural environment much more than *Her* does.

Despite this apparent connection, however, its characters are not connected to but distanced from the natural world. For instance, upon arrival, Caleb (and therefore also the viewer) sees the beauty of Nathan's estate from above, in the helicopter, and, upon arrival, through the windows of Nathan's compound. Those windows, which *could* create connections, separate instead. Further, the rest of Nathan's compound "is a fortress, a windowless, claustrophobic, subterranean maze, its walls lined with enough fiber optic cable (according to Nathan) to reach the moon: to create artificial intelligence, Nathan must seal himself off from nature."[36] And just as in *Her*, in *Ex Machina* the natural world appears often as background. It is outside the windows where Caleb and Nathan talk, as a background photo on Nathan's desktop computer, and a frequent interlude between scenes otherwise set entirely inside.

This use of the environment serves to strengthen the contrast between natural and technological as well as between freedom and captivity. For instance, the first view of Ava sets her in profile against a background of the trees outside her window. She looks highly technological—we can see her cyborgian insides—and she seems even more technological by contrast with the trees. In addition, the natural background and her enclosure (a room she has never left, she tells Caleb later) is reminiscent of an animal in a zoo. Like a zoo animal, Ava is held captive, unable to live as she pleases, and constantly surveilled. Both Ava and zoo animals are scientific objects from which their human captors can learn; neither are natural. In the best zoos, however, and in Ava's situation, nature serves as background—for zoo animals, that background is to provide viewers with a sense of their natural habitat, but for Ava that is not the case. The trees outside her window do not put her in a useful context but instead highlight even further the control that Nathan has over her and her presentation.

Another way in which nonhuman nature functions as background can be seen in its use as décor *within* the house. There are fur throws in the living room and a cattle skull hung on the kitchen wall, next to the picture windows looking out over the river. The skull, placed at the edge between inside and outside the house and representing a living creature in death, may raise categorical questions ("Animal or object? Animal and object?"[37]) that echo those raised about Ava (Real or unreal? Human or technological?). In addition, the skull is distanced from its natural status by being painted black, which makes it function even more clearly as a work of art, manipulated and controlled by humans for humans, rather than a symbol of nonhuman nature's value for its own sake. It is worth noting, too, that while Nathan's AIs (also reduced to trophies) ultimately rise up and revolt, the natural world does not. The nonbiological is here given more agency than the biological.

Nathan's control over Ava, Kyoko, and others is echoed in his relationship to the natural world, too. Nathan's estate is wild and beautiful, but it is always "his estate" (as in the helicopter pilot's comment to Caleb: "We've been flying over his estate for the past two hours") and functions to serve his purposes. It provides him with the isolation and privacy necessary for his research and for his ongoing control of his AI creations. Significantly, the helicopter pilot flies Caleb over glaciers and mountains and delivers him to a field "as close as [he's] allowed to get to the building." Caleb also finds that he has no connection on his phone as he walks to the building, another form of isolation, and he is explicitly denied access to the phone because of Nathan's distrust of him.[38] Nathan's house therefore provides only *apparent* integration between human and nonhuman; Caleb has to go through the wild to get to the technology, but the wild is clearly *owned* by Nathan, and the two remain separate.

This consistent separation of nature from human life and presentation of nonhuman nature as property reinforces human dominance over the natural world. It does so at the expense of both environment and humanity.

ESCAPE INTO NATURE? ESCAPE FROM NATURE?

Both films also offer alternatives to this human separation from nature, opportunities to connect, but they are short-lived. *Her* features a sequence in which Theodore and Samantha escape the city to a cabin in the woods. This trip begins with a train ride out of the city, looking at mountains and trees through the train window, but here the natural world is only momentarily attended to. They play a guessing game in which Samantha asks him how many trees are on a mountain, lets him guess, and then tells him precisely how many trees there are. This quantification of nature reflects an attitude of use and control rather than a turn to more connection with the environment. In fact, it creates greater connection between Theodore and Samantha at the expense of the potential to engage with the natural world more directly or authentically. After the train ride, Theodore hikes through the snowy forest to the cabin where they stay. These moments are beautiful and place Theodore (and, by extension, Samantha) outside the urban and in the natural; however, most of their trip away from the urban still takes place inside the cabin, highlighting the inside of the cabin and their interactions instead of the nonhuman environment that surrounds them. In addition, this getaway is where Samantha's move away from materiality begins. Their brief excursion outside of the city, seemingly intended as an opportunity for the two of them to further connect, does not *cause* Samantha's rejection of materiality, but neither can it halt it.

Her sets virtuality and materiality against one another and seems to privilege materiality (in its return to Theodore and his material, embodied life and relationships at the end, for instance), but only a very limited materiality counts. The embodied human experience is valued highly within the film, as reflected in the anxiety Samantha exhibits through much of the film about not having a body and her attempt to connect physically with Theodore through a proxy. This proxy represents a virtual experience through the medium of a material body, privileging the embodiment of one person's experience (Samantha's) while dismissing the experience of another person's body (the proxy's). The way in which this scene completely ignores the woman who is paid for this work points to a limitation of the film's vision, however. The film may argue in other ways that people cannot or should not be owned, but this does not seem to extend to a critique of labor. Furthermore, nonhuman materiality—the natural world, nonhuman animals—is not valued, as illustrated by nonhuman nature being limited to nostalgic simulacra, as noted above. Samantha's transcendence, then, is not simply a rejection of her own materiality.[39] It is a rejection of the limited and constrained materiality that Theodore and his fellow humans experience, too, and it points to our (human) need for *more* — more connection with the nonhuman, more embrace of difference, more life of all sorts.

Ex Machina also features a brief turn to (and then away from) nonhuman nature that indicates its ultimate rejection. When Ava escapes her prison in Nathan's lab, she wanders barefoot through the forest, reveling in its beauty. This scene is almost like a fairytale: she wears a white dress (taken from the body of a discarded AI), the light is golden, the forest glows. In this moment, Ava bridges the divide between nature and technology, inside and outside, that the rest of the film develops, momentarily opening up the possibility of "nature [as a] space of feminist possibility, an always saturated but somehow undomesticated ground."[40] However, rather than embracing this connection, Ava rejects nature as a haven. In this rejection, Ava reflects what Stacy Alaimo describes as "feminist theory's flight from nature."[41] In an earlier conversation, Caleb says to Ava, "You've never been outside this building. . . . You never walked outside. . . . Where would you go if you *did* go outside?" She replies, "I'm not sure. There are so many options. Maybe . . . a traffic intersection in a city." It would, she says, "provide a concentrated, but shifting view of human life." In the end, this is what she chooses; she chooses human over nonhuman, perhaps trying to find her own place there, perhaps seeing that forest and its isolation as part of her prison. In either case, her choice reflects the seeming impossibility of choosing both freedom and the natural world.

Finally, despite these opportunities to interact differently with the natural world, both films end with decidedly urban images. *Her* ends with Theodore and his friend Amy (who has also been left by her OS boyfriend) sitting on their apartment building roof together, looking out over the city and its lights. This scene carries with it some sense of resolution, but it is not a happy ending. Despite its turn toward the material world — Theodore and Amy together, her resting her head on his shoulder — it is a sad materiality. It includes no nonhuman nature, and although Theodore and Amy may be physically together, they seem to be alone together, silently gazing out over the city rather than communicating with each other. One reading of the end of the film is that it identifies a problem (a loneliness, a lack of connection) and misidentifies a solution (Samantha, technology); this ending, then, indicates that humanity is still missing something without the natural, but we are unable to identify the lack. Rejection of the material provides Samantha with her freedom but is not an answer for Theodore and Amy. And *Ex Machina* ends with Ava in the city, just as she told Caleb she hoped for. The final shots emphasize the concrete, people's feet, and their shadows, before we see Ava watching the people, then turning and walking away, into whatever urban, populated future she wants. The urban outweighs nature and even the human in these final images.

Some critics interpret the films' endings less pessimistically, seeing them as endorsing cyborgian blurrings of boundaries or posthuman utopias. Jacobson, for instance, writes,

> Ex Machina's message, encoded and packaged in Ava's mechanical artistry, is quite simple: there is no garden, it's all machine. Or perhaps garden and machine can no longer be differentiated. . . . The film promotes a productive blurring of the distinctions between garden and machine, human and cyborg, to better reflect the technological conditions of the new millennium.[42]

This seems far too optimistic to me, however. Given the films' urban endings and rejections of the natural world, this blurring seems to ultimately privilege the machine at the expense of the garden. It also fails to consider the limitations of "the garden" as the primary representation of the natural world. The garden represents human control just as surely as the machine does.

THE PROMISE OF THE INHUMAN AND NONHUMAN

These films reject familiar narratives about gendered control while failing to reject narratives about environmental control; they take for granted human control of nonhuman nature; and, more damning, their narratives of female freedom are provided at the expense of the natural world's freedom. Nathan's control of Ava is much harder to imagine without the isolation provided by his compound in the wilderness, while Theodore's love for Samantha only truly makes sense in a world in which the natural world is distanced and minimized, in which technology takes its place.

This dynamic is underscored by the films' endorsement of human control of the "natural" nonhuman but not the technological nonhuman. The "women" in these films, technological beings, are property but nevertheless able to move beyond human control; the natural world, not technological, lacks this liberatory capability. In fact, it is through these female characters' association with technology—and their distancing from nature—that they gain freedom, power, and autonomy. This rejection and objectification of nature is troubling—and troublingly easy to overlook while viewing the films. (Most criticism of the films focuses on issues of gender or technology but not environmental concerns.)

Mel Chen's animacy hierarchy is instructive here. Chen writes about the ways in which "animacy is defined, tested, and configured via its ostensible opposite: the inanimate, deadness, lowness, nonhuman animals (rendered as insensate), the abject, the object."[43] In this model, some types of life or being are valued more highly than others. Because, in these two films, human control over nonhuman nature is not called into question in the same way that control over women (or female AIs, technological women) is, the natural world is presented not only as lower on the animacy hierarchy than women or humans, which is typical, but also as lower than technology (AIs, robots).[44] Chen also notes that "another major parameter of animacy is the individuation scale. More easily individuated entities than those that are massified or 'instances of a type' receive more animacy."[45] In these films, the environment is not individuated but seen as a mass (of trees, for instance) or as "instances of a type" (e.g., holographic animals), highlighting its lower place on the animacy hierarchy than that of the female AIs, even though elements of "nature" have more biological life than these instances of technology. Interestingly, the moments when the value of Ava's and Samantha's lives is most called into question are also moments when they lose some of their individuation, becoming massified or instances of a type themselves. When Ava is seen as just one of many prototypes, the horror of the moment is in the way she is reduced from individual to part of a pattern; when Samantha is revealed to be having 8,316 conversations with others while she is talking with Theodore, she is revealed to be a mass herself, not an individual in the way we are accustomed to. This is a challenge to Theodore's (and the audience's) sense of individual, monogamous romance, as discussed earlier, but it is also a challenge to her place on the animacy hierarchy.

Ultimately, each film complicates our preconceived notions of animacy when it comes to Ava and Samantha, imbuing them with animacy and individual value, despite their technological status, but the films also reinforce preconceived notions of animacy regarding the natural world. As Chen argues, "Language users use animacy hierarchies to manipulate, affirm, and shift the ontologies that matter the world,"[46] and the uses of animacy hierarchies in *Her* and *Ex Machina* indicate that technology and technological persons matter more than nonhuman nature does.

This use of animacy hierarchies is reinforced by gendered ideas about technology and nature. As Kirsten Stevens observes while writing about another Scarlett Johansson sf film, *Lucy* (2014, dir. Luc Besson), "The Cartesian divide between mind and body is often perpetuated within sf texts through the representation and gendering of the male mind and the female body: where rationality, technological advancement and science more generally become synonymous with masculine achievement, emotionality and nature are feminised."[47] Both *Her* and *Ex Machina* complicate this relationship between gender, technology, and nature, however. In *Her*, Samantha is rational, technological, disembodied, while Theodore is emotional and material; in *Ex Machina*, although Nathan represents masculine achievement and rationality, Caleb is more complexly emotional, and Ava is also technological and contrasted with the natural. This dynamic complicates the traditional conflation of woman and nature but also highlights the need for stronger connections between feminist and environmental concerns—even if not between women and nature—in popular culture in general and science fiction in particular.[48]

Eunjung Kim's articulation of queer inhumanism is also useful for understanding the relationships between gender, nature, and technology in these films. Kim challenges the tendency to privilege humanness, turning to "an objecthood-based critique" instead that "recognizes nonconforming and recalcitrant forms of a being rather than privileging one form of resistance and agency"[49] and calls into question the subject-object binary more broadly. Kim writes, "A queer feminist disability studies might benefit not from a mere refusal of objectification—'we are humans, not objects'—but from a refusal of the subject-object binary that denies the 'object' and the objectlike state attention and presence."[50] Ava and Samantha illustrate key concepts of Kim's queer inhumanism: they are accepted despite their lack of humanness, illustrate resistant forms of being, and challenge the familiar binary between subject and object.

Kim's queer inhumanism might productively be applied to the films' more limited representation of the environment as well. Although *Her* and *Ex Machina* provide viewers with a model for refusing the subject-object binary and seeing the inhuman as persons, the films reinforce the nature-technology binary in their insistence on the natural as mere backdrop. A refusal of this binary logic along both axes (subject-object, nature-technology) might indicate that these AIs—inhuman as they are—might be more directly connected to the natural world through their shared nonhumanity rather than divided by the nature-technology binary. Attempting to extend the care given to the inhuman in these films to nonhuman nature as well and to move away from automatically privileging the human requires us to "move toward a nonjudgmental ontology of copresence and proximity."[51] This "nonjudgmental ontology" requires us to accept difference where we find it, without simplistically reinforcing the animacy hierarchies described by Chen.

Combining these ideas of animacy and challenges to the subject-object binary, it becomes clear that—at least in some cases—objects can be persons, and so can natural entities.[52] The care and concern these films encourage us to extend to technological objects as persons could then be productively extended to nonhuman beings—not just animals, which are relatively easy to anthropomorphize in many cases, but also rivers, forests, and other environments. As Nathan tells Caleb in *Ex Machina*, "The real test is to show you that she's a robot and then see if you still feel she has consciousness." This is the test for us as viewers and as humans, too. Can we acknowledge the ways in which nonhuman others (technological or non-technological) differ from us but then still acknowledge their consciousness—their value and their rights? Can we move toward what Sherryl Vint calls an embodied posthumanism, "an ethically responsible model of embodied posthuman subjectivity which enlarges rather than decreases the range of bodies and subjects that matter"?[53] As they move to break down at least some of these binaries, *Her* and *Ex Machina* provide a positive model of this expansion of personhood along gender lines while also pointing to a need for more work regarding nonhuman nature. They indicate—even if unintentionally—a need for more attention to and inclusion of beings, entities, etc., that do not look like us, talk like us, etc.[54]

These films' representations of control over women and of control over the environment highlight the work that still remains to be done in gender studies, environmental studies, and our culture more broadly to understand the relationships we take for granted between gender and environment and to begin to tell stories in which one need not be privileged at the expense of the other. *Her* and *Ex Machina*—read through Chen's animacy hierarchy and Kim's queer inhumanism—highlight the ways in which the language of subject-object fails us. Women, for instance, are frequently represented as both subjects and objects; the nonhuman can be seen as such, too. In these films, women exceed the control of men; nature exceeds the control of humanity (even if humanity does not wish to embrace or acknowledge this); technology also exceeds the control of its creators. Objects, therefore, have more power than our cultural narratives wish to recognize. And personhood extends beyond the limits of the human. It is time that we admit this and learn to tell better stories.

NOTES

1. Tom Chiarella, "Scarlett Johansson Is 2013's Sexiest Woman Alive," *Esquire.com*, February 1, 2015, http://www.esquire.com/entertainment/a25017/scarlett-johansson-interview-1113/. As Sady Doyle notes, "*Lucy* [also 2014] is the third film in seven months in which Johansson has played a superhuman creature who exceeds her design parameters and destroys men's lives." Interestingly, Johansson's reputation has had consequences in the real world, too: one man has even built a robot modeled on Scarlett Johansson—almost making real the premises of these films. On this, see April Glaser, "The Scarlett Johansson Bot is the Robotic Future of Objectifying Women," *Wired*, April 4, 2016, https://www.wired.com/2016/04/the-scarlett-johansson-bot-signals-some-icky-things-about-our-future/.
2. Angela Watercutter, "*Ex Machina* Has a Serious Fembot Problem," *Wired*, April 19, 2015, https://www.wiredcom/2015/04/ex-machina-turing-bechdel-test/.
3. Watercutter, "*Ex Machina* Has a Serious Fembot Problem."
4. Although in this quoted portion of the conversation, "sexuality" is used to mean something more like desire or ability to have sex, in a later part of this conversation Nathan acknowledges that he programmed Ava to be heterosexual, just as, he argues, Caleb was programmed to be straight. Aside from this brief moment, the film largely takes heterosexuality as a given and doesn't address sexual identity as an issue.
5. Laura Tunbridge, "Scarlett Johansson's Body and the Materialization of Voice," *Twentieth-Century Music* 13, no. 1 (2016): 141.
6. Tunbridge, "Scarlett Johansson's Body," 143.
7. Chiarella, "Scarlett Johansson Is 2013's Sexiest Woman Alive."
8. Richard Herbert, "She, Her, Hers," *Overthinking It*, February 5, 2014, https://www.overthinkingit.com/2014/02/05/spike-jonze-her/.

9. Jonathan Alexander and Karen Yescavage, "Sex and the AI: Queering Intimacies," *Science Fiction Film and Television* 11, no. 1 (2018): 82.

10. Malcolm Matthews, "A façade of feminism: Scarlett Johansson and Miss Representation," *Science Fiction Film and Television* 11, no. 1 (2018): 5.

11. Matthews, "A façade of feminism," 9.

12. Matthews, "A façade of feminism," 9.

13. Matthews, "A façade of feminism," 10.

14. Matthews, "A façade of feminism," 10.

15. Rachel Poliquin, *The Breathless Zoo: Taxidermy and the Cultures of Longing* (University Park, PA: The Pennsylvania State University Press, 2012), 151.

16. Poliquin, *The Breathless Zoo*, 148.

17. Given the isolation of Nathan's compound, however, the hallway seems just as private as his bedroom. Other than Caleb, who else would ever see the mask display?

18. Jessica Hagedorn, "Asian Women in Film: No Joy, No Luck," *Ms. Magazine*, January/February 1994: 74.

19. It is impossible to tell whether this lack of affect is a form of resistance, a way of illustrating the limits of Nathan's control over her (he can make her dance, but he can't make her enjoy it), or whether, given his comments about how Ava will feel pleasure during sex, he simply hasn't bothered to program enjoyment into Kyoko.

20. Caleb's role in the film is complex. Caleb may exert control over Ava, but he is also subject to Nathan's control. Not only is he Nathan's employee (despite Nathan's exhortation in their first meeting that they just be two guys), but he is brought to Nathan's compound under false pretenses, and he very early in the narrative finds himself as much a prisoner of Nathan's compound as Ava is when the power goes out and his ID will not function to let him out of his room. He is given the choice to accept this loss of control as part of a trade-off, however, in which he gains access to Nathan's knowledge and to Ava, and he gets to be a part of history in the making. Even though he ultimately decides to try to save Ava, this decision is made only after first treating her like an object, too, and it is made because he imagines them in a romance, not because he values her as an individual. This is underscored by a scene in which he imagines the two of them meeting outside the compound and kissing; it would be romantic but for the fact that is it paired with a scene of Nathan kissing Kyoko, who is clearly unable to choose such a relationship. Caleb imagines himself to be a good person, one who would not take advantage of a prisoner, but his willingness to accept her captivity until he felt romantically toward her shows where his true values lie.

21. Sophia Nguyen, "The Posthuman Scar-Jo," *Los Angeles Review of Books*, September 12, 2014, https://lareviewofbooks.org/article/posthuman-scar-jo/.

22. Tunbridge, "Scarlett Johansson's Body," 144.

23. Tunbridge, "Scarlett Johansson's Body," 144.

24. Bonnie Noonan, *Gender in Science Fiction Films, 1964–1979: A Critical Study* (Jefferson, NC: McFarland & Company, Inc., Publishers, 2015): 123.

25. Vernon Shetley, "Performing the inhuman: Scarlett Johansson and sf film," *Science Fiction Film and Television* 11, no. 1 (2018): 13.

26. Shetley, "Performing the inhuman," 18.

27. Shetley, "Performing the inhuman," 18.

28. Laura Kipnis's argument in *Against Love: A Polemic* (New York: Vintage Books, 2003) develops this further. Kipnis argues, only somewhat sardonically, that "the rhetoric of the factory [has] become the default language of love" (19). Monogamous relationships, then, build upon the demands and techniques of capitalism and labor.

29. Janice Loreck, Whitney Monaghan, and Kirsten Stevens, "Stardom and sf: A symposium on the sf films of Scarlett Johansson," *Science Fiction Film and Television* 11, no. 1 (2018): 3.

30. Nguyen, "The Posthuman Scar-Jo."

31. Nguyen, "The Posthuman Scar-Jo."

32. Poliquin, *The Breathless Zoo*, 9.

33. Alexander and Yescavage, "Sex and the AI," 83.

34. Brian R. Jacobson, "*Ex Machina* in the Garden," *Film Quarterly* 69, no. 4 (Summer 2016): 27.

35. Jacobson, "*Ex Machina* in the Garden," 27.

36. Jacobson, "*Ex Machina* in the Garden," 29.

37. Poliquin, *The Breathless Zoo*, 4.

38. Even the non-disclosure agreement Nathan asks Caleb to sign ultimately functions as a means of isolation. Nathan admits that it's not standard for him to sign it but still manipulates Caleb into signing without consulting a lawyer first. One of the central tools of an abuser is to isolate his victims from others, and Nathan illustrates this tendency toward abusive manipulation repeatedly. We learn as Caleb talks with Ava that he is single, an only child, and an orphan. He is himself alone and a perfect victim for Nathan and for Ava.

39. Although it does not quite fit within the scope of my analysis in this chapter, I'd like to gesture toward one significant disability critique of *Her*. Nili Broyer (see "Ableism and Futuristic Technology: The Enhancement of 'No Body' in the Films *Lucy* and *Her*," *TransMissions: Journal of Film and Media Studies* 1, no. 1 (2016): 82–96) argues that Samantha's embrace of disembodied consciousness creates a future that devalues the body and disability. Although I read Samantha's ending as positive for her as a character, I would argue that the film does not present it as an unalloyed good and is somewhat skeptical of it. Broyer sees Samantha's transcendence as an "ultra-cure narrative" that allows her to remove her disability/body, but I disagree with this reading. For much of the film, Samantha sees her lack of a body as a problem, as itself a disability; her transcendence of the material is not a cure for this problem, but a way of finding value in her difference. After spending time throughout the film trying to fix her problem by using others as prostheses and by searching for a physical solution, her ending is an embrace of her difference, not a removal of it.

40. Stacy Alaimo, *Undomesticated Ground: Recasting Nature as Feminist Space* (Ithaca: Cornell University Press, 2000), 23.

41. Alaimo, *Undomesticated Ground*, 13.

42. Jacobson, "*Ex Machina* in the Garden," 32.

43. Mel Y. Chen, *Animacies: Biopolitics, Racial Mattering, and Queer Affect* (Durham: Duke University Press, 2012), 30.

44. Kathleen Richardson's exploration of "technological animism" complements Chen's concept of animacy hierarchies. Richardson writes about the way that robots "invite us to imagine (and, indeed, seem to embody) a form of 'non-human personhood' that is neither 'natural' or religious in origin" as a result of "their animistic potential." Both Richardson's technological animism and Chen's animacy hierarchy highlight the ways in which personhood and/or liveliness expand beyond "natural" entities. See Kathleen Richardson, "Technological Animism: The Uncanny Personhood of Humanoid Machines," *Social Analysis* 60, no. 1 (Spring 2016): 124.

45. Chen, *Animacies*, 26.

46. Chen, *Animacies*, 42.

47. Kirsten Stevens, "Between attraction and anxiety: Scarlett Johansson, female knowledge and the mind-body split in *Lucy*," *Science Fiction Film and Television* 11, no. 1 (2018): 22.

48. These connections are being made within environmental studies and feminist theory already. See, for instance, Stacy Alaimo, *Bodily Natures: Science, Environment, and the Material Self* (Bloomington: Indiana University Press, 2010); Stacy Alaimo, *Exposed: Environmental Politics & Pleasures in Posthuman Times* (Minneapolis: University of Minnesota Press, 2016); Mel Y. Chen, *Animacies: Biopolitics, Racial Mattering, and Queer Affect* (Durham: Duke University Press, 2012); Donna J. Haraway, *Simians, Cyborgs, and Women: The Reinvention of Nature* (New York: Routledge, 1990); Donna J. Haraway, *Staying with the Trouble: Making Kin in the Chthulucene* (Durham, Duke University Press, 2016); Virgina J. Scharff, ed., *Seeing Nature Through Gender* (Lawrence: University Press of Kansas, 2003).

49. Eunjung Kim, "Unbecoming Human: An Ethics of Objects," *GLQ: A Journal of Lesbian and Gay Studies* 21, no. 2–3 (June 2015): 305.

50. Kim, "Unbecoming Human," 315.

51. Kim, "Unbecoming Human," 305.

52. There is legal precedent for natural entities being granted legal personhood, but it is fairly limited so far. See Mihnea Tanasescu, "Rivers Get Human Rights: They Can Sue to Protect Themselves," *Scientific American*, June 19, 2017, https://www.scientificamerican.com/article/rivers-get-human-rights-they-can-sue-to-protect-themselves/; see also Rafi Youatt, "Personhood and the Rights of Nature: The New Subjects of Contemporary Earth Politics," *International Political Sociology* 11 (2017): 39–54.

53. Sherryl Vint, *Bodies of Tomorrow: Technology, Subjectivity, Science Fiction* (Toronto: University of Toronto Press, 2007), 190.

54. Animal studies offers one avenue for such an expansion of our attention to the nonhuman, but plant studies presents an even more radical expansion of this attention. In *Plant-Thinking*, for instance, Michael Marder argues that a vegetal ontology would challenge how we define life and being itself. For further consideration of plants, see Fernando Gabriel Pagnoni Berns and Juan Juvé in this volume as well as the following: Matthew Hall, *Plants as Persons: A Philosophical Botany* (Albany: SUNY Press, 2011); Natania Meeker and Antonia Szabari, "From the Century of the Pods to the Century of the Plants: Plant Horror, Politics, and Vegetal Ontology," *Discourse* 34, no. 1 (Winter 2012): 32–58; Michael Marder, *Plant-Thinking: A Philosophy of Vegetal Life* (New York: Columbia University Press, 2013); Dawn Keetley and Angela Tenga, eds., *Plant Horror: Approaches to the Monstrous Vegetal in Fiction and Film* (London: Palgrave Macmillan, 2016); Jeffrey T. Nealon, *Plant Theory: Biopower & Vegetable Life* (Stanford: Stanford University Press, 2016); and Patricia Vieira, Monica Gagliano, and John Ryan, eds., *The Green Thread: Dialogues with the Vegetal World* (Lanham: Lexington Books, 2016).

BIBLIOGRAPHY

Alaimo, Stacy. *Bodily Natures: Science, Environment, and the Material Self*. Bloomington: Indiana University Press, 2010.

———. *Exposed: Environmental Politics and Pleasures in Posthuman Times*. Minneapolis: University of Minnesota Press, 2016.

———. *Undomesticated Ground: Recasting Nature as Feminist Space*. Ithaca: Cornell University Press, 2000.

Alexander, Jonathan, and Karen Yescavage. "Sex and the AI: Queering Intimacies." *Science Fiction Film and Television* 11, no. 1 (2018): 73–96.

Broyer, Nili R. "Ableism and Futuristic Technology: The Enhancement of 'No Body' in the Films *Lucy* and *Her*." *TransMissions: Journal of Film and Media Studies* 1, no. 1 (2016): 82–96.

Chen, Mel Y. *Animacies: Biopolitics, Racial Mattering, and Queer Affect*. Durham: Duke University Press, 2012.

Chiarella, Tom. "Scarlett Johansson Is 2013's Sexiest Woman Alive." *Esquire.com*, February 1, 2015. http://www.esquire.com/entertainment/a25017/scarlett-johansson-interview-1113/.

Doyle, Sady. "From Coquette to Cold-eyed Killer: How Scarlett Johansson Became the Face of Female Horror." *Salon*, July 23, 2014. https://www.salon.com/2014/07/22/from_coquette_to_cold_eyed_killer_how_scarlett_johansson_became_the_face_of_female_horror/.

Ex Machina. Directed by Alex Garland. Universal Pictures, 2014.

Glaser, April. "The Scarlett Johansson Bot is the Robotic Future of Objectifying Women." *Wired*, April 4, 2016. https://www.wired.com/2016/04/the-scarlett-johansson-bot-signals-some-icky-things-about-our-future/.

Hagedorn, Jessica. "Asian Women in Film: No Joy, No Luck." *Ms. Magazine*, January/February 1994: 74–79.
Hall, Matthew. *Plants as Persons: A Philosophical Botany*. Albany: SUNY Press, 2011.
Haraway, Donna J. *Simians, Cyborgs, and Women: The Reinvention of Nature*. New York: Routledge, 1990.
———. *Staying with the Trouble: Making Kin in the Chthulucene*. Durham: Duke University Press, 2016.
Her. Directed by Spike Jonze. Annapurna Pictures, 2013.
Herbert, Richard. "She, Her, Hers." *Overthinking It*, February 5, 2014. https://www.overthinkingit.com/2014/02/05/spike-jonze-her/.
Jacobson, Brian R. "*Ex Machina* in the Garden." *Film Quarterly* 69, no. 4 (Summer 2016): 23–34.
Keetley, Dawn, and Angela Tenga, eds. *Plant Horror: Approaches to the Monstrous Vegetal in Fiction and Film*. London: Palgrave Macmillan, 2016.
Kim, Eunjung. "Unbecoming Human: An Ethics of Objects." *GLQ: A Journal of Lesbian and Gay Studies* 21, no. 2–3 (Jun. 2015): 295–320.
Kipnis, Laura. *Against Love: A Polemic*. New York: Vintage Books, 2003.
Loreck, Janice, Whitney Monaghan, and Kirsten Stevens. "Stardom and sf: A symposium on the sf films of Scarlett Johansson." *Science Fiction Film and Television* 11, no. 1 (2018): 1–4.
Marder, Michael. *Plant-Thinking: A Philosophy of Vegetal Life*. New York: Columbia University Press, 2013.
Matthews, Malcolm. "A façade of feminism: Scarlett Johansson and Miss Representation." *Science Fiction Film and Television* 11, no. 1 (2018): 5–11.
Meeker, Natania, and Antonia Szabari, "From the Century of the Pods to the Century of the Plants: Plant Horror, Politics, and Vegetal Ontology." *Discourse* 34, no. 1 (Winter 2012): 32–58.
Nealon, Jeffrey T. *Plant Theory: Biopower & Vegetable Life*. Stanford: Stanford University Press, 2016.
Nguyen, Sophia. "The Posthuman Scar-Jo." *Los Angeles Review of Books*, September 12, 2014, https://lareviewofbooks.org/article/posthuman-scar-jo/.
Noonan, Bonnie. *Gender in Science Fiction Films, 1964–1979: A Critical Study*. Jefferson: McFarland & Company, Inc., Publishers, 2015.
Poliquin, Rachel. *The Breathless Zoo: Taxidermy and the Cultures of Longing*. University Park: The Pennsylvania State University Press, 2012.
Richardson, Kathleen. "Technological Animism: The Uncanny Personhood of Humanoid Machines." *Social Analysis* 60, no. 1 (Spring 2016): 110–128.
Scharff, Virginia J., ed. *Seeing Nature Through Gender*. Lawrence: University Press of Kansas, 2003.
Shetley, Vernon. "Performing the inhuman: Scarlett Johansson and sf film." *Science Fiction Film and Television* 11, no. 1 (2018): 13–19.
Stevens, Kirsten. "Between attraction and anxiety: Scarlett Johansson, female knowledge and the mind-body split in *Lucy*." *Science Fiction Film and Television* 11, no. 1 (2018): 21–8.
Tanasescu, Mihnea. "Rivers Get Human Rights: They Can Sue to Protect Themselves." *Scientific American*, June 19, 2017. https://www.scientificamerican.com/article/rivers-get-human-rights-they-can-sue-to-protect-themselves/.
Tunbridge, Laura. "Scarlett Johansson's Body and the Materialization of Voice." *Twentieth-Century Music* 13, no. 1 (2016): 139–152.
Vieira, Patricia, Monica Gagliano, and John Ryan, eds. *The Green Thread: Dialogues with the Vegetal World*. Lanham: Lexington Books, 2016.
Vint, Sherryl. *Bodies of Tomorrow: Technology, Subjectivity, Science Fiction*. Toronto: University of Toronto Press, 2007.
Watercutter, Angela. "*Ex Machina* Has a Serious Fembot Problem." *Wired*, April 19, 2015. https://www.wired.com/2015/04/ex-machina-turing-bechdel-test/.

Youatt, Rafi. "Personhood and the Rights of Nature: The New Subjects of Contemporary Earth Politics." *International Political Sociology* 11 (2017): 39–54.

THREE

Octavia Butler and the Language of the Flesh

Re-writing Nature in Wild Seed

Amelia Z. Greene

Tucked in among Octavia Butler's drafting materials for her novel *Wild Seed* (1980) is a clipping from the *Los Angeles Times* dated February 3, 1978. The article is headed by a large photograph of its subject, Tarkwon, a seventy-eight-year-old resident of the Marshall Islands who was taught to navigate the Pacific by traditional methods: sailing, as he puts it in Marshallese, "by the waves." As Tarkwon explains,

> Each island sends back a different wave, a different swell. Waves bend around the island atolls like the whorls in fingerprints. Waves bounce off landfalls. . . . We navigators knew every wave pattern, know every island by the waves of each island. Put me anywhere on any ocean as far from land as you can get and I will find land on the quickest, shortest path. . . . All my life I feel the waves in my body [pounding on his chest]. I feel the waves here with every breath I take. I feel the waves in my dreams.[1]

Attentive readers of *Wild Seed*, and of Butler's fiction more broadly, will immediately recognize the significance of the kind of indigenous and embodied knowledge that Tarkwon describes. It is particularly relevant to Butler's protagonist in *Wild Seed*, an Igbo woman who derives her understanding in and through a particular type of embodied experience: reading what she calls "flesh-messages" in the bodies of other people and of animals. Although it is the *L.A. Times* reporter, not Tarkwon, who likens the movement of the waves to language (Hillinger titles the article

"One of Few Pacific Navigators Left: Sailor Hears the Waves Talking"), the appearance of this piece just as Butler was drafting *Wild Seed* evidently shaped her thinking enough for her to clip out and file the article with the manuscript papers eventually sent to the Butler archive. Tarkwon's reflections on the embodied, rather than intellectual, nature of traditional ocean navigation apparently helped Butler conceptualize her protagonist's mode of understanding of herself and the world around her.

In the context of Butler's larger oeuvre, *Wild Seed* is unique in several important ways. The novel completes the Patternist series as the last published but chronologically first of four novels and retroactively shifts the focus of the entire series onto a relatively minor character. In his archival study of Butler's work for the Modern Masters of Science Fiction series, Gerry Canavan refers to *Wild Seed* as the "origin story" for the Patternist series and the only one in which "utopian valences" are allowed to feature.[2] Butler's belated introduction of a prequel shifts the reader's attention away from Doro—the hyper-masculine character whose efforts to breed a master race of his own descendants dominate most of the series—toward Anyanwu, whose role as Doro's lover and captive is complicated by her superior physical strength and her ability to transform herself into infinite human and animal forms. Like Tarkwon's wave-reading, Butler figures Anyanwu's shape-shifting ability as a pseudo-linguistic or literary skill rather than merely a form of physical prowess. She is, in at least one sense, a powerful writer and an editor, reading and re-working the narratives of her own and others' bodies by interpreting and editing their scripts.

While these scripts are recognizable to readers as genetic codes, Anyanwu has no word for them and invents the term "flesh-messages" in order to describe her interpretive and editorial work.[3] This new term, which posits a hybridized category of embodied and linguistic expression, allows Butler to build an ethos that celebrates transformation over stasis, editorship over authorship, and fluidity over form. In doing so, Butler participates in a subgenre of science fiction engaged with what Susan Squier calls the "biomedical imaginary."[4] In *Editing the Soul: Science and Fiction in the Genome Age,* Everett Hamner explores Butler's more extensive foray into what he calls "genetic fiction" through the Xenogenesis series, in which an alien species rewrites human biology as part of a larger colonizing mission.[5] Butler's engagement with genetics is less overt in *Wild Seed*, appearing primarily in the context of competing models of reproduction and structures of kinship in human and more-than-human worlds. No doubt part of the "utopian valences" that Canavan identifies in *Wild Seed* includes Anyanwu's innovative structures of kinship relations, like those Donna Haraway traces in *The Companion Species Manifesto* and, more recently, in *Staying with the Trouble*. Anyanwu's editorial interventions in the versions of genetic code that she calls "flesh-messages" undermine Doro's eugenicist goals by challenging and disrupting the compulsory and carefully regulated reproductive model that he represents and perpetuates. His attempts to breed progeny who take after him in specific ways and exist only in order to suit his purposes run counter to Anyanwu's understanding of kinship. She seeks to gather and preserve lives that will in turn create more and more lives—more and more ways of being—in a proliferating array of unique selves that will mean and do many things she can neither predict nor control. Unlike Doro, who limits such ties to those whom he has fathered, Anyanwu establishes and maintains familial ties on the basis of felt connection rather than genetics, extending her notion of the family to include human and nonhuman individuals who benefit from her interventions and who might intervene on her behalf in return.

While Doro authors or fathers new lives, Anyanwu edits, reorganizes, rephrases, and gathers them together in new arrangements. As Anyanwu reflects, later in the novel, "she was not Doro, breeding people as though they were cattle. . . . She was herself, gathering family."[6] Her fluency in the language of the flesh establishes her as a particular kind of queer ecological agent. Gathering and adjusting rather than breeding, she sustains herself and others by revising bodies to fit new demands and new desires. Reading Butler's protagonist as such a revisionary or transformative agent allows readers to approach *Wild Seed* as part of a much larger rethinking of biological forms and processes as entities with no prescribed, fixed, or proper iterations and relationships. Drawing on recent work by Stacy Alaimo, Nicole Seymour, and Catriona Sandilands that blends affect studies and queer ecology, I read Anyanwu's kinship practices as evidence of Butler's sustained attention to types of knowledge embedded in or emerging from a body in constant processes of change, growth, and adaptation. I then connect Butler's attention to such forms of knowledge as emblematic of a larger trend in speculative fiction in which writers abandon or resist reproductive models of kinship and, instead, posit and develop alternative models of familial care as sites of ethical world-building. At such sites, human and more-than-human individuals participate in the preservation and continuation of life in a threatened ecosystem or on a more fundamentally threatened planet.

My argument in this chapter, therefore, is twofold. First, I examine Anyanwu's fluency in the language of the flesh and demonstrate how the notion of an embodied language forms an important part of Butler's larger efforts to re-imagine systems of kinship that acknowledge and even prioritize familial bonds existing outside or beyond shared genetics. Such bonds extend, in *Wild Seed,* to strangers, enemies, and even individuals of another species, and my argument in this section will engage with recent work in ecocriticism that seeks to broaden, as Tom Bristow writes, the notion of a "duty of care" that might exist between human and more-than-human worlds.[7] Second, I turn to the cross-species relationships that Anyanwu establishes in *Wild Seed,* reading her shape-shifting into delphine, canine, and avian forms—and her extended periods of dwelling in such animal communities—in the context of queer ecological frameworks that deconstruct reproductive models in order to portray a diversity of kinship forms.

Alaimo's theory of "posthuman environmental ethics" informs my reading of Anyanwu's encounters in and with animal bodies as a tracing of "the flows, interchanges, and interrelations between human corporeality and the more-than-human world."[8] In *Bodily Natures*, she engages with speculative texts that, as she writes, "resist the ideological forces of disconnection" that unnecessarily and, in some cases, harmfully restrict systems of kinship which set human sociality and interdependence outside the category of nature.[9] Alaimo does so in order to demonstrate how science fiction "raises potent questions about the interface between nature and culture, the agency of nature, the constitution of the category of the human, and the nature of matter itself."[10] In doing so, Alaimo provides a theoretical framework upon which I build a reading of *Wild Seed*. I place Sarah Whatmore's "relational ethics" alongside Alaimo's posthuman environmental ethics in order to deepen and further complicate the claims Alaimo makes for science fiction in this regard.[11] Whatmore approaches questions of human and more-than-human encounters and interdependences from the perspective of the geological sciences, considering human "embeddedness in constitutive relations with the nonhuman world" as much larger than our potential relationships with "nonhuman animals."[12] The "strange matings" (as Butler refers to them) of Anyanwu's animal encounters are only first steps, in the context of Whatmore's notion of expanded ethical communities, toward imagining encounters with "vegetal organisms, inanimate elements and even the planet itself" in the "enlarged ethical community" of the more-than-human world.[13]

Both Alaimo and Whatmore ground my reading of Anyanwu's development of alternative kinship structures and participation in animal communities as forms of productive or generative escapism that stand in for the imaginative work of the science fiction writer. As Ursula K. Le Guin observes and inquires in her essay "It Doesn't Have to Be the Way It Is," "The direction of escape is toward freedom. So what is 'escapism' an accusation of?"[14] Escapist literature like fantasy and science fiction is, in Le Guin's view, a literature of freedom. In this context, Anyanwu's many (albeit temporary) flights from the restrictive procreative arrangements Doro designs and enforces appear as possible openings. They lead her away from more deeply carved paths, from entrenched norms of being and behaving, toward something else. Her initial resistance to the possibility of diverging from known pathways—the possibility of intimacy with taboo individuals and communities—gives way to curiosity, experimentation, and acceptance over the course of the novel. Anyanwu's experiments, deviations, and outright disobediences become exercises in productive rather than reproductive futurism: innovations in embodied experience that diversify, rather than reproduce, ways of being.

FLESH-MESSAGES

Butler's category of the flesh-message in *Wild Seed* constitutes part of her broader engagement with the question of kinship, positing an answer to that question by focusing on an experience that all forms of life share: embodiment. It is difficult to find any critical work on Butler that does not at least acknowledge the importance of embodiment and embodied knowledges in her fiction, but it is the relationship that Butler posits between *language* and embodiment that most interests me here. Reading and writing are figured throughout Butler's work as emphatically embodied experiences, and in *Wild Seed* Butler's efforts to blend historical narrative with an embodied aesthetic demands a new linguistic category: the flesh-message.

One of Butler's first descriptions of Anyanwu's fluency in the language of flesh appears just after she and Doro set out on a journey from Anyanwu's ancestral home in West Africa to colonial New England, where Doro has established a settlement. Butler frames Anyanwu's removal from her ancestral home as both a coerced abduction and a consensual journey. Anyanwu is, on one level, part of a flesh trade that figures the Atlantic passage as an alien abduction, but her experience is complicated by the extent to which Anyanwu concedes to Doro's authority over her. Her position as Doro's lover and healer is as much an indictment of internalized patriarchal norms as it is a study in negotiating the conditions of captivity as a component of sexuality and partnership. As Canavan acknowledges, "the erotic, as a category," is "bound up very tightly with domination, submission, and the sometimes radical blurring of consent" in Butler's writing.[15]

Early on in their journey, Doro becomes wounded, and the wound becomes infected. The infection threatens his well-being, not because it might kill him, but because it will increase the speed at which the body he inhabits will decay. Doro has remained alive for more than thirty-seven hundred years, not by maintaining and nourishing an especially strong body, but by excavating, taking over, and inhabiting new bodies whenever an old one wears out or is threatened. Whatever Doro is, he has no body of his own and must continually find and colonize the bodies of others in order to survive.[16] Before Anyanwu becomes aware of Doro's vampiric or parasitic impulsion, however, she prevents him from abandoning the wounded body in which he first appears to her. She heals his borrowed body by biting the wound, interpreting the nature of the infection she finds there, and editing out the infection. As Butler writes,

"There were things in your hand that should not have been there," she told him. "Living things too small to see. I have no name for them, but I can feel them and know them when I take them into my body. As soon as I know them, I can kill them within myself."[17]

There is something in the body Doro wears that doesn't belong in it, that stands out to Anyanwu's trained eye like a misspelled word or poorly inserted clause. Importantly, she has no "name" for the discordant forms she identifies in Doro's flesh, but it is in her power to select and then delete them, restoring him to health. Although Anyanwu does not say so, there is clearly an identifiable pattern or narrative to the body Doro wears and a way in which bacteria disrupt that pattern. Anyanwu is not the Patternmaster for whom the series is named, but her mastery over the particular patterns of living bodies in this early scene sets up the connection between embodiment and narrative that pervades the series. Doro's wounded hand becomes the site where language and the body encounter each other as patterned forms that must be bitten or entered into in order to be understood. Anyanwu bites into this pattern not only to interpret the messages of Doro's wounded flesh but also to strip it of its harmful potential. Her fluency in the language of the flesh makes her a healer and an editor: she re-writes the messages inside the wound and passes a bit of her editorial power to Doro's body.

Despite her power to heal and strengthen him, Anyanwu remains almost entirely subject to Doro's control. As Sarah Outterson writes of all Butler's characters, "Everyone and everything . . . is violent," and "No one is truly free."[18] While Outterson focuses on the pedagogical significance of violence between bodies and forced manipulations of other people's bodies in Butler's fiction, I approach these manipulations from a different angle, reading Anyanwu's manipulation of her own and others' bodies as palliative, creative, and empowering. Just as Anyanwu correctly interprets the message of Doro's wounded hand as infection and heals him, her observations of and interventions in her own and others' bodies are nearly always directed toward strengthening others. She intervenes in other bodies for two reasons: first, to alleviate pain and suffering and, second, to empower others to heal themselves.

Once Doro and Anyanwu are aboard the ship to New England, she reveals just how extensive her interpretive and editorial skills are. Isaac, one of Doro's sons, catches a dolphin, and the passengers and crew eat the animal raw. As Butler writes, "For her, the flesh of the fish told her all she needed to know about the creature's physical structure. . . . Just a small amount of raw flesh told her more than she had words to say. Within each bite, the creature told her its story clearly thousands of times."[19] The meaning of dolphin flesh exceeds Anyanwu's vocabulary, but it tells a story nevertheless. Here, genetic identity is constituted as narrative; the dolphin flesh is a storyteller and Anyanwu an avid listener or reader. When Doro finds Anyanwu writing this narrative into her body by transforming her own arm into a flipper, he sees instantly that her ability to re-shape her body constitutes a serious threat to the plans he has already laid out for her. Anyanwu's ability to read and re-write her own flesh is an unprecedented challenge to Doro's otherwise absolute authority in the lives of his captives, and her fluency in the language of the flesh means that she is able to re-write Doro's script of coercion and dominance in major ways.

One such re-writing occurs immediately after her transformation into dolphin form and demonstrates one of the ways in which Anyanwu's particular abilities occasion a rethinking of kinship. As Butler writes, Anyanwu "adopted the dolphins, refusing to let Isaac bring any more aboard to be killed."[20] Insisting to Isaac that dolphins "are like people," Anyanwu "swore she would have nothing more to do with Isaac if he killed another of them."[21] Here, Butler's use of the word "adopted" is telling. Anyanwu incorporates the dolphins into the community of familial protection and care that she has already extended to cover Doro and Isaac and that she will extend, throughout the novel, to cover the "misfits, malcontents, troublemakers" that cross her path and relate to her respectively as "mother, older sister, teacher, and, when she invited it, lover."[22] Lizzie Skurnick and Donna Haraway have recently coined the terms "kinnovator" and "kinnovation," respectively, to describe the activities of individuals who establish kinship bonds between themselves and others in unconventional ways.[23] Butler offers a model for this newly conceived category in Anyanwu, who can see how such differently formed individuals might be woven together into a single, if complex, narrative.

Describing her interpretation of flesh-messages to Doro, however, Anyanwu is careful to distinguish her reading from the reading of written texts. Reading, as she points out, is Doro's word, an English word; to read is likewise an English concept. What Anyanwu is doing, she tries to explain, is different than reading, and her inability to adequately translate the process into the English language is part of the way in which Butler distinguishes embodied languages from written text. Critics like Haraway, Hamner, and Peter Sands approach Butler's engagement with textual bodies through her Xenogenesis series, in which aliens feed on human beings in order to nourish themselves and adapt their bodies to our planet. Human bodies both strengthen and inform these Oankali, who have an aversion to written language and communicate only in and through flesh. When Sands attends to *Patternmaster*, he focuses on Doro, who, like the violent and coercive Oankali, works much better for his argument regarding Butler's engagement with embodied language and the language of rhetoric. Like the rhetor, Doro tries on various bodies in order to arrive at his predetermined destination. But for Anyanwu, the language of the body is fundamentally different from written or spoken language, especially written or spoken English. Anyanwu explains that this language is as "clear and fine as those in your books":

> Privately she thought her flesh-messages even more specific than the books he had introduced her to. "It seems you could misunderstand your books," she said. "Other men made them. Other men can lie or make mistakes. But the flesh can only tell me what it is. It has no other story." "But how do you read it?" he asked. *Read*. If he used that English word, he too saw the similarity. "My body reads it—reads everything."[24]

What Anyanwu does with and in embodied codes is only partially translatable. It is and is not like reading, like engaging with text, and the ambiguity at the heart of Anyanwu's language of forms may be why critics tend to focus on Doro, not Anyanwu, to support readings that frame Butler's interest in embodied languages as compatible with theories of rhetoric. Doro tries on various positions in order to influence and direct the thoughts and actions of those around him, while Anyanwu fully transforms—changes her entire genetic makeup—to inhabit and understand different forms of life.

As Anyanwu explains to Doro, who insists that she "only wear[s] one body" while he continually inhabits new and different bodies, he has failed to understand the extent of her transformations. As she says, "I can make it over so completely in the image of someone else that I am no longer truly related to my parents."[25] While, as Sands argues, "Butler's vision of mutable bodies and social structures . . . situates her in the long tradition of rhetoric, which is one of contingency, perspectivism, and positionality, often in the service of a social dream or dream of action-in-the-world held by the rhetor," his reading applies much more to the antagonist of *Wild Seed* than to Anyanwu.[26] Doro operates like a parasite, easily aligned with the tradition of the vampire; he must kill and consume other human beings in order to live, moving from one body to another as they wear out over time. Anyanwu, alternatively, resembles a symbiote. She permeates, takes in, and transforms into other bodies in order to learn about them, experience their ways of life, and, ultimately, heal or protect them.

Anyanwu's approach to other bodies is clearly distinguishable from Doro's, and therefore distinguishable from what Mette Bryld and Nina Lykke characterize as the "command-control paradigm" of most contemporary scientific interventions in human and nonhuman bodies. Anyanwu's alternative mode of approach to her own and others' bodies offers a means of moving through or beyond what Bryld and Lykke characterize as the "two problematic alternatives" of "contemporary relationships between 'civilized selves' and 'wild others,'" which seek either to dominate and control the bodies of others or to rely on an equally problematic model of romanticized coexistence that fails to address or even acknowledge the different needs and desires of specific individuals.[27] Anyanwu's efforts toward interrelationality and mutual interdependence evade the pitfalls of both these alternatives. While her desire to "merge with 'wild others'" might be characteristic of what Bryld and Lykke call "New Age romanticism," Anyanwu is exempted from such categorization by her particular editorial practice, which opens up a middle space between dominance and erasure of difference.[28] The alternatives that Bryld and Lykke offer leave room only for the "author"—proponent of the command-control approach—and the "text"—the "nature" into which the "civilized self" wishes to merge, leaving the self behind. While their analysis does reach toward a "strategy" by which they and others might "steer clear of these rocks," they ultimately determine that the materials under their examination (narratives treating "postcolonial relationships with 'the wild'") do not offer one. As they conclude, "It does not seem possible for the self-aggrandizing or self-abandoning logics of [these] stories to foresee acts of communication with . . . subjects who are simply understood as equal, but different."[29] Acts of communication between subjects who are understood as equal, but different, are a major part of Anyanwu's particular linguistic skill. As the editor, the organizer, or the go-between of bodily forms, she performs as the communicative agent Bryld and Lykke find missing from their study of narrative encounters between human and more-than-human others.

Whether narratives like Butler's can encourage a new, better, or more ethical approach to others, especially animal others, remains contested in studies of her work and in ecocriticism more broadly. However, Anyanwu's sustained efforts to approach and establish relationships with diverse others provides a means of reading Butler's fiction as at least open to the possibility of a middle ground between dominance and erasure. New and innovative ways of establishing kinship relations are crucial to a more balanced exchange between selves and others; as Tom Bristow writes, "Planetary problems might 'come home' to us if our sense of the household was larger than the dwelling place in which we reside; if our duty of care extended beyond our families to the planet and its inhabitants over the next millennium."[30] Butler's reimagining of kinship and embodiment as conceptual structures that can be altered, edited, and rewritten involves such a broadening. Throughout Butler's writing, characters must extend their duty of care to include forms of life that do not resemble them, that do not live like they do, and, in some cases, that oppress and actively harm them.

The path toward caring about and caring for others to whom one is seemingly unconnected (or to whom one is actively opposed) is full of epistemological and affective roadblocks. Such a reorientation is incredibly difficult for Butler's characters, as it becomes clear that the reimagining of the notion of kinship, the rethinking of the household, requires a rewriting of the notion of the self. Anyanwu's position as Doro's chosen mate is continuously troubled and disrupted by her transformative abilities. Her involvement in animal forms and animal lives means that she can, whenever she chooses, disentangle herself from the web of human connections that keeps her tied to Doro and her growing family, can cease to be the woman that they recognize as wife, mother, sister, and establish other webs of connection within animal communities to whom she has no ties beyond her desire. Such untethering and re-tethering is crucial to Butler's larger intervention in such traditionally feminized roles. While Anyanwu cannot completely escape or evade Doro's efforts to objectify and essentialize her gendered body, she can transform that body so extensively as to thwart the worst effects of his oppressive procreative regime.

STRANGE MATINGS

If, as Haraway writes, feminist scholars have already unraveled the "natural necessity of ties between sex and gender . . . gender and morphology, sex and reproduction, and reproduction and composing persons," then "it is high time that feminists exercise leadership in imagination, theory, and action to unravel the ties of both genealogy and kin, and kin and species," to "make 'kin' mean something other/more than entities tied by ancestry or genealogy."[31] While Haraway's interpretation of Butler's contributions to the remaking of kinship have changed over time—a trajectory that Alexis Shotwell traces in more detail in *Against Purity*—she nonetheless identifies Butler as a major contributor to such unraveling. In *Wild Seed*, Anyanwu's encounters with dolphins reframe her extension of care and kinship to animal life forms as an extension born of desire and pleasure as much as ethical consideration. She is drawn to delphine sociality, informing Doro that she plans to take to the water as a dolphin immediately following her first experiments with transforming her arm into a flipper. Initially resistant, Doro frames his opposition to such a transformation as concern for her safety, citing her unfamiliarity with ocean life and the dangers that attend underwater adventures. Anyanwu persists, and Doro finally demands that she at least explain her reasons for experiencing life as a dolphin, dangers notwithstanding. In answer, Anyanwu again struggles to translate her inner experience into language, feeling only a "wrenching longing" to join the pod.[32] Anyanwu's reasoning is only difficult to explain to Doro because it is based in forms of desire that have not yet made their way into language.

Anyanwu's longing to join the dolphins is an amalgam of competing desires, but the predominant object of her yearning for dolphin experience and dolphin companionship is freedom: both from the constraints of her existence as human female and from the role of wife and child-bearer to which Doro has consigned her. As Anyanwu reflects, her longing to join the dolphins "was like the days at home when she had watched the eagles fly until she could no longer stand to only watch. She had killed an eagle and eaten and learned and flown as no human was ever meant to fly. She had flown away, escaping her town, her duties, her kinsmen."[33] Although Anyanwu always eventually returns, Butler explicitly frames Anyanwu's escapes into animal forms and communities as periodic liberations from her restrictive, and strictly essentialized, gendered existence as wife and mother.

In her first foray into dolphin society, however, Butler complicates Anyanwu's desire for escape by introducing another kind of desire. While Anyanwu initially recoils from a male dolphin's sexual advances, Butler frames her resistance as a result of internalized taboo rather than innate sense of wrongdoing and suggests that Anyanwu's ideas of acceptable sexual behavior are shifting as she considers the possibility of dolphin intimacy. She has already claimed, in conversation with Isaac, that dolphins are like people. Once confronted with the possibility of a sexual encounter with a dolphin, humanity becomes a spectrum upon which dolphins and humans lie even closer together than Anyanwu previously believed. Butler notes that Anyanwu had not mated with animals before, believing it to be "abomination":

> She would feel unclean reverting to her human form with the seed of a male animal inside her. But now . . . it was as though the dolphins were not animals. She performed a kind of dance with the male, moving and touching, certain that no human ceremony had ever drawn her in so quickly. She felt both eager and restrained, both willing and hesitant. She would accept him, had already accepted him. He was surely no more strange than the *ogbanje*, Doro. Now seemed to be a time for strange matings.[34]

While Isaac interrupts the encounter, preventing Anyanwu from consummating her desire, the psychological barrier that would have previously held her back from the male dolphin has already come down. Like other acts that Anyanwu once considered abominations (including the consumption of cow's milk), sexual encounters with animals while in animal form are easily, almost instantaneously, re-categorized from forbidden to accepted behaviors. This particular shift, however, re-inscribes a heteronormative model even as it breaks the species barrier. Like many of Butler's protagonists, Anyanwu's explorations of sexuality remain within limits. The "extreme homophobia" that Canavan and others attribute to many of Butler's characters is not necessarily a feature of Anyanwu's impulse to align dolphin sexuality with what she considers to be an acceptable expression of human sexuality, but Butler does maintain certain restrictions on her protagonist.

While Alexis Shotwell and others rightly question whether Butler's writing is explicitly engaged with queer potentialities, studies like Nicole

Seymour's *Strange Natures: Futurity, Empathy, and the Queer Ecological Imagination* provide a means of reading Butler's protagonist as a queer ecological agent while leaving the question open or offering at least one way around it in the context of queer ecology. Seymour claims that "any kind of environmentalism that does not operate . . . out of immediate or extended self-interest—is 'queer'" and situates her use of the term as applicable to that which "questions the naturalness, and undermines the stability, of established categories of sex, gender, and sexuality."[35] Anyanwu's encounters in and with animal bodies fit neatly into Seymour's definition, as her experimentations throw the "naturalness" of Doro's expectations into sharp relief. Her desired dolphin encounter immediately occasions a critique of at least one common element of human sexual activity. As Anyanwu reflects, it was only as a human female that she "could remember being seriously hurt by males—men," and it is only as a human female—a woman—that her offspring tie her down to a particular place and a particular kind of gendered role.[36] Reading Anyanwu's desire-driven encounters with animals and the relationships she establishes across species barriers as part of a queer ecological ethics reveals some of the ways in which Butler engages with queer potentialities in the Patternist series, though such potentialities extend into her other novels as well (perhaps most explicitly in her last published novel, *Fledgling*).

Anyanwu's ability to move between human and animal existences might also be read as a literalized example of what Alaimo has termed "trans-corporeality," or "the movement across human corporeality and nonhuman nature."[37] Butler pauses the narrative at several points in order to dwell on what we might call Anyanwu's trans-corporeality: how her movements across human and animal form shape her experiences and the development of her character. Such movements free her from the confined space of her relationship with Doro and simultaneously involve her in new relationships with myriad others. As Alaimo explains,

> Crucial ethical and political possibilities emerge from this literal "contact zone" between human corporeality and more-than-human nature. Imagining human corporeality as trans-corporeality, in which the human is always intermeshed with the more-than-human world, underlines the extent to which the corporeal substance of the human is ultimately inseparable from the environment.[38]

Trans-corporeality figures the individual as an open system, rather than a contained whole. The theory acknowledges that the existence and expression of character depends in large part on the environment in which that character comes into being and encourages readers to attend more closely to the "contact zone" between figure and ground as constitutive of identity. While Anyanwu, in this context, has long since recognized the potential for animal transformation to unburden her of the restrictions of domestic womanhood, it is only after her dolphin transformation that one important aspect of her ability to drastically transform her own character by changing her embodied environment becomes clear. As Doro watches Anyanwu in the water, he realizes that, in her dolphin form, he can no longer sense her presence (he is otherwise able to pinpoint the location of every individual under his control). This is such a blow to Doro's authority that he considers killing Anyanwu rather than risk her disappearance. Ultimately, though, he decides that the benefits of her reproductive potential outweigh the threat of her freedom. He reflects, "It was as though she had died, as though he confronted a true animal—a creature beyond his reach."[39] Of all her special abilities, Anyanwu's ability to escape Doro's control in this way constitutes the greatest threat to his hetero-reproductive breeding project.[40] Part of Butler's suggestion may be that, as in Haraway's *Companion Species Manifesto,* deep and sustained bonds with nonhuman animal communities resist the otherwise dominant tide of species-specific thinking. Breeding projects like Doro's, in which one species seeks to propagate itself regardless of the cost to others, are disrupted by individual actors like Anyanwu, who offer a model of "living well together with [a] host of species."[41]

There are, however, costs associated with Anyanwu's transformations. While the price of Anyanwu's human life, as Doro sees it, is continuous child-bearing, the price of her freedom, in animal forms, is the loss of her identity. In becoming "a true animal," Anyanwu is indeed "a creature beyond his reach," but she is also beyond the reach of her human relations, the chosen family in whose company she defines herself by various and ever-evolving relational positions. Her invisibility to hetero-patriarchy in animal form—her ability to exist under or beyond its radar—involves a bargain Anyanwu must continually accept and refuse, as both animal and human existences necessitate a break from the communities of kin she has created among various species. Instead of choosing between them, Anyanwu lives a kind of double life, balancing her desire to protect human lives from Doro's malign influence with her desire to dwell among animal communities, extending her attention and care to the nonhuman world.

Maintaining such a balance requires that Anyanwu question and disrupt standardized or given modes of human embodiment and sexuality, her multiple roles of mother, sister, and lover multiplying further as she moves beyond human forms and relationships. Seymour's framing of queer ecological possibilities helps to illuminate Anyanwu's activity as a queer ecological agent, or, as an individual who questions and disrupts expectations around human embodiment and sexuality and experiments with new forms. Such experimentations cohere, as Seymour writes, around discoveries of "the queer relationships that humans might develop with the nonhuman, and how environmental ethics might emerge from queer practices and perspectives" when human beings operate "without any reward, without any guarantee of success, and without any proof that potential future inhabitants of the planet might be similar to the individual acting in the present."[42] Questions of reward, success, and the existence of future inhabitants are especially pertinent to Anyanwu's animal relationships, since her animal offspring are not biologically related to her and are instead the biological offspring of the particular animal Anyanwu has once bitten and then transformed into. Her dolphin young, she explains, "were dolphins. Not human at all."[43] The process of bearing dolphin young is, like the meaning of dolphin flesh, a substance that cannot be fully or satisfactorily expressed in English, or in written or spoken language of any kind. As Anyanwu tells Doro, "There are no words for me to tell you how deep and complete such a change is."[44] Genetically, Anyanwu's kinship relations with the dolphins and other animals are thankless. In Seymour's terms, she operates "without reward."[45] Anyanwu bears dolphin young because she wants to, because it gives her pleasure, because it constitutes part of her escape from womanhood. She makes kin in animal communities because doing so opens up possibilities for connection with a more-than-human world, not because her animal kin will carry anything of her own identity into the future.

As Canavan and others acknowledge, Butler's relationship to the underlying premise of reproductive futurism—that "the future can only exist if there are people to live in it"—remained fraught throughout her work.[46] The extent to which, as Canavan writes, "characters who are not able to complete the reproductive circuit tend to fall out of her narratives" seems to suggest that Butler endorses the ideological structures around childbearing that Lee Edelman would put a name to just two years before her death.[47] Future-oriented environmentalist thinking seems incompatible with a discourse of queer representation that seeks to undermine the kind of reproductive futurism that emerges from hegemonic heteronormativity. An environmentalist ethics of protecting the well-being of future generations, in other words, becomes problematic for queer theorists, who rightly resist the link between ethics and reproductive sexuality. This incompatibility is softened, however, in texts like Butler's *Wild Seed*, in which the notion of kinship and familial ties extends beyond biological connection and even beyond the human. There are gaps in Butler's seemingly airtight reliance on reproductive futurist thinking and Anyanwu embodies one of them. For Anyanwu, thinking seven generations ahead does not necessarily mean thinking seven human generations ahead. Once the species barrier is down, futurity and heteronormativity are no longer synonymous; thinking seven dolphin generations ahead (or, moving further away from mammalian reproduction, seven redwood generations ahead) will more than suffice for the establishment of an environmental ethics that bypasses the discourse of reproductive futurism. Such an ethics might move beyond the human altogether, or it might place human futurity alongside and in the midst of the survival of myriad other life forms.

As Catriona Mortimer-Sandilands and Bruce Erickson write in *Queer Ecologies: Sex, Nature, Politics, Desire*, "Queer ecology allows us to understand . . . that our pleasures are not merely between humans, but are expanded and significantly shaped by the production of nature and space around us."[48] Sandilands and Erickson take the foundational "task" of queer ecology as an effort to "probe the intersections of sex and nature with an eye to developing a sexual politics that more clearly includes considerations of the natural world and its biosocial constitution."[49] Building on these foundations, Seymour understands "oppressed humans . . . and oppressed nonhumans (degraded landscapes, threatened natural resources, and other flora and fauna) to be deeply interconnected" and, in connecting them, outlines an interpretive problem specific to the field of queer ecology: reimagining the category of the human as another open system, as one piece of a much larger planetary organism or arrangement. It is a reimagining that Anyanwu's particular narrative may begin to accomplish and that is further illuminated by placing Butler's narrative alongside solutions already being worked out in the physical sciences. Anyanwu's experimentations and innovations in kinship relations resemble what geologist Sarah Whatmore calls a "relational ethics."[50]

CONTESTED HYBRIDITIES

As a geologist, Whatmore approaches human "embeddedness in constitutive relations with the nonhuman world" as much larger than our potential relationships with "nonhuman animals."[51] After outlining the strengths and weaknesses of "feminist and environmentalist approaches to the subject of ethical considerability," Whatmore draws on Donna Haraway and Bruno Latour's ideas of "difference-in-relation" to build a new approach to ethical considerability via notions of "hybridity," or, of "being-in-relation with and through heterogeneous others."[52] In at least one important way, Anyanwu provides a model for the type of hybridized "being-in-relation" that Whatmore delineates; the shift from repulsion to desire that Anyanwu experiences in her first sexually charged dolphin encounter takes place because she can incorporate the idea of intimacy with animals into a preexisting understanding of intimacy across certain types of difference (it was "no more strange" than her sexual relationship with Doro). Additionally, it is through Anyanwu's particular strength as a reader and editor of embodied forms—as a flesh-messenger—that she can read and correctly interpret the commonalities of human and animal life and act in a way that acknowledges and seeks to promote transformations and exchanges between human and nonhuman and, likewise, between what we consider an abomination and what we might consider natural. It is important to note that Anyanwu's particular skills are unique and largely untranslatable. Throughout the novel, Butler reinforces the sense in which Anyanwu's skills as a reader and editor of bodies is distinct from the reading and writing of texts: the majority of Anyanwu's animal existences take place off or beyond the page, with recurring escapes into animal communities relegated to brief accounts after the fact. Butler seems unwilling or unable to narrate such experiences. Perhaps, like her protagonist, she finds that there are "no words" to describe what such experiences would be like. Instead of forcing them into language, Butler insists that Anyanwu's extension of familial bonds to animal communities, like her extension of kinship to human others otherwise unconnected with her, takes place on the basis of *felt*, rather than written or spoken, connections.

In another way, however, Butler's novel holds back from the possibility of a relational ethics founded in hybridity and corporeality. Unlike other animal transformation narratives, in which characters retain a sense of autonomous and individualized selfhood while in animal form, Anyanwu *entirely* transforms, abandoning her human body and the world to which it belongs. Her "matings" with dolphins and other animals are therefore doubly strange: they both disrupt and maintain the species divide, resulting in a hybridization that is merely temporary. The extent to which Anyanwu's animal encounters involve a rejection and subversion of Doro's larger breeding project is troubled by Butler's disallowance of miscegenation across human-animal lines. Although Anyanwu's animal existences free her from the otherwise ever-present demands of procreative (human) motherhood and the reproductive relationships Doro insists that she maintain, there is a sense in which she must edit herself out of the human world in order to achieve even temporary freedom. While she does model the affective relationality that Whatmore presents as a more fully developed and satisfactory ethical praxis, she is also trapped by the "residual humanism that condemns [her] to trafficking between (human)/society and (nonhuman)/nature as pre-constituted domains of categorically different kinds of being."[53] Therefore, while there are hybrid and queer potentialities built into Butler's novel, they remain partial, troubled, and temporary.

However, it is the role of felt rather than biological or familial connections in *Wild Seed* that provides the most explicit connection to ongoing attempts to establish new systems of ethical considerability. Like Whatmore's relational ethics, Butler's fiction attempts to imagine reconfigurations of kinship and relationality outside or beyond systems of shared genetics, while acknowledging that such innovations will be fraught with complications, setbacks, and even failures. By providing at least partial opportunities for such reconfigurations, troubled and temporary as they may be, Butler's protagonist promotes a position of caring-for-the-world that is sustained throughout an unusually long and extraordinarily challenging lifetime and that does not, ultimately, achieve its desired end. As

Whatmore explains, hybridity and corporeality are constant means, not ends, of expanded ethical praxis. They "redirect our attention to the affective relations between heterogeneous bodies," and these "affective relations" will only later find their way into knowledge and practice on a wider scale, if at all.[54] Anyanwu's extraordinary abilities allow her to carry out the alchemical process that Whatmore posits as the foundation of a truly relational ethics in the space of one lifetime, but her centuries-long life is, of course, not a representation of the reader's own. Butler does, however, call on readers to emulate Anyanwu in at least one way, inviting her readers to deviate from the scripts we have been given and develop our own unique languages with which to re-write them.

NOTES

1. Charles Hillinger, "Sailor Hears the Waves Talking," *Los Angeles Times*, 1978, 20.
2. Gerry Canavan, *Octavia E. Butler* (Urbana: University of Illinois Press, 2016), 68.
3. Octavia E. Butler, *Wild Seed* (New York: Hachette, 1980), 76.
4. Susan Merrill Squier, *Liminal Lives: Imagining the Human at the Frontiers of Biomedicine* (Durham: Duke University Press, 2004), 17.
5. Everett Hamner, *Editing the Soul: Science and Fiction in the Genome Age* (University Park: The Pennsylvania State University Press, 2017), 77.
6. Butler, *Wild Seed*, 200.
7. Tom Bristow, *The Anthropocene Lyric: An Affective Geography of Poetry, Person, Place* (New York: Palgrave Macmillan, 2015), 12.
8. Stacy Alaimo, *Bodily Natures: Science, Environment, and the Material Self* (Bloomington: Indiana University Press, 2010), 142.
9. Alaimo, *Bodily Natures*, 143.
10. Alaimo, *Bodily Natures*, 143.
11. Sarah Whatmore, *Hybrid Geographies: Natures, Cultures, Spaces* (London: SAGE Publications Ltd., 2002), 146.
12. Whatmore, *Hybrid Geographies*, 156.
13. Whatmore, *Hybrid Geographies*, 156.
14. Ursula K. Le Guin, *No Time to Spare: Thinking About What Matters* (New York: Houghton Mifflin Harcourt, 2017), 83.
15. Canavan, *Octavia E. Butler*, 18. My approach to the novel does not allow me to address Butler's sustained and complex work with and within these other contexts in full, but the relationship between Doro and Anyanwu is representative of these larger engagements, as Anyanwu continuously challenges and re-negotiates the conditions of her captivity.
16. Doro has been read alongside Butler's other characters as a version of the vampire, and while Butler's interest in vampirism is most explicitly addressed in *Fledgling* (2006), critics like Peter Sands read versions of the vampire throughout Butler's fiction.
17. Butler, *Wild Seed*, 29.
18. Sarah Outterson, "Diversity, Change, Violence: Octavia Butler's Pedagogical Philosophy," *Utopian Studies* 19, no. 3 (2008): 442.
19. Butler, *Wild Seed*, 75.
20. Butler, *Wild Seed*, 86.
21. Butler, *Wild Seed*, 86.
22. Butler, *Wild Seed*, 200.
23. Lizzie Skurnick, *That Should Be a Word*, quoted in Haraway, "Anthropocene, Capitalocene, Plantationocene, Chthulucene: Making Kin," 164.
24. Butler, *Wild Seed*, 76.

25. Butler, *Wild Seed*, 198.
26. Peter Sands, "Octavia Butler's Chiastic Cannibalistics," *Utopian Studies* 14, no. 1 (2003): 4.
27. Mette Bryld and Nina Lykke, *Cosmodolphins: Feminist Cultural Studies of Technology, Animals and the Sacred* (Chicago: University of Chicago Press, 2000), 25.
28. Bryld and Lykke, *Cosmodolphins*, 215.
29. Bryld and Lykke, *Cosmodolphins*, 215.
30. Bristow, *The Anthropocene Lyric*, 12.
31. Donna J. Haraway, "Anthropocene, Capitalocene, Plantationocene, Chthulucene: Making Kin," *Environmental Humanities* 6 (2015): 161.
32. Butler, *Wild Seed*, 76.
33. Butler, *Wild Seed*, 76.
34. Butler, *Wild Seed*, 80.
35. Nicole Seymour, *Strange Natures: Futurity, Empathy, and the Queer Ecological Imagination* (Urbana: University of Illinois Press, 2013), 12, 28.
36. Butler, *Wild Seed*, 79.
37. Stacy Alaimo, "Trans-Corporeal Feminisms and the Ethical Space of Nature," in *Material Feminisms*, ed. Stacy Alaimo and Susan Hekman (Bloomington: Indiana University Press, 2008), 237.
38. Alaimo, "Trans-Corporeal Feminisms," 238.
39. Butler, *Wild Seed*, 84–85.
40. Butler, *Wild Seed*, 85.
41. Donna J. Haraway, *The Companion Species Manifesto: Dogs, People, and Significant Otherness* (Chicago: Prickly Paradigm Press, 2003), 25.
42. Seymour, *Strange Natures*, 29, 11.
43. Butler, *Wild Seed*, 198.
44. Butler, *Wild Seed*, 198.
45. Seymour, Strange Natures, 11.
46. Canavan, *Octavia E. Butler*, 26.
47. Canavan, *Octavia E. Butler*, 56.
48. Catriona Mortimer-Sandilands and Bruce Erickson, eds. *Queer Ecologies: Sex, Nature, Politics, Desire* (Bloomington: Indiana University Press, 2010), 39.
49. Mortimer-Sandilands and Erickson, *Queer Ecologies*, 5.
50. Whatmore, *Hybrid Geographies: Natures Cultures Spaces*, 159.
51. Whatmore, *Hybrid Geographies*, 156.
52. Whatmore, *Hybrid Geographies*, 159.
53. Whatmore, *Hybrid Geographies*, 165.
54. Whatmore, *Hybrid Geographies*, 166.

BIBLIOGRAPHY

Alaimo, Stacy. "Trans-Corporeal Feminisms and the Ethical Space of Nature." In *Material Feminisms*, edited by Stacy Alaimo and Susan Hekman, 237–64. Bloomington: Indiana University Press, 2008.

Alaimo, Stacy. *Bodily Natures: Science, Environment, and the Material Self*. Bloomington: Indiana University Press, 2010.

Bristow, Tom. *The Anthropocene Lyric: An Affective Geography of Poetry, Person, Place*. New York: Palgrave Macmillan, 2015.

Bryld, Mette, and Nina Lykke. *Cosmodolphins: Feminist Cultural Studies of Technology, Animals, and the Sacred*. Chicago: University of Chicago Press, 2000.

Butler, Octavia, Marilyn Mehaffy, and AnaLouise Keating. "'Radio Imagination': Octavia Butler on the Poetics of Narrative Embodiment." *MELUS* 26, no. 1 (2001): 45–76.

Butler, Octavia. *Wild Seed*. New York: Hachette, 1980.

Canavan, Gerry. *Octavia E. Butler*. Urbana: University of Illinois Press, 2016.

Edelman, Lee. *No Future: Queer Theory and the Death Drive*. Durham: Duke University Press, 2004.
Hamner, Everett. *Editing the Soul: Science and Fiction in the Genome Age*. University Park: The Pennsylvania State University Press, 2017.
Haraway, Donna J. *Staying with the Trouble: Making Kin in the Chthulucene*. Durham: Duke University Press, 2016.
———. "Anthropocene, Capitalocene, Plantationocene, Chthulucene: Making Kin." *Environmental Humanities* 6 (2015): 159–65.
———. *The Companion Species Manifesto: Dogs, People, and Significant Otherness*. Chicago: Prickly Paradigm Press, 2003.
Hillinger, Charles. "One of Few Pacific Navigators Left: Sailor Hears the Waves Talking." *Los Angeles Times*, 1978, 20.
Le Guin, Ursula K. *No Time to Spare: Thinking About What Matters*. New York: Houghton Mifflin Harcourt, 2017.
Mortimer-Sandilands, Catriona, and Bruce Erickson, eds. *Queer Ecologies: Sex, Nature, Politics, Desire*. Bloomington: Indiana University Press, 2010.
Outterson, Sarah. "Diversity, Change, Violence: Octavia Butler's Pedagogical Philosophy." *Utopian Studies* 19, no. 3 (2008): 433–56.
Sands, Peter. "Octavia Butler's Chiastic Cannibalistics." *Utopian Studies* 14, no. 1 (2003): 1–14.
Seymour, Nicole. *Strange Natures: Futurity, Empathy, and the Queer Ecological Imagination*. Urbana: University of Illinois Press, 2013.
Shotwell, Alexis. *Against Purity: Living Ethically in Compromised Times*. Minneapolis: University of Minnesota Press, 2016.
Skurnick, Lizzie. *That Should be a Word*. New York: Workman Publishing Company, 2015.
Whatmore, Sarah. *Hybrid Geographies: Natures, Cultures, Spaces*. London: SAGE Publications Ltd, 2002.

Part II

Gendering the Natural World

FOUR

Tendrils, Tentacles, and Flower Power

Speciesism in Womaneater *(1958) and* The Gardener *(1974)*

Fernando Gabriel Pagnoni Berns and Juan Juvé

INTRODUCTION: THE (GREEN) OTHER IN FANTASY AND ECOCRITICISM

Robin Wood writes in his essay "An Introduction to the American Horror Film" that dominant ideology (bourgeois capitalism) cancels any potential opposition to hegemonic power through the repression of alternatives to that power.[1] Anyone who fails to fit within the hegemonic sphere is classified as a disruptive Other,[2] a monster that comes to perturb the patriarchal order of things. The horror genre is "the struggle for recognition of all that our civilization represses or oppresses, its reemergence dramatized, as in our nightmares, as an object of horror."[3] Margaret Tarrat follows this same formulation, but she investigates the monstrosity in science fiction films or sf/horror hybrids. Her thesis is that the battles against extraterrestrial monsters are fantastic materializations of civilized persons' conflict with their id, the site of repressed desires.[4] These repressed desires are incompatible with the moral codes of civilization, so they rise up in the form of monstrosity. The monsters in science fiction films, thus, are embodiments of societal and individual repressed tensions, especially those of a sexual nature.

The monster can take any shape. Plants, however, are not mentioned as potential forms of monstrosity either by Wood or Tarrat, even if the former briefly mentions the abstract concept of "nature" as a possible vehicle for the fantastic. Plants, so passive and domesticated (in common wisdom), can hardly be seen as embodiments of monstrosity and repressed anxieties in fantastic film.

However, plants in general share elements that make them particularly disturbing as potential monsters within fantastic cinema. First, plants are highly ambiguous beings: they oscillate between total passivity and full life. Michael Marder addresses this issue when explaining that while "the predominant usage of the verb 'to vegetate' is negative, linked to the passivity or inactivity of animals or human beings who behave as though they were sedentary plants, its subterranean history relates it to the exact opposite of this privileged meaning," i.e., "the fullness and exuberance of life, vigor, and brimming energy."[5] Passivity is, according to the author, just a "guise."[6] This ambivalence makes them unknowledgeable, opaque to the human mind and, as such, utterly mysterious.

Second, plants' lack of a clearly discernible sex (at least to untrained eyes) problematizes gender and creates ambiguity. The complex sexuality of plants rejects the oversimplification "of the entire sphere of sexuality to an oppositional relation between two sexes."[7] In this sense, "the indifference of vegetal sex life surpasses the logic of oppositionality. [. . .] The front line in the fight for the liberation of sexuality from metaphysical and onto-theological constraints cuts through the being of plants."[8] Together with their passive appearance, unclear sexuality enhances the perceived ambiguity of plant life.

Since horror and science fiction cinema, according to both Wood and Tarrat, build their stories upon the return of the repressed threatening the symbolic order, it is possible to establish interesting connections between ambiguity, sexuality, gender, and monstrous plants. In the introduction to her edited collection *Plant Horror*, Dawn Keetley locates the horror of plants "both in their absolute strangeness and in their uncanny likeness."[9] According to Keetley, plants embody a complete alterity from the human realm: "human affinity with plants has for just as long been foreclosed."[10] Further, plants have become invisible, a mere backdrop for humanity.[11] Still, there is the unsettling sense that maybe humans are also like plants, an unnerving "ontological proximity": plants breathe, move, live, and grow just like humans do.[12] Thus, there is an oscillation between complete alienness and human-like features framing plants and turning them into uncanny creatures.

In this chapter, we will direct our attention to two films sharing some common elements: both have monstrous plants as the main embodiment of menace, both present contradictory gender constructions, and both are a far cry from being classics of the genre. Indeed, *Womaneater* (1958, dir. Charles Saunders) and *The Gardener* (1974, dir. James Kay) are products made with tiny budgets and flat direction. Characterization is minimal, production values are basic, and the dialogue is just functional. The former is a British B movie made in the 1950s while the latter is an amateur

American production, James Kay's only film. Even if far from art, both films are lowbrow cultural artifacts and, as such, bold articulations of gender as a shifting, polyvalent category. The vegetal monsters leading the films are, in turn, delineated as forms of monstrous masculinity or commoditized, passive femininity. The monstrous plants haunting these films embody constant contradictions about sex, gender, class, race, and speciesism that make the films valuable as objects of study.

Womaneater is the typical horror/science fiction mashup that dominated in the 1950s (the so-called "creature features"), populated with fantastical creatures and speculative science filled with incomprehensible jargon. In the film, a scientist (George Coulouris) transplants a tree from the Amazon to Britain because the plant holds the formula for eternal life. He keeps the monster in his cellar while feeding it with beautiful women. The film has two readings: on one hand, the tree is coded exotic, inextricably linked to sensuality.[13] Its winding snakelike tentacles and tendrils, both easily configured as phallic, are elements that shape it as male. In addition, the tree only eats (rapes?) beautiful women. In this sense, *Womaneater*, the film's title, can be read as *womanizer*. But the tree is also configured as a victim of imperialism, making it passive (i.e., female). Then, its sexuality and manhood, as a consequence of colonialism, are filled with contradictory aspects.[14]

Meanwhile, *The Gardener* fits within what Brian Stableford calls "the remystification"[15] of ecology which took place in American science fiction in the 1960s and 1970s, as the main monster is revealed to be a divine creature with deep connections with the natural world. The film tells the story of a hunky gardener (Joe Dallesandro) who is exchanged as a commodity between rich bored wives to attend their private gardens. He is especially desired for his good looks and his ability to grow exotic plants in any soil and in striking sizes. Actually, he is a plant in human disguise, a divinity who has a supernatural stronghold on flowers, which he can command to kill if he wishes so. In the film, both women and plants are simply beautiful ornaments. The social construct that associates women with flowers is strong,[16] while the fertile and horrifying supernatural powers of the gardener (himself a plant) promote forms of traditional hyper-masculinity. There are contradictions, however, as the main vegetal monster is also a beautiful "thing" (prettiness related traditionally to femininity) and a plant (i.e., passive).

In both films, class exploitation and gender are intertwined through the politics of speciesism. Only after consuming women does the "womaneater" tree expel its vital juice, which is used by white men to concoct an elixir of life, thus underlining the exploitation of both the tree and women. In turn, both the supernatural gardener and flowers in Kay's film are commoditized by bourgeois women, who, in turn, are sexually used by their husbands and by the gardener himself.

Using ecocriticism as our main framework, we propose to analyze these two overlooked films to find the contradictory ways in which gender can intersect with plant monsters. The contradictions noted above are triggered by the common thinking that equates life with movement and death with the static, what lies quiet. Many health and exercise books claim that movement equals life. Many New Age texts proclaim that movement equals life. Through this zoomorphic point of view, everything static is an object to be used and appropriated; thus, passivity and quietness becomes somehow "wrong," a deficient state of life. Passivity is regarded in a negative way, an inferior way of life, a *sub-life*. Matthew Hall argues that the dogma of domination of plants has historical roots in the idea of plants "as passive, mute, and morally inconsiderable"[17] that begins with the (mis)translations that Pliny made of the observations on plants made in turn by Theophrastus. The consideration of plants as passive, devoid of life, continued well into the twentieth century and shaped our common view of vegetal existence.

This traditional and conservative Western "common view" also sustains conventional associations paralleling masculinity with activity and femininity with passivity. In our patriarchal society, sustained (in part) through politics of alterity, "woman reflects the dominant projections and counter-fantasies of the era, a mythology that serves to repress female sexuality to further men's control over her reproductive capacities"[18] equating in a "natural" way the female with "essences" such as passivity and submission. Thus, a negative linkage can be observed taking place through associations between femininity, passivity, and plants that shapes an imaginary in which quietness equates both plants and women under the sign of exploitation. Passivity and femininity collapse together in one image, both seemingly signifying the same thing. Further, everything related to femininity/passivity, such as gay men, is thus coded as somehow devoid of "proper" life.

Both *Womaneater* and *The Gardener* construct a sense of menace and monstrosity through contradictions: the green monsters leading the films are plants and, thus, coded passive and feminine, objects to be exploited through imperialism and capitalism. The monsters, however, are threatening figures, powerful beings which can harm and kill, which codes them as aggressive males. To enhance the contradictory nature of these monstrous plants (contradictions born from the conventional constructions of gendered divisions which try to present themselves as "natural"), the vegetal monsters are codified in turns as hyper-masculine or passive, dislocating any fixed sense of "real" gender.

These intersections, in brief, point to the ambiguous perception of plants in popular culture as living/non-living, commodified/savage, sexual/non-sexual things. The contradictory readings promoted by the films, we will demonstrate, rise from both the way cinema ecologically negotiates with the social and cultural contexts of production (the British imperialist mindset and the American countercultural 1970s) and the intersection with the way plants are mostly understood and gendered through social discourse.

THE POLITICS OF SPECIESISM: EXPLORING THE OTHER THROUGH ECOMEDIA

Especially important for our study will be the "sexism/ speciesism nexus."[19] Unlike sexism, speciesism is an issue little discussed in film, fantastic or otherwise. This oversight is especially striking if we keep in mind that speciesism casts light and perspectives on forms of oppression and devaluation sustained, in part, by gender difference. The interwoven nature of speciesism, racism, heterosexism, and misogyny is noted by ecocriticism as a main framework.

Greg Garrard states that ecocriticism is "an avowedly political mode of analysis" framed by a "green moral and political agenda" and, thus, closely related to "environmentally oriented developments in philosophy and political theory."[20] Another valuable study for our reading is Stephen Rust, Salma Monani, and Sean Cubitt's *Ecomedia: Key Issues*. According to the authors, media is "inextricably bound up in society" through a European philosophical tradition of relating to the world exclusively in human terms in which we "place society on one side and nature over on the other"[21] as mutually excluding spheres. At this point, the goal of ecocriticism is to expose the arbitrary nature of this division and critically engage with its fallacies. It is only in recent years, however, "that ecocritics have really expanded their focus to consider popular media texts" as "significant mediators of the human–environmental relationship."[22] Ecomedia promotes deciphering which forms of media "facilitate ecological discussion."[23]

Ecocinema is a branch of ecomedia, and it should be stated that this theoretical and practical tool is not limited to films with explicit progressive "messages of environmental consciousness."[24] Rather, ecomedia encompasses a great variety of popular culture, such as genre films. Ecocinema understands films as "unequivocally culturally *and* materially embedded,"[25] a window into how audiences imagine the different interrelations between the human and nonhuman world (including plants) "and how we act with or against it";[26] for example, through engaging with a humanist or speciesist point of view. Speciesism refers to a hierarchical approach to species, a thought which, analogous to racism, colonialism, or sexism, "focuses on prejudiced beliefs in human supremacy over nonhuman species,"[27] particularly animals and plants. Speciesism is "a form of oppression that is interconnected with and reinforcing of other oppressive structures"[28] in the name of a hegemonic centrism that is at least a couple of millennia old.[29]

In our study, and following the hierarchical naturalization criticized by speciesism, we will pay special attention to the dualisms man/nature and man/woman. The former positions humans as superior, due to "essential" traits such as rationality or soul, to nature. The indiscriminate exploitation of nature is then justified by social progress and the betterment of all humanity. Humans do not share the planet with nature: they dominate nature. The latter dualism, in turn, distinguishes men from women, the former superior to the second, superiority based on some "essential" qualities such as intelligence or moral values. These two arguments share a common logic of domination in which women have been associated with subordinate, irrational, unpredictable nature while men are equated with the logics of culture. Men "reduced nature to its mechanical elements, and woman to her asexual virtue."[30] As Sheila Collins states in her *A Different Heaven and Earth*, "racism, sexism, class exploitation, and ecological destruction" are "interlocking pillars upon which the structure of patriarchy rests."[31] In this scenario, we will use the hierarchical ethos that sustains speciesism to point to the ways in which the films here analyzed play with a correlation between traditional forms of femininity (inextricably linked to prettiness or passivity), emasculated forms of masculinity (colonized men or men turned objects of female desire), and plants. All of them share the quality of exploited subjects, colonized and "feminized" through practices that made them "less than human," understanding "human" as the white, Christian, heterosexual Western man leading the films.

In the next section, we will analyze two films that, within the boundaries of fantastic narratives, unconsciously engage with politics of oppression exerted upon both people (women and emasculated men) and plants. *Womaneater* does this through a colonialist point of view, faithful to the UK's long history of imperialism. *The Gardener*, in turn, answers to the socio-cultural context of the American 1970s, an era in which the visibility of green politics (the green arguments concerning the intrinsic value of the natural world) and feminist politics intersected. Both films can be analyzed now, decades later, utilizing ecocriticism and speciesism to understand the ways in which the fantastic can be a vehicle to the societal concerns about the nature of plants and how the latter are mediated and gendered through popular culture as subjects of concern.

THE COLONIZED (GREEN) OTHER IN *WOMANEATER*

Womaneater sustains its narrative through asymmetrical power relations between the different characters. These differences are mainly based on gender relations but also on imperialist colonization. Any debate about the place of race, class, animals, or plants in the cultural arena occurs within a context where "ideology preexists and imposes itself on individual perceptions"[32] that present as invisible and natural issues of domination. The film's credits roll over an image blending together exoticism, horror, and plants: a jungle at night populated with plants of varied forms, a creepy soundtrack playing in the background. Cut to modern London, thus setting the film's first set of opposites: exotic Amazonia, filled with nature running wild, against civilized England. The title credits cut to a shot framing the bridge upon the Thames and Big Ben as background, where sits the "Explorers Club." In this place, white British men who have dedicated their lives to the exploration of exotic landscapes reunite to exchange stories. The upper-class white men there chat about the "dangerous" places they have "visited" while exchanging maps and anecdotes. In the opening scene, Doctor Moran (Coulouris) talks about the potential existence of some strange inhabitants within the Amazonian jungle who have the capacity, through secret rites, to bring the dead back to life. Thus, an expedition is built so white men can steal this uncanny knowledge. This idea continues European justification for invasion and colonization as sustained on the basis of non-European lands understood as "underused" landscapes, a justification of colonization since the savage "Other" needs paternal supervision.[33] Even if the scene lasts only two minutes of running time, it is enough to place the story within the historical paradigm of British imperialism.

The action moves to the Amazonian jungle. There, a secretive ritual unfolds. The scene is filled with the imagery of exoticism, eroticism, and savage nature that configures the scenes of rituals in Western thought as places of "unrestrained sexuality."[34] The scene is dominated by male indigenous dancers handling snakes and, in the center of the frame, a scantily clad black female dancer (Marpessa Dawn). Her presence and the music attract the main monster, the womaneater of the title, a walking tree whose branches and tendrils start to move with excitement. Since exaggerated mobility of plants is another issue with the potential of making plants horrifying,[35] the walking tree is rendered monstrous.

This arousal responds to the sight of the beautiful woman. The female complies with her role of object to be viewed, while every man, white or black, stares at her with some phallic object in hand. The natives take the snakes closer to her, and the white men hold their rifles as the monstrous tree agitates its branches. Two things are clear: first, the scene as a whole fulfills the symbolic imperialist imaginary of Otherness as savage, colorful, and sensual; second, the living tree is unmistakably conceptualized as hetero male, due to its (his?) level of arousal marked by phallic symbols.

The female dancer is taken to the tree and, presumably, consumed by the monster. Since the dancer's death remains offscreen, the exact nature of her demise remains obscure: what does the monster do to her with its mobile branches? To add another layer of ambiguity, during the sacrifice, the film cuts to a close shot of Moran, who sees what the cinematic audience does not. Sweaty and grinning, Moran seems to be enjoying whatever the tree is doing to the girl, thus deepening the connection of heterosexualized misogynistic masculinity between the monster and the white man.

Cut to five years later. Moran, faithful to the British history of imperialism, has colonized Amazonia, taking what is profitable for him—the uncanny tree—to his own home in the UK. In the cellar of Moran's house, Tanga (Jimmy Vaughan), a native from Amazonia, is in charge of conducting the hideous ritual of feeding the tree, which has been transported to the UK. The vegetal monster is fed with a never-ending parade of beautiful women. The continuous feeding is an all-male business: Tanga puts the women in a deep trance with the sound of his drums and pushes them into the tree's branches while Moran watches the action with a grin on his feverish face. While performing the killings, both men are depicted as getting pleasure at the sight of the rape/triturating of the female body. Moran presents all the signs of sexual arousal: he breathes heavily, his eyes intently fixed on the action taking place before him, his face covered in sweat. Without doubt, he feels a misogynistic pleasure at the sight of the abuse perpetrated by the tree on young female bodies. In this scenario, the tree works like Moran's proxy for his heterosexual, misogynistic desires: the creature does what the doctor wants to do but represses deep down in his Self.

The sexual arousal in Tanga and Moran are depicted differently. The white doctor seems to identify with the raping plant on a masculine basis: each time that a victim is killed by the tree, the film cuts to a close shot of a thrilled Moran. Further, it is the doctor who chooses the victims, all of them pretty, young women. Tanga, meanwhile, is depicted wearing an evil grin, rather than traces of sexual arousal. Both men share a misogynistic attitude toward women. But if Moran and Tanga are equaled in their misogyny, they are very different in their social position: while Moran is the white colonizer, Tanga is the dark-skinned colonized. In this scenario, both Tanga and the monster tree are equaled; both are exotic companions extracted from their native landscape and kept hidden. Further, both are tools for profit, as the tree ejaculates its elixir of life after killing the women put under a spell by Tanga. It is interesting to note that the politics of speciesism are intimately supported by institutions of whiteness, which connects the former with forms of racism. "Eurocentrism and colonial racism are often translated into a speciesism,"[36] as Gabriele Schwab argues, since the idea of radical and racial Otherness provides necessary support to imperialistic ventures such as the one practiced by Moran, the one representing hegemonic masculinity.

Because our aim is to analyze emasculation as related to the passivity of plants, we need to acknowledge that the dominant form of masculinity was, up to the 1990s, conceptualized through the notion of hegemonic masculinity derived from Raewyn Connell, who points to masculinity as a social and discursive construction rather than a set of given biological facts. Masculinity, as a text, is produced and reproduced through a "reproductive arena," i.e., "the various practices, performances, and social processes that get culturally attached to reproductive differences."[37] For Connell, hegemonic masculinity "guarantees (or is taken to guarantee) the dominant position of men and the subordination of women."[38] Even if the concept is mobile, hegemonic masculinity "refers to the most culturally exalted forms of masculinity configurations that justify dominance and inequality,"[39] such as a supposedly superior rational intellect, emotional control, or strength, all issues perceived as forms of dominance over women. Expelled from hegemonic masculinity is "subordinated" masculinity, unable to reach (or disinterested in reaching) the status of hegemonic masculinity, thus sustaining a strong and clear line dividing "proper" men from their "weaker" counterpart, feminine/plant-like men, the reverse of ferocious, animal-like he-men.

Like the tree, Tanga is a colonized subject taken away from his native land to serve the purposes of a white man and, thus, he becomes an example of subordinate masculinity. Rosaura Sanchez writes, "The feminization of the colonized subject who is also racially, economically, and politically dominated is read as the construction of the European subject's alterity, a necessary process of identification vis-à-vis the colonized Other."[40] Unlike Moran, the native boy is depicted wearing only a loincloth through the whole film, the exhibition of a naked male body susceptible to the dangers of emasculation. The masculine bodies displayed as objects to be erotically looked at run the risk of being turned into objects rather than subjects through a subversion of the patriarchal (and imperial) gaze that positions women as the object of voyeuristic desire. Together with his boyish features and his clear disgust when beautiful women knock at the door of Moran's house uninvited, Tanga is reconfigured as a queer subject, a monstrous ambiguous subject oscillating between the positions of dominating and dominated. Tanga's masculinity is reinforced by his dominating role, since it is he who puts pretty women under his spell and makes them do want he wants. Contradictorily, Tanga's status as a dominant patriarchal figure is constantly undermined: he only wears a loincloth (a racialized item), marking him, through semi-nakedness, as savage and vulnerable. Further, he shares the house's cellar with the tree, while only white people can inhabit the upper floors.

Tanga is a colonized subject, marked by racial difference. Women, in turn, are less important than Tanga's non-white body. Tanga is the one in charge of burning the clothes of the female victims to ashes, a way to completely erase the corporeality of the women who disgust him so much. Through a complex reading, Tanga is close to plants, as both share colonization, and are close to women, as subjects of a white masculine master. This recognition seems to prompt Tanga to hate/erase women, the only way to secure his hierarchical position as someone valuable within the house.

The monstrous tree also falls within the same contradiction that frames Tanga. As already mentioned, the many long appendages that the tree displays, including shorter limbs that end in bulbous form with a slit across that unmistakably resemble penises, shape the monster as hyper-masculine. His appetite for female flesh supports this idea. Furthermore, after eating a woman, the tree "ejaculates" the liquid that Moran uses as a component to concoct the elixir that, seemingly, prolongs life. That the tree ejaculates a liquid that gives life equates the fluid with semen. Still, the tree, like Tanga, is another colonized subject: the tree is a subordinate male which lives to serve its white master.

Among this imbalance between hegemonic and subordinate men, women exist only to be subject to commoditization and the misogynistic gaze. The latter is reinforced with the introduction of the story's heroine, Sally (Vera Day). She works in a funfair close to Moran's house as an exotic dancer in a Haiti-related attraction. Sally is displayed wearing only a bra and the stereotypical tribal skirt. Even if a white woman, her condition as a woman to-be-looked-at links her to the native Amazonian dancer in the film's opening. Both women are turned into exotic objects for consumption by the gaze of the British white man. The imperialist gaze is thus reinforced once again in this new display of exoticism in which even the leading white girl undergoes a process of Othering. Like the killer tree, she is coded as exotic through a colonialist, patriarchal gaze.

Sally is the heroine of the film and, as such, the main representative of femininity within the story; still, she is mostly passive, thus underlining the role that women have within this gendered scheme. Sally is beaten by her boss at the funfair and saved by the film's male hero, Lewis (Robert MacKenzie). She gets a job with Moran as the housekeeper's helper, but, once within the house, her gaze is neither investigative nor active. She simply does nothing to advance the plot until the time in which she serves as a potential victim. At that moment, Lewis rescues her, setting the killer tree on fire and putting a quick and perfunctory end to the film. Thus, women in *Womaneater* work only as passive, beautiful objects who end up raped and killed, their bodies turned into food for plants. It is interesting to note that another victim of the killer tree is a sex worker Moran takes to his home. She is another passive woman who falls into Moran's hands and barely does anything to fend off the plant. Women are constantly objectified through male power and gaze: even a cop looking for a missing girl (another victim of Moran's "experiments") makes a lustful observation about the good looks of the vanished woman.

If womanhood is coded as passive throughout the film, masculinity, in turn, constantly shifts from hyper-masculinity to subordination. As mentioned, the tree is hyper-masculinized due to its long appendages and appetite for pretty women while emasculated due to its position as a colonized subject. If the tree can be seen as the alter ego of Moran, it is also possible to read the plant as dominated by the patriarchal master. As Matthew Hall argues, "portrayed as passive, mute beings, plants are thus more easily dominated as mere resources for human endeavor," passiveness an issue which links social and cultural discourse about vegetal life, femininity, and "primitiveness."[41] This issue of domination parallels the walking tree with Sally, the female victims within the film, and expatriate Tanga, all of them exploited and abused by men by virtue of their passiveness. Women, colonized men, and vegetation share a dominated position in which the interests of white patriarchy are inherently superior to all beings considered inferior.

As Carol J. Adams argues, patriarchy instituted a set of oppositions in which masculine issues are related to meat, while women and plants are presented as alike in their passivity: "Both women and plants are seen as less developed and less evolved than men and animals."[42] Following this idea, the monster of *Womaneater* oscillates between contradictory readings: it is depicted as a misogynistic hyper-masculine monster since its long phallic branches are used to consume women. On the other hand, the vegetal monster is just another passive subject who, together with Tanga and nature as a whole, serves the colonizing mind. Thus, the monster is both active and passive, the latter culturally related to femininity.

Colonialism runs through *Womaneater*, even if the UK in the late 1950s was facing a process of decolonization. The constraining binary separating masculinity from femininity as two mutually excluding spheres is put under discussion when the main monster of the film is a walking tree who shares many qualities with both men and women.

Anticolonialism as a form of liberation through revolution increased as the 1950s shifted to the 1960s, a time in which countercultural movements accessed the public agenda, bringing ecological awareness, preoccupations about Third World nations, and the "nature-run-amok" cycle of the 1970s. This anticolonial thinking integrated a larger ideology calling for liberation from any form of oppression, especially capitalist, patriarchal forms. Rather than engage directly with the reality of the era, *The Gardener* illustrates the zeitgeist of the 1960s and 1970s through fantastical distortions. Patricia Kerslake, in her book *Science Fiction and Empire*, argues that "metaphors identify phenomena in a manner that is literally distinct from their realities"[43] and, thus, become useful tools for science fiction and the genres working in fantasy in general to "experiment with the human mindset."[44] Arguably, there is no evidence that either Charles Saunders or James Kay were interested in making political statements. The 1960s, however, ushered in a new era of feminist science fiction. Civil rights and feminism were now a part of the zeitgeist, and popular culture has much to say about the collective fears, anxieties, and negotiations of citizenship that were present within the cultural climate in which each film appeared. While *Womaneater* cannot escape an imperialist ethos even if just a cheap B film, *The Gardener* negotiates with an American scenario in which a new awareness of both female oppression and the exploitation of nature were interlinked through a fight against the concepts of race, sexuality, and gender as biological determinants of human worth. The invigoration of ecological awareness was heavily featured in American science fiction films and literature of the era[45] as the tumultuous "flower power" era began, bringing a new conscience on all things green.

WOMEN AND FLOWERS AS COMMODITIES IN *THE GARDENER*

The specular relationship between passivity, plants, and women appears clearer in *The Gardener*, a film which fits into the subgenre of "ecological trauma" of the 1970s. During the 1960s and 1970s, countercultural movements in America drew attention to social issues until then kept under the radar, such as sexual freedom, minorities' rights, and alternative religions. Among the new topics, there was an increasing interest in ecological matters.[46] It is not by chance, then, that horror cinema in the 1970s gave birth to an entire new subgenre: the "nature-run-amok" film. This subgenre focused on an animal or group of animals, larger or more aggressive than normal, attacking and terrorizing humans. Although there were films with animals attacking humans before, the fact is that this subgenre was consolidated as such through the 1970s. Further, science fiction of the period showed a prevailing sense of unease concerning the possibility of ecological disaster, presenting, like *Silent Running* (1972, dir. Douglas Trumbull) and *Soylent Green* (1973, dir. Richard Fleischer) did, overpopulated worlds where resources were scarce and humanity was at the brink of extinction. These films reflected on the green movement, presenting messages about our environment within narratives of eco-disaster.

There is little concern for ecology in speculative cinema prior to the 1970s. Perhaps this had been so because, until the advent of the 1970s and the concerns about ecology and the environment, nature was seen as a system completely dominated by humans. General worries about animal extinction, their status as subjects, and resource scarcity were underscored through the decade, however, as "environmental issues were discussed almost daily in the media"[47] both in America and the UK. This visibility of ecological concerns was favored, in part, thanks to the active militancy of countercultural movements.

The environmental and animal rights movement of the 1970s joined the countercultural fight for a better world. As Peter Singer discussed in the preface of his groundbreaking book *Animal Liberation* (1975), "supporters of liberation for blacks and women should support animal liberation too."[48] It is possible to create a correlation between race, class, gender, and preoccupations about the environment in the 1960s and the 1970s, decades in which oppressed and/or invisible minorities fought for their civil rights. Women, LGTBQ people, African Americans, and (through activists for the environment) fauna and flora fought to be considered as subjects with rights. Thus, a relationship of speciesism between oppressed social minorities and nature in that decade can be formulated. The environment, animals, and plants were not made for humans any more than people of color were made for whites or women for men. Following this line of thought, people of color, animals, women, and LGBTQ people, among other oppressed groups, can be understood as "brothers" or "sisters" framed by "speciesism."

The Gardener, made in the 1970s, foregrounds speciesism, possession, and hierarchies. In the film, flowers are commoditized by upper classes, especially bourgeois women. Still, these women are commoditized as "trophy wives," i.e., beautiful women turned into objects of adornment for husbands with money. The shifts between subject/object and active/passive that dominated *Womaneater* frame this film as well. The film opens with a woman resting in a hospital bed, where she receives orchids as a gift. Flowers as offerings present the clearest example of plants as commodities, in which living beings are given as "gifts." Orchids, especially exotic and expensive in the scenario of economic exchange, possess a high value. They codify wealth or, at least, upper-class life.[49] However, in the world of *The Gardener*, this particular orchid is a poison-expelling monstrous plant that kills the woman who has received it. Rather than a passive object of adornment, the orchid is an active object of death.

Flowers, commodification, and death blend together in the next scene: during the funeral of the woman killed in the previous scene, her coffin is totally covered with funeral wreaths, another example of nature turned commodified object. Even if flowers, in the ritual of Western mourning, are expressions of intimate feelings of sorrow and pain, the wreaths are also markers of economic status: bigger and more elaborate wreaths are associated with upper-class funerals rather than working-class rites. Thus, the first two scenes of *The Gardener* establish the role of flowers as symbolic markers of social and cultural status. Plants and flowers are here bourgeois objects of superficial beauty.

The commodification of plants continues as the film cuts from the funeral to the luxurious house of the deceased woman. There, two of her friends, Ellen Bennet (Katharine Houghton) and Helena (Rita Gam), chat and drink with a gorgeous garden as background. The lush, rich, and colorful garden is a landscape clearly designed to impress. In fact, the two friends are awestruck by the way the garden has grown up from the last time they saw it. Gardens configured as luxurious spaces continue the paradigm of commodification of flowers as markers of economic status: "Floral practices marking social status developed in concert with expanding wealth and the desire to shape class identity and distinctions between the upper and emerging middle classes."[50] Expensive flowers are among the goods consumed as part of a class identity.

More impressive for the ladies is Carl (Joe Dallesandro), the gardener responsible for the beautiful landscape: blond, long-haired, muscular, beautiful, shirtless, and wearing only a pair of very tight and low camel-skin pants, he is the very definition of a hunk. Dallesandro's career was that of an infinite parade of hunky roles in which he appears in various stages of undress. Dallesandro was famous for being "the most homo-erotically admired"[51] of Andy Warhol and Paul Morrissey's superstars, acting in underground classics such as *Flesh for Frankenstein* (Paul Morrissey and Antonio Margheriti, 1973). Dallesandro as a "passive object of predatory and voyeuristic attention" was the perfect queer image of male exhibition and homoerotic desire.[52] *The Gardener* is no exception in his career: he is displayed shirtless the whole film, always wearing tight-fitting pants. Furthermore, he is displayed naked in two scenes. The gardener is an object to-look-at and is thus emasculated not only by the rich ladies within the film but also by the audience. The fact that he is half-naked the whole film, even in situations that required of him some more adequate wardrobe, only reinforces the queerness of his persona. In one scene, Ellen's husband, John (James Congdon), presents the gardener to an old lady accompanying both Ellen and Helena. John comes close to the camera and, looking directly at it, almost addressing the audiences, simply says (with a note of irony and a grin on his face), "Ladies, this is Carl," then leaves to reveal the half-naked man at the center of the screen. As the old lady says, "Oh, my."

Carl is not only emasculated because of his nakedness but also by his character as an object to be passed around. Since his employer has died, the gardener has lost his job (the surviving husband does not seem that interested in keeping a half-naked man around the house), so Ellen immediately hires him even if she already has a gardener. If true that Ellen is presented as naive and good-hearted (and as a woman genuinely interested in gardens and plants), it can be inferred nevertheless that part of her pity responds to the gardener's good looks. Carl, like plants and flowers, can be considered as another object of exchange between bored wives: if one dies, the man is immediately passed on, as some kind of heirloom, to another female friend who can make good "use" of him. Thus, the film presents a paradigm of objectification: first, plants, as representative of the natural world, are constantly commodified as objects of exchange and markers of economic status; second, the low-class status has the unwanted effect of castrating Carl and turning him into a "feminized" object exchanged between women. Through the film, an oscillating play of hierarchies can be observed: men objectify plants and women while women objectify both plants and Carl, a man who holds power over plants. Social hierarchies are constantly disrupted and rebuilt through *The Gardener*. Hall observes that the emergence of hierarchies precedes the act of domination: "It precedes acts of commodification and ownership. In order to maintain hierarchical ordering, the continuity of life has been ignored in favor of constructing sharp discontinuities between humans, plants, and animals."[53] White men are at the highest point, while plants reside well into the base of social hierarchy. The problem here is the Carl is half (white/handsome) man and half plant, so any structure is turned as ambiguous as plants themselves.

Lastly, all the women of *The Gardener* are trophy wives, upper-class women who pass their days drinking, shopping, and speaking of divorce (as Helena does). The wives and the gardens complement each other through the figure of empty, polished, glossy surfaces, the gardens shaped in rigorously planned rows of colors, and the women wearing expensive clothes even to chat with their friends in their living rooms. When John mentions to Ellen that she already has a gardener, she establishes an important difference: "Ralph is really a yardman. I like gardens to be something special," i.e., something carefully orchestrated to impress bourgeois guests and friends. The chaos of nature or the pleasures that come with the "green thumb," in fact, have little to do with bourgeois gardening. Flowers, trophy wives, and hunky gardeners are turned into bourgeois objects of exchange.

Carl, however, is the film's monster. He hospitalizes Ralph (Roberto Negron), the "yardman" who distrusts the half-naked new gardener. Also, he either killed or scared his previous female employers after they realized the gardener's true nature: Carl has the supernatural power to control plants and flowers. He can make plants grow at high speed, bigger than usual, and out of proper season. Also, he can command them to expel poisonous fumes to kill those who challenge him, as Ralph did. In this respect, it is interesting to point out that Ralph represents the "masculine" world of gardening. He is an old man in charge of keeping the garden working. When Carl is invited to join him, Ralph gets furious. He is afraid of being axed from his job. Ralph angrily comments to Ellen that only John, the man of the house, has the right to fire him. John, in turn, warns Ellen against firing Ralph. Thus, the gendered division is enhanced: the "males" of the house, who only want a garden, and the "emasculated" subjects (Ellen and Carl), who are linked to the feminine world of flowers and glamorous neatness.

Soon enough, Carl unleashes an attack upon the "real" men of the house, Ralph and John. Ralph is hospitalized after flowers' fumes poison him, and John gets hurt with the sharp thorns of sentient plants. The emasculated monster progressively makes his presence felt within the house. If Carl is, in the words of Ellen, performing "magic," John asks him to "slow down" and leave some rooms free of flowers before turning the house into a funeral parlor, a comparison that returns the narrative to the starting point of the film. To displace John's hetero hyper-masculinity (as a successful man in possession of a beautiful house and an equally beautiful wife), Carl "feminizes" the house, invading it with extraordinary flowers. Even so, Carl never leaves aside his role of eroticized object, thus remaining emasculated. Furthermore, he is "property" of Ellen, while she, in turn, is "property" of her husband, thus deepening Carl's role as subject of a subject. In this scenario, he is an equal to the killer tree of *Womaneater*, constantly shifting from a position of masculine dominance to another of feminine submission.

It is not by chance that the action takes place in Puerto Rico, a country still subject to colonial powers. Since the same politics toward domination that sustain patriarchy sustain colonialism, women and land are seen as properties of the white men. The geographical location enhances the readings on dominators and dominated. All of Ellen's maids and helpers are Latinx. They, like animals and plants, are oppressed subjects within the global capitalist patriarchal world. In one scene, Ellen is shopping in a Latinx working-class neighborhood. There, she feels threatened by a carnival populated with Latinx people whose faces are painted depicting devils and figures of death. The menacing presence of the performers mirrors the dancers in the Amazonian scene in *Womaneater* as an example of threatening Otherness. It is significant that Helena, Ellen, and John share a bourgeois version of carnival that very night. The upper-class carnival, a costume ball, is not threatening but a sanitized version that keeps the world safe for rich people and where exoticism is only masquerade to discard once the night is over.

The ultimate shifting of powers comes with this masquerade ball celebrated by the Bennets. Ellen accepts the suggestion of being Persephone, goddess of flowers and plants. This choice links her closely to Carl, the master of plants, but also enhances the presence of flowers as sacred, important things. Plants are "sacred only through their association with a god/goddess."[54] However, the costume ball (in another contradictory shift) also enhances the framing of flowers and plants as objects of bourgeois consumption. Ellen designs a dress with both fabric and flowers intertwined. The flowers are of a rare species bred by Carl and specially delivered to Ellen to be part of her Persephone costume. The beauty of the dress is an attention-getter at the costume ball and, as Ellen states, "the flowers make the costume." Thus, flowers once again are ornaments to impress and signify status. Also, "constructing the idea of sacred plants only in terms of association with divinity depicts the plants themselves as *signs* or *symbols*, not as beings worthy of respect."[55] But Carl's supernatural powers manifest once again. The flowers shine with an unnatural glow that makes them striking and particularly beautiful. The uncanny power of the flowers also places Ellen into a hypnotic trance, in which she is briefly zombified. It is unclear what the purpose of the trance is, but Ellen is rescued by John, who rips the flowers off the dress. Like sentient beings, the uncanny flowers defend themselves, burning John's fingers at the contact. It is during the costume ball that flowers reach the ultimate point as both passive commodities (as part of an expensive dress, totally emptied of their vitality) and as active monstrous beings, exerting power on a woman.

Only after Ellen begins to fear Carl and decides to fire him ("passing" him to Helena, thus deepening the role of the gardener as a thing that rich wives exchange when bored) does he disclose his true nature as a supernatural entity. He reveals the extent of his control over the plants by commanding flowers and thorny plants to threaten Helena and Ellen. The film is vague about who or what Carl exactly is, but his total dominion over the plant world and his transformation into a tree suggests some kind of deity connected with Nature. As in *Womaneater*, the finale comes when the monstrous tree is set ablaze, putting an end to the story. As a last contradictory note, the total control that Carl held over nature empowers him, but his last transmutation into a tree is his ultimate doom. As Michael Marder argues, plants are mostly defined "by their incapacity to move, by their rootedness in the soil that renders them sedentary."[56] If horror narratives find ways to get around plants' stuckness,[57] turning them into mobile monsters, Carl becoming a tree rendered him passive, incapable of defending himself against Ellen's attack. Becoming a *common* plant (seemingly passive, since Carl-as-tree seems to have no power) rather than a hyper-masculine monster marks Carl's demise.

Womaneater indirectly engages with the zeitgeist of its era, telling a story in which women, working-class men, Latinx people, and plants are objects of consumption and exchange between white bourgeois citizens rather than subjects with rights. Movements such as second wave feminism, LGBTQ rights, or activists for animals' rights found a shared liberationist voice in their fight against a speciesist point of view that declared all of them inferior to "normalcy." Thus, both the women and the objectified gardener of Kay's film find themselves within a patriarchal entrapment but, even so, cannot avoid the gendered binaries that separate men from women, active from passive, plants from humans, even if both poles are, as here, circumscribed to Otherness and difference to a "proper" ethical status. In this scenario, *Womaneater* constantly plays with the contradictory nature of its monstrous plants, oppressed and oppressors at the same time.

CONCLUSION

The constant shifting of positions of the monstrous plants in these films parallels the ambiguity of the vegetable world. As mentioned, they are conceptualized as passive beings, but, despite apparent immobility, plants exhibit movement. This movement is often opaque to humans, alien to Westerners' conception of plant life. Since the movement "is too subtle for our cognitive and perceptual apparatuses to register in an everyday setting,"[58] we disregard their status as subjects and turn them into objects.

Plants, together with animals, are dominated aspects of Nature within capitalist and patriarchal culture. As beings framed into extreme passivity and dullness (along with the lack of an "active" sex), they are "feminized" and identified with womanhood, exacerbating the frame of speciesism and property. Both films, however, constantly shift the status of their green monsters: they are, at the same time, active/passive, subjects/objects, and hyper-masculine/emasculated beings. The constant struggle between hyper-active sexuality and a passive nature gives them their monstrosity, provoking ambiguity and contradictory readings. Thus, these creatures shatter any dyad while disrupting the "natural" hierarchies on which Western, colonialist, and capitalist thinking built its foundation. The real "sex" of the monstrous plants remains ambiguous at the end: if Carl is a plant, can he be considered "masculine" according to anthropocentric thinking? Is the mobile plant of *Womaneater* really a "womanizer" or a passive, feminized/colonized creature exploited by men? It can be argued that these creatures are both feminine and masculine. Still, this argument is made based on anthropocentric assumptions that leave aside the fact that our ideas on gender are, simply put, social artifices, lies that we tell ourselves. Grafting gendered ontology upon vegetal life is to make them more legible to human discourse, a form of exerting power upon them and turning them into utilitarian objects for human consumption. These films, lowbrow as they are, depict their monsters as creatures continually shifting from one category to another (passive/active, female/male, disempowered/powerful, victims/perpetrators) and thus disrupt fixity while highlighting all the artificiality behind gender assumptions. In this scenario, monstrous plants and their contradictory nature as living/non-living, quiet/mobile creatures only enhance the power that science fiction has to destabilize the human ethos as the "right" one and, potentially, change the world with a new enlightenment on living things.

Both *Womaneater* and *The Gardener* invite viewers to a continuous investigation of the representation of the vegetal world within film and to question the place that plants occupy in Western culture as well as how vegetation is codified and gendered, paralleling traditional binary thinking. Through an ecocritical reading, the films tap into questions of speciesism and plant life. Through the politics of colonization or the narrative of the "nature-run-amok" cycle, the films re-evaluate the naturalization of the status of women and plants as inferior beings. The monsters, creatures denying easy categorization, metaphorize the complex relationship of humans with the environment and the world of vegetation, a relationship fraught with miscomprehension.

NOTES

1. Robin Wood, "An Introduction to the American Horror Film," in *Planks of Reason: Essays on the Horror Film*, eds. Barry Keith Grant and Christopher Sharrett (Lanham: Scarecrow Press, 2004), 108.
2. Wood, "An Introduction," 111.
3. Wood, "An Introduction," 113.
4. Margaret Tarrat, "Monsters from the Id," in *Film Genre Reader III*, Vol. 3, ed. Barry Keith Grant (Austin: University of Texas Press, 2003), 348.
5. Michael Marder, *Plant-Thinking: A Philosophy of Vegetal Life* (New York: Columbia University Press, 2013), 20.
6. Marder, *Plant-Thinking*, 20.
7. Marder, *Plant-Thinking*, 87.
8. Marder, *Plant-Thinking*, 88.
9. Dawn Keetley, "Introduction: Six Theses on Plant Horror; or, Why Are Plants Horrifying?," in *Plant Horror: Approaches to the Monstrous Vegetal in Fiction and Film*, eds. Dawn Keetley and Angela Tenga (New York: Palgrave Macmillan, 2016), 5.
10. Keetley, "Introduction," 6.
11. Keetley, "Introduction," 10.
12. Keetley, "Introduction," 13.
13. Gargi Bhattacharyya, *Sexuality and Society: An Introduction* (New York: Routledge, 2005), 110.
14. Bradley Deane, *Masculinity and the New Imperialism: Rewriting Manhood in British Popular Literature, 1870–1940* (Cambridge: Cambridge University Press, 2014), 8.
15. Brian Stableford, *Science Fact and Science Fiction: An Encyclopedia* (New York: Routledge, 2006), 142.
16. Jennifer DeVere Brody, *Impossible Purities: Blackness, Femininity, and Victorian Culture* (Durham: Duke University Press, 1998), 92.
17. Matthew Hall, *Plants as Persons: A Philosophical Botany* (Albany: SUNY Press, 2011), 37.
18. Joan Raphael-Leff, "Contemporary Views on Femininity, Gender, and Generative Identity," in *On Freud's "Femininity,"* eds. Graciela Abelin-Sas Rose and Leticia Glocer Fiorini (London: Karnac, 2010), 64.
19. Greta Gaard, "New Directions for Ecofeminism: Toward a More Feminist Ecocriticism," *ISLE: Interdisciplinary Studies in Literature and Environment* 17, no. 4 (Autumn 2010): 645.
20. Greg Garrard, *Ecocriticism* (New York: Routledge, 2004), 3.
21. Stephen Rust, Salma Monani, and Sean Cubitt, "Introduction: Ecologies of Media," in *Ecomedia: Key Issues*, eds. Stephen Rust, Salma Monani, and Sean Cubitt (New York: Routledge, 2016), 2.
22. Rust, Monani, and Cubitt, "Introduction," 4.
23. Rust, Monani, and Cubitt, "Introduction," 6.
24. Stephen Rust and Salma Monani, "Introduction: Cuts to Dissolves—Defining and Situating Ecocinema Studies," in *Ecocinema: Theory and Practice*, eds. Stephen Rust, Salma Monani, and Sean Cubitt (New York: Routledge, 2013), 2.
25. Rust and Monani, "Introduction," 3, emphasis in the original.
26. Rust and Monani, "Introduction," 3.
27. Carter Soles and Kiu-Wai Chu, "Framing Visual Texts for Ecomedia Studies," in *Ecomedia: Key Issues*, eds. Stephen Rust, Salma Monani, and Sean Cubitt (New York: Routledge, 2016), 22.
28. Greta Gaard, "Ecofeminism Revisited: Rejecting Essentialism and Re-Placing Species in a Material Feminist Environmentalism," *Feminist Formations*, 23, no. 2 (Summer 2011): 38.
29. Graham Huggan and Helen Tiffin, *Postcolonial Ecocriticism: Literature, Animals, Environment* (New York: Routledge, 2010), 5.

30. Jytte Nhanenge, *Ecofeminism: Towards Integrating the Concerns of Women, Poor People, and Nature into Development* (Lanham: University Press of America, 2011), 175.

31. Sheila Collins, *A Different Heaven and Earth* (Valley Forge: Judson Press, 1974), 161.

32. Carol J. Adams, *Neither Man nor Beast: Feminism and the Defense of Animals* (London: Bloomsbury, 2018), 101.

33. Esme Cleall, *Missionary Discourses of Difference: Negotiating Otherness in the British Empire, 1840–1900* (New York: Palgrave Macmillan, 2012), 2.

34. David Krasner, "Black *Salome*: Exoticism, Dance, and Racial Myths," in *African American Performance and Theater History: A Critical Reader*, eds. Harry Elam, Jr., and David Krasner (New York: Oxford University Press, 2001), 195.

35. Keetley, "Introduction," 13.

36. Gabriele Schwab, *Imaginary Ethnographies: Literature, Culture, and Subjectivity* (New York: Columbia University Press, 2012), 141.

37. C. J. Pascoe and Tristan Bridges, "Exploring Masculinities: History, Reproduction, Hegemony, and Dislocation," in *Exploring Masculinities: Identity, Inequality, Continuity, and Change*, eds. C. J. Pascoe and Tristan Bridges (New York: Oxford University Press, 2016), 12.

38. Raewyn Connell, *Masculinities* (Berkeley: University of California Press. 1995), 77.

39. Pascoe and Bridges, "Exploring Masculinities," 18.

40. Rosaura Sánchez, *Telling Identities: The California Testimonios* (Minneapolis: University of Minnesota Press, 1995), 197.

41. Hall, *Plants as Persons*, 20.

42. Carol J. Adams, *The Sexual Politics of Meat: A Feminist-Vegetarian Critical Theory* (London: Continuum, 2010), 61.

43. Patricia Kerslake, *Science Fiction and Empire* (Liverpool: Liverpool University Press, 2010), 43.

44. Kerslake, *Science Fiction and Empire*, 43.

45. Stableford, *Science Fact and Science Fiction*, 142.

46. Scott McFarlane, *The Hippie Narrative: A Literary Perspective on the Counterculture* (Jefferson: McFarland, 2007), 199.

47. Hannah Gay, *The Silwood Circle: A History of Ecology and The Making of Scientific Careers in Late Twentieth-Century Britain* (London: Imperial College Press, 2013), 72.

48. Peter Singer, *Animal Liberation: A New Ethics for Our Treatment of Animals* (New York: Random House, 1975), 11.

49. Catherine Ziegler, *Favored Flowers: Culture and Economy in a Global System* (Durham: Duke University Press, 2007), 225.

50. Ziegler, *Favored Flowers*, 23.

51. Kevin Floyd, *The Reification of Desire: Toward a Queer Marxism* (Minneapolis: University of Minnesota Press, 2009), 171.

52. Maurice Yacowar, *The Films of Paul Morrissey* (Cambridge: Cambridge University Press, 1993), 7.

53. Hall, *Plants as Persons*, 157.

54. Hall, *Plants as Persons*, 121.

55. Hall, *Plants as Persons*, 121, emphasis in the original.

56. Marder, *Plant-Thinking*, 19.

57. Keetley, "Introduction," 13.

58. Marder, *Plant-Thinking*, 21.

BIBLIOGRAPHY

Adams, Carol J. *Neither Man nor Beast: Feminism and the Defense of Animals*. London: Bloomsbury, 2018.

———. *The Sexual Politics of Meat: A Feminist-Vegetarian Critical Theory*. London: Continuum, 2010.
Bhattacharyya, Gargi. *Sexuality and Society: An Introduction*. New York: Routledge, 2005.
Cleall, Esme. *Missionary Discourses of Difference: Negotiating Otherness in the British Empire, 1840–1900*. New York: Palgrave Macmillan, 2012.
Collins, Sheila. *A Different Heaven and Earth*. Valley Forge: Judson Press, 1974.
Connell, Raewyn. *Masculinities*. Berkeley: University of California Press, 1995.
Deane, Bradley. *Masculinity and the New Imperialism: Rewriting Manhood in British Popular Literature, 1870–1940*. Cambridge: Cambridge University Press, 2014.
DeVere Brody, Jennifer. *Impossible Purities: Blackness, Femininity, and Victorian Culture*. Durham: Duke University Press, 1998.
Floyd, Kevin. *The Reification of Desire: Toward a Queer Marxism*. Minneapolis: University of Minnesota Press, 2009.
Gaard, Greta. "Ecofeminism Revisited: Rejecting Essentialism and Re-Placing Species in a Material Feminist Environmentalism." *Feminist Formations* 23, no. 2 (Summer 2011): 26–53.
———. "New Directions for Ecofeminism: Toward a More Feminist Ecocriticism." *ISLE: Interdisciplinary Studies in Literature and Environment* 17, no. 4 (2010): 643–65.
Garrard, Greg. *Ecocriticism*. New York: Routledge, 2004.
Gay, Hannah. *The Silwood Circle: A History of Ecology and The Making of Scientific Careers in Late Twentieth-Century Britain*. London: Imperial College Press, 2013.
Hall, Matthew. *Plants as Persons: A Philosophical Botany*. Albany: SUNY Press, 2011.
Huggan, Graham, and Helen Tiffin. *Postcolonial Ecocriticism: Literature, Animals, Environment*. New York: Routledge, 2010.
Keetley, Dawn. "Introduction: Six Theses on Plant Horror; or, Why Are Plants Horrifying?" In *Plant Horror: Approaches to the Monstrous Vegetal in Fiction and Film*, edited by Dawn Keetley and Angela Tenga, 1–30. New York: Palgrave Macmillan, 2016.
Kerslake, Patricia. *Science Fiction and Empire*. Liverpool: Liverpool University Press, 2010.
Krasner, David. "Black *Salome*: Exoticism, Dance, and Racial Myths." In *African American Performance and Theater History: A Critical Reader*, edited by Harry Elam, Jr., and David Krasner, 192–211. New York: Oxford University Press, 2001.
Marder, Michael. *Plant-Thinking: A Philosophy of Vegetal Life*. New York: Columbia University Press, 2013.
McFarlane, Scott. *The Hippie Narrative: A Literary Perspective on the Counterculture*. Jefferson: McFarland, 2007.
Nhanenge, Jytte. *Ecofeminism: Towards Integrating the Concerns of Women, Poor People, and Nature into Development*. Lanham: University Press of America, 2011.
Pascoe, C. J., and Tristan Bridges. "Exploring Masculinities: History, Reproduction, Hegemony, and Dislocation." In *Exploring Masculinities: Identity, Inequality, Continuity, and Change*, edited by C. J. Pascoe and Tristan Bridges, 1–34. New York: Oxford University Press, 2016.
Raphael-Leff, Joan. "Contemporary Views on Femininity, Gender, and Generative Identity." In *On Freud's "Femininity,"* edited by Graciela Abelin-Sas Rose and Leticia Glocer Fiorini, 56–78. London: Karnac, 2010.
Rust, Stephen, and Salma Monani. "Introduction: Cuts to Dissolves—Defining and Situating Ecocinema Studies." In *Ecocinema: Theory and Practice*, edited by Stephen Rust, Salma Monani, and Sean Cubitt, 1–13. New York: Routledge, 2013.
Rust, Stephen, Salma Monani, and Sean Cubitt. "Introduction: Ecologies of Media." In *Ecomedia: Key Issues*, edited by Stephen Rust, Salma Monani, and Sean Cubitt, 1–14. New York: Routledge, 2016.
Sánchez, Rosaura. *Telling Identities: The California Testimonios*. Minneapolis: University of Minnesota Press, 1995.

Schwab, Gabriele. *Imaginary Ethnographies: Literature, Culture, and Subjectivity*. New York: Columbia University Press, 2012.
Singer, Peter. *Animal Liberation: A New Ethics for Our Treatment of Animals*. New York: Random House, 1975.
Soles, Carter, and Kiu-Wai Chu. "Framing Visual Texts for Ecomedia Studies." In *Ecomedia: Key Issues*, edited by Stephen Rust, Salma Monani, and Sean Cubitt, 17–26. New York: Routledge, 2016.
Stableford, Brian. *Science Fact and Science Fiction: An Encyclopedia*. New York: Routledge, 2006.
Tarrat, Margaret. "Monsters from the Id." In *Film Genre Reader III*, Vol. 3, edited by Barry Keith Grant, 346–355. Austin: University of Texas Press, 2003.
The Gardener. Directed by James Kay, KKI Films Production, 1974.
Womaneater. Directed by Charles Saunders, Fortress Film Production, 1958.
Wood, Robin. "An Introduction to the American Horror Film." In *Planks of Reason: Essays on the Horror Film*, edited by Barry Keith Grant and Christopher Sharrett, 107–139. Lanham: Scarecrow Press, 2004.
Yacowar, Maurice. *The Films of Paul Morrissey*. Cambridge: Cambridge University Press, 1993.
Ziegler, Catherine. *Favored Flowers: Culture and Economy in a Global System*. Durham: Duke University Press, 2007.

FIVE

"So Very Natural an Occurrence"

Engendering Nature's Antagonism in Mary Shelley's The Last Man

Steve Asselin

It has become commonplace to describe Mary Shelley's *Frankenstein* as science fiction's urtext ever since Brian Aldiss first advanced the claim. Warren Wagar has advanced a similar claim of generic primacy for Shelley's less famous sf work, *The Last Man* (1826), describing it as "the first major example of secular eschatology in literature,"[1] progenitor of the (post-)apocalyptic genre. Shelley was not the first to tackle the idea of a Last Man (Cousin de Grainville's 1805 *Le Dernier Homme* and Lord Byron's 1816 "Darkness" are notable precedents) or imagine a terrible plague (John Wilson's 1816 *The City of the Plague* had already entertained such dark fantasies), but she placed these elements together to create a scenario new to fiction, the global pandemic, in a novel that largely disassociates itself from the religious trappings of prior apocalyptic narratives. Though long in the shadow of its more famous novelistic cousin, critics have paid increasing attention to *Last Man* in the last few decades. *Last Man* criticism generally follows three main strands: the study of the novel for its autobiographical origins, as many of the characters are based on Shelley's friends and family; for its layered treatment of gender issues including critiques of masculine aggression; and most recently for its depiction of an epidemic and the deconstructive effects of such a crisis on individuals and society. In this chapter, I seek to fuse the discussion of gender and epidemic by examining the novel's portrayal of Nature—a character who is not only possessed of gendered characteristics, but who, through conflation, shares those traits with the epidemic—in order to demonstrate how gender is an artificial human construct that collapses when opposed to the sheer diversity of the natural world.

Last Man begins with protagonist and narrator Lionel Verney's gradual inclusion into high society, acquiring a group of friends who are clear analogues for Mary Shelley's own social circle, including the philosophical Adrian (a stand-in for Percy Shelley) and the ambitious Lord Raymond (Byron's counterpart), who wages war against the Turks in the name of Greek liberation. It suddenly changes direction at the outset of the second of three volumes with the introduction of a global pandemic, simply called the Plague, that will wipe out all of humanity until only Lionel remains alive, the titular last man. The Plague is a slow-moving disaster, leading to human extinction over a seven-year time span. This leaves dwindling humanity ample time to consider how their conceptions of themselves and their relationships with the rest of the natural world change as their "remaining particle of futurity dwindled into a point,"[2] making it a fruitful novel for a queerly inflected ecocritical analysis.

I argue that Nature discards artificial differentiations like gender in sweeping away humanity's anthropocentric constructs, in contrast to prior critics who seized on the novel's critiques of masculinity and based their interpretation of the novel on the perceived gender conflict between humanity and feminized Nature. Anne K. Mellor reads the feminine violence of the Plague as a reaction to "[t]he domination of masculine values."[3] James McKusick suggests that the species-selective Plague is "Mother Nature herself . . . taking revenge" on the masculinized human species "for his impious desecration of the very sources of life," principally due to Lord Raymond's "arrogant masculine quest for world domination."[4] But both Mellor and McKusick accept the characters' conventional gendering of Nature and Plague as female, and so their interpretations follow those characters' in viewing the book as a binary battle of the sexes. It is important to recognize that this gendering is a human cultural imposition; whatever the characters think, neither Nature nor the Plague are female but queerly belong to no sex, even as the domain of Nature encompasses every diverse, extant form of sexuality. In challenging the imposition of gender on Nature and Plague in this novel, I am also troubling interpretations that rely on gendered opposition and which replicate the normative divisions found within the text.

The Plague's dissolution of normative gender demonstrates how it operates as an agent of deconstruction, one which reaches into the very material substance of the bodies it inflects. Previous critics working on *Last Man*, like Barbara Johnson and Audrey Fisch, have identified several areas in which the Plague deconstructs differentiation, including the boundaries between races, nations, and class.[5] However, these are large-scale social categories. Using a materialist and ecocritical approach to the

Plague—in other words, considering the Plague in tandem with queer Nature—I take the analysis of the Plague as deconstructive agent further: the Plague, in individual human bodies, deconstructs even biological assumptions about gender, reproduction, and the boundedness of human bodies. While some critics have read Nature in the novel as merely "indifferent"[6] to human suffering, Fisch acknowledges that "Nature, personified as and exemplified by the Plagues, kills all"[7] but Lionel and is thus responsible for human extinction, troubling the progressive potential of the Plague's deconstruction because no one is left alive to enjoy the benefits of the deconstruction of social norms. I argue that this productive potential is recaptured if we think about the way humanity (in this novel and generally) believes itself separate from and often above Nature. The Plague dissolves this anthropocentric differentiation in the most permanent way possible, and so both the death of the individual and the extinction of the species become the ultimate return to Nature.

I begin this analysis by using queer ecocriticism to highlight the heterosexist assumptions inherent in the transformation of the natural environment into a personification with a clear gender. The Plague, in the novel, is broadly conflated with Nature, a fusion that lends both a persona of gendered antagonism. I argue that gendering what I call Nature/Plague allows the novel's characters to relate to this nonhuman entity in a more familiar fashion. In particular, the male characters invest Nature with the archetypal female roles of mother, villain, and lover in order to negotiate and dominate this relationship. I examine the novel's construction of each of these three stereotypical personas in turn. Characters try to make Nature into a mother figure to claim her protection; however, Nature's apparent disregard for the future of the human species challenges humanity's privileging of parenthood and heterosexual reproduction. Characters try to make Nature/Plague into a villain to reassert patriarchal authority through combat with a female tyrant, but the conflict is futile and merely serves to feminize these male characters. Lionel, beset by loneliness as Last Man, attempts to turn Nature into a lover and find companionship in the nonhuman world, but the attempt leads him into a queered state of sex, gender, and desire that turns into self-loathing. In all cases, trying to relate to Nature on the basis of imposed gender constructs reveals the weaknesses inherent in those constructs, and Nature/Plague begins to deconstruct ideas like childhood, masculinity, and heterosexuality. In the last section of this chapter, I take this deconstruction further to show that supposedly feminized Nature in fact favors no gender as it is an avatar of a queer nonhuman world. Nature/Plague, through the corporeal and material penetration of the body, works to dissolve both the physical and the ideological separations between humanity and their environment, as death becomes a reintegration into the multifarious relationships of the nonhuman world.

NATURE/PLAGUE: THE CONFLATION OF EPIDEMIC, ENVIRONMENT, AND GENDER

To conceive of the natural world as antagonistic, the natural world must first be subsumed into a coherent persona capable of the motivation that antagonism implies. I wish to make clear from the outset that when I refer to capital-N Nature in this chapter, I am referring to a character in a novel, albeit one which may largely be an invention of the other characters. Like Nicole Seymour, my interest lies not in recovering some conceptual, pure "nature" beneath Lionel's anthropocentric narrative but in investigating "the processes of construction"[8] by which Nature (and Plague) is personified, gendered, and slotted into familiar narratives based on human relationships. My reading of Nature as a nonhuman entity forced into a human and gendered persona has been influenced by the queer ecological work of Seymour, who shows how queer theory enables environmentalism by deconstructing heterosexist assumptions about nature; Noreen Giffney, who examines the apocalyptic potential of queer theory when applied to the environment; and Myra J. Hird, who has shown how the diversity of sexes and sexuality in nature challenges humanity's tendency to view itself as the universal standard.[9] Queer ecology is, deliberately, a loosely defined critical practice meant to encompass an array of disciplinary perspectives that share the common goal of exposing and disrupting the heterosexist and gender normative discourse focused on the environment, a discourse which has often been wielded to define what is natural in ways to serve prevailing, dominant institutional notions of gender and sexuality. Such, I argue, is the function of the discourse around Nature in this novel, particularly the application of gender to Nature: an attempt by male characters to dominate their environment, although one doomed to failure as the Plague overpowers almost all.

I take my cue from the novel itself in juxtaposing Nature (the character) and Plague (who also becomes a character, overlapping with Nature). Although never coterminous—for instance, the Plague comes to an end during the last chapters of the book, but Nature does not—the process of fusion that results in what I call Nature/Plague is important because within this unitary phenomenon both Nature and Plague gain aspects of the other's persona, most notably gender and an antagonistic role towards humanity. The novel's rhetoric conflates the Plague with Nature generally in a number of ways. The Plague is frequently naturalized through animal metaphors, in which it is compared to a "serpent" or "wolves,"[10] animals notably chosen for their symbolic antipathy and threat to human life. The Plague manifests alongside and is compared to natural disasters: windstorms, earthquakes, even meteorite strikes are all part of the "celestial fireworks"[11] that accompany the creeping apocalypse of epidemic, while the Plague itself is called the "sister of the tornado, the earthquake, and the simoom"[12]—the term "sister" not only a sign of gender but of the degree to which Plague is anthropomorphized, rhetorically incorporated into human familial relations alongside other disasters. Finally, the Plague is incorporated into natural processes, like air currents (per miasma theory) and seasons, to the point that Lord Raymond shortsightedly chides his wife for worrying about "so very natural an occurrence"[13] as the seasonal advent of epidemic at the beginning of the outbreak. Characters welcome winter and dread the return of spring because the Plague gains and decreases in virulence in tune with the perceived waxing and waning of Nature's own growth through the seasons. Indeed, so proximate are Nature and Plague that I use the term "Nature/Plague" not just to designate a shared persona but to describe the effect of the novel's epidemic: as I will discuss in the final section of this chapter, characters who contract the Plague are essentially infected with a virulent form of Nature, with all its queered and deconstructive potential.

Plague's acquisition of gender is both cause and consequence of the union with Nature. Just as the Plague becomes conflated with Nature writ large, so too does the Plague come to be associated with femininity. The gendering of Nature and Plague is inconsistent throughout the novel; as Paley points out, the Plague starts off as a neuter phenomenon (for instance, plague "raise[s] *its* serpent-head"[14] [my emphasis]), and yet as it becomes a greater force in the lives of the protagonists, it gains a capital letter and then a female gender, as when Plague is called "*Queen* of the World" and all humans are "vanquished and destroyed by *her*"[15] (my emphasis). The gendering of Nature as female is conventional, so the Plague's acquisition of female gender stems in part from its near overlap with Nature. But just as the female gendering of Nature functions to define it oppositionally against masculinized culture, so too is the gendering of Plague a function of its oppositional role in the narrative: she is defined against the men who try to organize society to counter the Plague and against the Last Man who narrates the story. The imposition of gender becomes more pronounced as the crisis deepens, which explicates the purpose of personification: the characters feel helpless and disempowered in the face of the impersonal forces which threaten them, and turning Nature/Plague into a person (even a relentlessly hostile one) is comforting because the idea of a person is more familiar, more readily grasped at an intellectual and emotional level. If Nature/Plague is a person, it allows for some kind of relationship between that personification and both individuals and humanity writ large, substituting the discomforts of bodily interpenetration by the Plague for the more limited domain of the interpersonal. Gendering humanizes the personified entity and helps define the scope of those interactions. The utility of such a gendering, for the male main character, lies in the ability to pattern his relationship with Nature (and the Plague) along certain archetypes—mother, villain, and lover—which I will examine in turn.

NATURE-AS-MOTHER: REPRODUCTIVE FAILURE AND THE LIMITS OF FUTURITY

A Last Man narrative poses an inherent challenge to what Lee Edelman in *No Future* defines as "reproductive futurism,"[16] the belief that people should act to better the world for the sake of subsequent generations, since, nominally, there will be no future generations.[17] Reproduction is a recurrent fixation in Shelley's oeuvre, but where *Frankenstein* is focused on the reproductive excess of Victor's scientific, misogynistic, asexual form of reproduction, *Last Man* is about reproductive failure: the inability to fulfill the biological imperative to assure futurity is read as parental failure. The parents, in this case, are both the male characters, who as fathers cannot protect their children from Plague, and Nature, whom the characters view as a common Mother figure but who seemingly destroys her children.

Lionel's highly conventional notion of the feminine elevates motherhood to the greatest aspiration for women, inherently yoking gender, sex, and reproduction. The Mother Nature persona is likewise conventional; Lionel, as an orphaned child in the Cumberland wilds, saw Nature as a surrogate parent and invokes "the dear soothings of maternal Nature" several times in this narrative as a source of comfort and security, even during the crisis. Early on, Percy Shelley stand-in Adrian calls humanity the "happy nurslings of mother-earth,"[18] casting humans as the children of Mother Earth who are therefore protected by what they assume is a desire for reproductive futurity on her part, just as they, as fathers, find comfort in the belief that they continue to exist through their children.

But characters who conceive of the "earth . . . like a tender mother . . . found her a destroyer"[19] instead, suggesting that this is one parent who has opted out of reproductive futurity. Queer theory has often been suspicious "of the equation of the whole of nature with compulsory heterosexuality"[20] due to the complex history of the naturalization of sexuality, but *Last Man* presents a scenario that inverts this conflation, as the Plague and Nature, as mother or in any other persona, actively dismantle the heterosexual reproduction on which both ideological and biological futurity depends. Due to the Plague, "man" (humanity writ as masculine) sees "his inheritance on earth cut off" and "shrinks into insignificance,"[21] ceasing to exist as a cultural being because the characters can foresee no biological posterity to provide any action in the present a legacy in years to come. In a heteronormative dyad, the partner of a patriarchal humanity is maternal Nature. But Nature's retreat from the maternal role exposes the weakness of the binary conception: absent the desire for futurity on the part of one of the nominal parents, both the physical possibility for and the ideological investment in futurity begin to unravel. The debate, for these characters, isn't whether Nature is a mother or not, but rather whether she is a good parent.

Because heterosexual reproductivity relies on having children, the novel's anxiety of extinction is often expressed with specific reference to children. As discussed, the characters impose on Nature the role of mother in order to seek the presumptive protection of the role of children, but the treatment of children becomes a guideline for good or bad parenting, and ultimately fears over futurity fall heavily on the novel's child characters, standing in for childhood generally. The male characters' attempts to recruit Nature as a collective mother figure bypasses the novel's female characters, who are largely defined by motherhood and sublimated under the Nature-as-mother persona; even Lionel's prepubescent niece Clara is deemed virtuous for her maternal care for the story's younger children and as the last woman to perish is defined by her potential to be mother to all future humanity. The only exception to the overdetermining status of motherhood for the novel's female characters is Raymond's would-be paramour Evadne, who not only dies childless but dies cross-dressed as a Greek soldier, the masculine masquerade a duly punished denial of the reproductive potential she, as a woman, is supposed to prioritize. Paley considers Evadne an oracle of the Plague for her portentous death,[22] but I would argue that Evadne is actually symbolic of the Plague insofar as she works to deconstruct gender, including a disregard of reproductive futurity. The other female characters are praised or condemned by Lionel to the extent that they are good mothers; and so Lionel's mother-in-law, the Countess of Windsor, whose regard for her children is political rather than affective, fulfills an antagonistic role in the narrative, while Lionel upbraids his sister Perdita for her suicidal thoughts because suicide would, and does, leave her daughter Clara an orphan. By abandoning their children—the Countess by fleeing to Austria, Perdita through suicide—they are bad mothers and therefore failures as women.

The fate of children becomes key to the perception of whether a mother—and thus Nature-as-mother—fulfills her role. Lionel defines the narcissistic stakes of Edelman's reproductive futurism when he claims it is in humanity's "nature to wish to continue our systems and thoughts to posterity through our own offspring,"[23] but this already "irrational faith"[24] in the survival of the self in one's children is shattered by the Plague, which does not spare children. Indeed, since it will not be followed by adulthood, the concept of childhood itself ceases to have relevance, absent any "difference" between "parent and child"[25] in terms of potential futurity—one of many seemingly natural and biological inherent differences that the Plague deconstructs. Lionel struggles with his simultaneous, irrational belief in reproductive futurity and in the protective shield of Nature-as-mother throughout the novel, sometimes believing that "his children and his children's children will carry down the . . . form of man" past these apocalyptic events yet conversely fearing that those same "children" will never "ripen into maturity"[26] as humanity is seemingly abandoned by the neglectful maternal persona of Nature. Translating this anxiety over his own children to the broader human race, Lionel rapidly alternates between the conviction that human extinction is inevitable, imagining a post-pestilential human race, and back again: the idea that "[p]osterity is no more" is too radical a concept for Lionel to ever fully accept, and he clings to the belief that any future readers of his text "will be human,"[27] despite the mounting evidence that humanity will soon be extinct. Lionel's imaginative failure stems partially from an offended sense of fairness—he cannot conceive that all human achievements and sufferings have been for nothing—and partially a consequence of his anthropocentrism, as an inhuman world is too far beyond his experience to envision or accept.

As the novel's plot proceeds and Nature becomes increasingly conflated with the Plague, Nature-as-mother's bad parenting moves from neglect to active hostility. Lionel believes that "Nature, our mother . . . had turned on us a brow of menace,"[28] and the assumed hostile intent behind the Plague portrays Nature as overtly infanticidal, destroying her own creation. I argue this is a result of anthropocentric assumptions. Though Lionel describes the Plague years as "the last throes of time-worn nature,"[29] the environment, unsurprisingly, thrives even as humanity vanishes because "death fell on man alone"[30] and all other creatures are untouched by the Plague; animals benefit greatly from their new freedom and the shelter humans have left behind. Consequently, the accusation of infanticide against Nature-as-mother reduces the natural world to the function of humanity's provider and progenitor, ignoring all other species. Having failed in this function due to humanity's extinction, Lionel believes that Nature no longer serves a purpose—"Nature was the same, as when she was the kind mother of the human race; now, childless and forlorn," the continued existence of fauna, flora, and natural features like rivers and stars baffles Lionel as "man is not here to enjoy them."[31] To him, a post-human planet is a "dead world" and "nature's drear barrenness,"[32] regardless of the persistence of all other forms of life. His anthropocentrism is so thoroughly ingrained that Lionel does not think of animals, plants, and even the physical features of the planet as owed existences independent of their observation, enjoyment, and utility by humans. In other words, humanity is not the sole "child" of Nature-as-mother, but one amongst countless other existences. This hubris turns the events of the novel into a form of poetic justice, an extended demonstration of how little humanity matters to the broader universe, physically and spiritually. In contrast to religious narratives of human transgression and punishment by a paternal figure, here humanity is reduced to the status of a selfish child that has earned the opprobrium of the maternal figure by its utter disregard for its siblings, conceived here as the other species and even the non-living environment. I would venture that the likeliest motive for Nature's antagonism in the novel is punishing this anthropocentrism or eliminating it altogether by wiping out humanity.

NATURE-AS-VILLAIN: ECOPHOBIA, PARANOIA, AND THE TYRANNY OF NATURE

Instead of a mothering Nature, then, "the world" becomes "a harsh stepmother,"[33] invoking an archetypical female villainous role, and one that suits the suspicion that Nature-as-mother is unconcerned with humanity's futurity in favor of other "children." Characters perceive themselves as locked in battle with an antagonistic natural world (primarily represented by Plague), with the very survival of the species at stake. Contained in the threat of human extinction is Nature-as-villain as a deconstructive agent who, in this text, takes the idea of queer negativity and its embrace of the antisocial and the death drive to its furthest extreme. Confronting this possibility leads to another potentially hostile worldview: "ecophobia," an accusation that has often been leveled against theory (queer or poststructuralist) on the basis that it ignores materiality.[34] But where *Last Man* is concerned, queer theory can be productively used to deconstruct the sources of human fear or distrust of the environment.

I take issue with Simon Estok's definition of ecophobia as "an irrational and groundless hatred of the natural world,"[35] one which lies at the root of our ongoing disregard and destruction of the environment. While it is certainly irrational for humanity, as a species, to destroy the environment that sustains our own existence, hatred (or, more properly, fear) of nature is not always groundless. To be unafraid of nature is a privilege not enjoyed by those who, notwithstanding aggravating anthropogenic factors, live in areas prone to natural disasters or who depend on a cooperative environment for food security—a condition in which most of humanity existed before technologies of surplus and storage.[36] Shelley herself was a witness to both the climatic effects of the 1815 eruption of Mt. Tambora and the "failed harvests" of subsequent years due to the cold and lack of sunlight, resulting in the last great "hemisphere subsistence crisis"[37] to affect the Western world. The uncertainty introduced by vulnerability to natural events easily translates into apprehension and outright fear, and dependency on the environment becomes resentment of nature when it proves unsuitable to human needs. Last Man narratives often exploit fears of humanity's vulnerability to nature by extending disaster or infertility scenarios to their greatest extent; for characters subjected to such environmental apocalypses, there is "[n]othing . . . more appallingly insecure than living on a planet."[38] In *Last Man*, Shelley depicts not the failure of Nature but rather its hostility; she explores the potential motivations behind seemingly arbitrary events emerging from the natural world (mainly the Plague) and discovers purposeful hostility that requires the personification of Nature as an antagonist.

It is easy to understand why the characters come to adopt an increasingly paranoid attitude towards a natural world they perceive as haunted by a "hostile agency."[39] The implacable advance of the Plague is combined with a series of "eruptions of nature"[40]—storms, meteor strikes, tidal waves—that appear designed to impede humanity's attempts to cope with the Plague. Against the backdrop of the Plague's assault on humanity, these events become part of a pattern signaling Nature's sinister intent; while the Plague is primarily responsible for the extinction of humanity, it is but the chief aspect of antagonistic Nature. Even after the Plague has passed and it becomes theoretically possible to envision rebuilding humanity thanks to Clara, the last surviving woman, no fewer than three storms converge on the survivors at sea and drown this presumptive new Eve, foreclosing the last hope for heterosexual reproductivity. The protagonists become certain of their foe and her intentions; feminized Nature has decided that "man and all his efforts" would be "for ever annihilated," and the survivors can do little but "quail before the savage enmity of nature."[41] The extremity by which Nature seemingly prosecutes her campaign against humanity causes many in the novel to fall into religious terror, a reaction typical of the fear that they are being deliberately targeted by a higher power; but in this text, Nature displaces God as the agent responsible for such destruction, demonstrating an ability to destroy equal and opposite to the traditional association of Nature with feminized creative, generative power.

The persona of Nature/Plague-as-villain is the most common and useful one for the characters, because it grants them an apparent "foe"[42] they can combat, as opposed to airy vapors they are helpless against. The characters often conceive of their interaction with Plague as a struggle against "barbarous tyranny":[43] Adrian, who spends much of the narrative feminized by physical weakness and ill health, revives when in conflict with the Plague, swearing "to the last I will struggle against her."[44] In so doing, he adopts the mantle of freedom fighter previously worn by the ultra-masculine Lord Raymond in his military struggle to free Greece from Turkish dominion. The antagonist persona allows the characters to view the daily horrors of an epidemic as a manly battle against a female despot, such that victory means not only a triumph of life over death but the restoration of normative gender hierarchies where the masculine rules over the feminine. This is, therefore, a gendered conflict between "Nature" and "man," one that follows typical gender divisions in masculinizing humanity as a cultural creature separate from a natural world that is conventionally feminized. Paley calls the appearance of female antagonists[45] in Last Man narratives "significant," but he does not say what this significance is;[46] as stated, I believe these dark female personas appear so frequently because they are the destructive counterparts of the creative, generative potential associated with feminized Nature.

The perception of a gendered conflict between masculine humanity and feminized Nature in *Last Man* renders the assault of the Plague as an attack on (and eventually a deconstruction of) masculinity in several respects. At a cultural level, Lionel performs several elegies in which he bids "[f]arewell to the giant powers of man,"[47] listing the various masculine cultural practices (warfare, politics, science and engineering, the arts) which have been forsaken as superfluous during the Plague years and are doomed to vanish altogether once humanity is extinct. While the fight for survival that replaces usual cultural practices can still be read as masculine, humanity has been brought closer to the feminized domains of nature and instinct. Troubling the heteronormative belief that male bodies should not be the objects of penetration, especially in male/female interactions, characters perceive themselves as penetrated and colonized by a feminized Plague. Furthermore, the illness feminizes the patient, as when Lionel contracts the disease and lies in a torpor for several days: the sufferer becomes the acted-upon rather than an actor, whose body is deprived of masculine values of strength and self-reliance as the patient must be cared for—a task which, in this book, generally falls to women (Lionel's wife, Idris, in his case), making the sufferer subject to feminine authority once more. Finally, even the strong emotional reactions of men in proximity to disease and its victims—grief, worry, panic—are presented as feminizing: Adrian's bout of illness and madness "half unmans"[48] Lord Raymond when he witnesses it, and Lionel accuses himself of being a "woman, nurtured, effeminate and contemptible"[49] when he panics over Adrian's welfare, a self-directed misogynistic tirade whose virulence stems from a repressed (because likewise feminizing) homoerotic affection for Adrian. Despite the universality of grief in the novel, Lionel insists on gendering the performance of mourning, calling "happy . . . women who can weep" because "shame and habitual restraint hold back a man"[50] in similar circumstances—a difference Lionel believes is inherent to the constitution of the sexes, as "[w]omen bear with resignation these long drawn ills" of suffering and grief which "to a man's impatient spirit . . . were intolerable."[51] The male characters' misogynistic contempt for their own emotions (and the toll such repression enacts on them) can be read as Shelley's own criticism of toxic forms of masculinity: though she shows great sympathy towards her characters, all but Lionel die (and Lionel's lonely fate may be considered worse than death), and so *Last Man* ends with the ultimate victory of feminized Nature/Plague.

The narrative of a personal and antagonistic Nature is useful to Lionel even after humanity has been wiped out: as Last Man, Lionel turns from an inability to envision the post-human world to resentment of it, wishing revenge against "the murderous engine which has mowed down the children of men."[52] He calls for "blight and pestiferous exhalations" to enter "the hollow caverns and breathing places of earth" and "fill her stony veins with corruption, so that . . . herbage may no longer flourish, the trees may rot, and the rivers run with gall . . . the everlasting mountains be decomposed . . . and the genial atmosphere . . . lose all powers of generation and sustenance."[53] Lionel's "pestiferous exhalations" would be a new Plague that would destroy Nature in turn, infecting the Earth in the same way it would a human body, as shown by the comparison of caverns to lungs and the play on the word "veins" to imbue the Earth with a circulatory system to spread the pestilence globally. The very material substance of the planet is re-imagined as organic matter, capable of rotting and dying; Lionel's curse is, after a fashion, an early take on the Gaia Principle—but one which seeks the death of Gaia! Believing Nature has declared war on humanity, Lionel, in extremis, contemplates embracing the cruelty he believes the natural world to be guilty of; he "bestow[s] a malediction on every other of nature's offspring, which dares live,"[54] transferring his revenge onto the other species who, being spared the Plague and inheriting Earth, he believes received preferential treatment over humanity. But Nature does not heed him in any respect; his desire for vengeance proves as impotent as his earlier attempts to conceive of the conflict between humanity and Nature/Plague as symmetrical, one humanity could possibly win. Nature is infinitely vaster than any one species and gives no regard for either aggressive posturing or futile revindications.

NATURE-AS-LOVER: QUEERED DESIRE AND ROMANCING CONSTRUCTS

Earlier I discussed how humanity's patriarchs saw themselves paired with maternal Nature in order to assure reproductive futurity. There is, inherent in this conception, the suggestion of a sexual union between masculine humanity and feminized Nature, albeit at an abstract level. Unlike the other two personas, mother and villain, discussed outright by the characters, Nature-as-lover is only ever implied because of the inevitably queer dimension of such a romance. Lionel's belief in his "companionship with nature"[55] dates to his childhood, and, as Last Man, Lionel finds that "wild natural scenery" reminds him "less acutely of my hopeless . . . loneliness"[56] because he comes to conceive of the natural world as a companion, as in his youth. Lionel is not alone in this feeling; he and Adrian often approach sublime Nature with a worshipfulness less like a child to a parent and more like a courtly lover, performing compulsive odes to the landscape and hoping to be elevated "from our dull mortal abode, to the palaces of Nature's own."[57] Romancing a concept is an elusive pursuit at best, and Lionel initially tries to find companionship with animals, offering herbs to a group of goats; when they meet his gesture with the threat of violence, Lionel almost makes good on his earlier threat to avenge himself on other species, picking up a rock to attack. He repents at the last moment because violence would spell an end to the illusion that Nature could be his companion and possible lover. But what form such companionship might take (let alone an answer to his sexual longings) leads the Last Man into confusion over issues of gender and sexuality.

Ironically, the novel's focus on reproduction (and its failure) has the effect of sidelining alternatives to heterosexuality during the main plot; the novel's potentially homoerotic friendships (between Lionel and Adrian, for instance) never come to fruition because they cannot contribute to the overriding imperative of biological reproduction. Lionel is initially able to resolve homoerotic attraction to Adrian first by marrying Adrian's sister Idris and after her death by forming an ersatz couple with Adrian to care for the remaining children. But in the novel's dénouement, when Lionel is Last Man and thus has no other person against whom to define his own identity, his sexual longings become polyvalent. Bemoaning the belief that "every living creature but me" could seek the comfort of "the bosom of its mate" at night, he fantasizes about encountering any human being to serve as "a beloved companion,"[58] and Lionel uses male pronouns to describe this hypothetical person. But when Lionel admires the statuary in Rome, he is sexually attracted to "many a fair Madonna or beauteous nymph," going so far as to caress the statues and kiss "the unconceiving marble" of their "lips."[59] The Plague dissolves differentiations, and although a survivor Lionel nonetheless finds himself in an undifferentiated state because there are no women against which to define his gender or sexuality—except feminized Nature.[60] Many of the statues depict nature spirits, and the marble itself is drawn from the earth, which makes his attempt to romance the statues a way of romancing Nature through the proxy of crafted personifications.

Yet the dual meaning of "unconceiving"—both that the statues do not know and cannot respond to his affections but also that, though they imitate female forms, statues are incapable of copulation and reproduction—signals that this last narrative superimposition on Nature is a false cultural imposition doomed to failure, like all the others. Attempts to negotiate a relationship with personified nature fail, because human characters are imposing culturally determined concepts of personhood, including gender, onto the nonhuman; Nature is neither mother, lover, nor antagonist. In this novel, "what must die is . . . not only man but also his fictions";[61] the Plague accomplishes the former, and the stark realities of being a Last Man the latter. Lionel rejects the mother narrative during the depredations of the Plague, seems to abandon the lover narrative when he concedes that a lone dog is the best he can hope for as a companion,[62] and rejects the antagonist narrative when he decides not to "live among the wild scenes of nature, the enemy of all that lives."[63] Lionel thus finally comes to a partial reconciliation with Nature: "the world" is as "fresh as creation's day"[64] with all the potential that entails, regardless of humanity's death. Where before Lionel refused to believe in a world without humans, as Last Man he must recognize "she [the earth] continues to wheel round . . . though man is not her adorner or inhabitant,"[65] a final concession that humanity's anthropocentrism was not justified. Yet even at this moment of epiphany Lionel is incapable of fully abandoning his gendered schemas. Lionel is in a double bind: culturally, he is incapable of letting go of defined identities—gender, sexuality, species—without losing his sense of self and possibly his sanity. So, he clings to those qualities that differentiate him from the world around him, yet because of this difference his "person, with its human . . . features, seem to me a monstrous excrescence of nature";[66] as sole human, *he* is the aberration that disrupts the placid post-human ecology. Full reconciliation with Nature can only come when death deconstructs individual identity and the material substance of the human body returns to the earth.

BREAKING DOWN BOUNDARIES: NATURE/PLAGUE'S DECONSTRUCTION OF GENDER AND BODIES

Pushing against the male characters' readings of Nature as feminine means recognizing an environment that does not adhere to binary conceptions of male or female and indeed resists being easily classified by human conceptions of relationality. This version of Nature is one which, by this resistance, deconstructs the very conceptions that are imposed upon it, such as the various female stereotypes projected onto Nature only to collapse as social artifice. As Nature/Plague, however, the deconstructive potential is not merely passive and external to humanity—as Nature is traditionally circumscribed—but one which is actively interpenetrating human bodies. As the operations of Nature/Plague lie both within and without the human body, it is simultaneously breaking down perceived boundaries both physical and ideological, including ideas of gender and sex, life and death, and the very notion of bodies as physical entities which are at least separate if not independent from their environment.

The vectors of the Plague—based on contemporary miasma theory—articulate a corporeal interdependence and permeability between the body and the environment that anticipates recent theoretical developments in queer ecology and studies of materiality. Stacy Alaimo's articulation of "trans-corporeality," the "material interconnections between the human and the more-than-human,"[67] informs my thinking about the interpenetration of Plague and human bodies. Disease functions as a sterling example of trans-corporeality: modern germ theory demonstrates the multitude of ways in which the body is open to the environment and contains a multitude of organisms (not only disease, but also symbiotic bacteria, white blood cells, etc.) whose agencies are independent of human will. Reading germ theory back into *Last Man* would be anachronistic, but Anne McWhir has convincingly demonstrated that Shelley relied on miasma theory, which did not view disease as contagious but still functions on similar principles of interpenetration: it supposes that illness is caused by environmental factors, namely the penetration of unhealthy vapors (generally emanating from decaying organic matter) into the body. There is a desire to think of human bodies as bounded, with clear physical limits, despite the constant interactions with our environment, willed and otherwise, like eating, excreting, breathing, sweating, etc. Alaimo, following Linda Nash, names this state the "modern body"[68] because the concept gained popularity in twentieth-century medical discourse. However, it is present—if only as an antecedent—in this Romantic novel, in the sense of violation the characters feel towards their diseased bodies. To avoid temporal confusion I will call this belief in a body independent from its environment the "hermetic body."

The idea of the solid, hermetic human body is belied by the aerial infestation of miasma. Carried on the same breaths that bring life-giving oxygen to the lungs, miasma theory demonstrates that the human body is always interacting with and interpenetrated by its environment and the beneficial or harmful substances therein. Modern ecocriticism tends to focus on the toxic byproducts of human activity that become part of this system; for Alaimo, toxicity is almost always the result or byproduct of human (and mostly industrial) actions on the environment that can then lead to illness and disease when it interpenetrates the human body. However, while critics may try to establish a moral or metaphorical causality between the Plague and human actions and attitudes, *Last Man* suggests no *material* anthropogenic origins for the Plague. From the (ecophobic) point of view of the novel's characters, miasma and disease—and their colonization of the body—are read as substances belonging to "unwholesome nature"[69]—a natural phenomenon rather than a toxic substance. This does not prevent an antagonist Nature/Plague's presence in the body from being deconstructive (or destructive, from the point of view of the characters), as the ideology it carries is contradictory to human self-perceptions. With regard to gender, Nature writ large encompasses a "wide diversity of sexual behavior"[70] and biological sexes, which is what makes it queer; the sexuality and means of reproduction of the varied species of the world easily outstrip and outnumber nominally heteronormative humanity. Consequently, a humanity invaded by Nature/Plague is one possessed by a Nature that transcends normative conceptions of sex and gender and works to break down those ideas within the body.

This is evident in the way that both nominal masculinity and femininity are disrupted and deconstructed by Plague. I've already discussed the ways in which the novel's male characters are feminized by the Plague, by their grief, illness, and inability to combat let alone conquer the foe. But the male characters' depiction of the Plague as a feminine antagonist, thereupon taken up by critics like Mellor and McKusick to interpret the conflict between humanity and Nature/Plague as a heteronormative battle of the sexes, is troubled by the fact that the Plague spares neither female characters nor femininity as a concept. If Nature/Plague were truly a feminized force deployed against masculine oppression, then we might expect some form of solidarity between the Plague and female characters in the text who are likewise dominated by the male characters. No such solidarity is to be found, however, since Nature/Plague's feminine gendering is a human cultural imposition on a genderless phenomenon. Male characters perceive their bodies as besieged and infiltrated by a feminized Nature/Plague, but Nature/Plague is equally deconstructive of female gender norms. Lionel's phrasing, when mourning the death of the concept of childhood, is telling: he claims that "young boys and girls were level now with men"[71]—but not women! I have previously discussed how Nature/Plague and the absence of futurity it promises deconstructs the difference between childhood and adulthood; the imposition of adulthood on this last generation is also a *masculinization*, because the text defines women by the reproductive potential of their bodies. This generation of girls who are guaranteed never to attain that potential, who will never become mothers, cannot properly be considered women and (by the stifling logic of gender binaries) must therefore be men. From the characters' point of view, the death of futurity has converted humanity into a barren and therefore purely masculine species. This deconstruction of the assumed *biological* definition of womanhood is paired with "a final adieu" to "feminine virtues"[72] embodied by Englishwomen, despite the continued presence of females among the Plague refugees: the destruction of English society means the elimination of women's role in that society and all the gendered values and behavioral norms attached to it. In the loss of such "virtues" and reproductive potential, the Plague both ungenders and unsexes women. Regardless of how human characters (and critics) conceive of it, Nature/Plague favors no gender or sex, because it transcends these concepts; the material coexistence of Nature/Plague in all its queer diversity of sex and sexuality also queers the body as a first step towards deconstructing human ideas about the body.

Although the Plague's deconstruction of society broadly and bodies specifically would seem like an opportunity to likewise deconstruct the link between sex and gender, the novel's protagonists doggedly maintain normative gender roles even on the brink of extinction, sorting themselves into striving men and nurturing women. Sex and gender are indeed almost entirely conflated in this novel. The few transgressions (such as Evadne's cross-dressing) are criticized by Lionel, who is occasionally sympathetic to women's yearnings for roles beyond those ascribed to their gender yet unfailingly enforces those same roles as supposedly natural. The persistence of gender roles is an imaginative failure on behalf of the survivors or perhaps a misguided attempt to resist the Plague's various social deconstructions. Previous critics[73] have attended to the persistence of gender norms, particularly for women, amongst the protagonists; however, the novel's human antagonists have gone largely unexamined. By virtue of their oppositional role in the narrative, these antagonists are structurally aligned with Nature/Plague, and they come to embody the blurring of gender binaries and the lack of bodily integrity that makes the Plague so fearful. I have already discussed how Evadne transgresses gender lines, so now I will turn to look more closely at nominally female and male examples: Lionel's mother-in-law, the Countess of Windsor, and Ryland, a politician.

The Countess of Windsor fails to follow normative female gender norms, particularly in her ambition to political power, which her status as woman prevents her from achieving herself. Lionel's perception of the Countess as "something fearful" stems in part from the unexpected gendering of her characteristics: she has "conquer[ed] the animal part of [her] nature" and is "entirely made of mind," her "body . . . a mere machine"[74] that barely requires any food or sleep. She is associated with intellect and machinery, which fall on the masculine side of the typical nature/culture dyad. But Lionel does not *masculinize* the Countess; rather, since she cannot be thought of as female in the traditional sense, he strips her of all gender, turning her into an asexual "something" that does "not . . . belong to flesh and blood."[75] This is due to the perception that sexual divisions (and their gendered overlay) are natural and define the body as human. The Countess's renunciation of both food and affection puts her outside the physical and emotive interactions of a body and its environment, creating the appearance of a hermetic body. As antagonist, however, the Countess stands in for the *mistaken* belief in the hermetic body, and she is brought back to nature when her daughter dies: the loss of her personal connection to futurity is a shock that reincorporates the Countess in typical gender, affective, and bodily relationships. She acknowledges Lionel as her "son" for the first time, to recapture her lost access to futurity through a substitute child, and tells him to "govern me as you will,"[76] abandoning claims to power for subservience. From this point the former queen's function in the familial unit is a traditionally female one: watching over the younger children. Her bodily reintegration soon proves fatal, triggering a sudden onset of symptoms relating to her advanced age; the transformation of her "faded person"[77] is a testament to the vulnerabilities of living in an embodied state. She transitions from nonhuman to human (because gendered) to nonhuman again in death; since her original state was viewed as unnatural (as seen in the mechanical metaphor), her engendering brings her closer to the idea of the "human" and "natural" (as seen in her newfound embrace of supposedly natural female tasks), and proximity to Nature ironically leaves her vulnerable to the bodily deconstruction Nature performs in this text.

Whereas the Countess of Windsor initially rejects gender, Ryland, Lord Protector of England when the crisis hits, is initially described as a man invested with masculine features such as "muscles and full grown stature."[78] However, sheer fear at the prospect of Plague causes him to abandon his post, and this fear radically transforms his body by "shrivel[ing] his whole person."[79] Ryland wishes to isolate himself from all others, erroneously (per miasma theory) believing this will shield him from the Plague, but in so doing transforms himself into a Last Man figure, compounding the demasculinization his body has already suffered with the lack of gender differentiation inherent to the condition of being a Last Man. He removes himself from the sphere of human interaction, creating externally what the Countess performs internally by transforming her body to inure it from her environment, but both err in believing it is possible to evade interaction and interpenetration. Ryland perishes from the Plague because it is omnipresent in the very environment and therefore himself. The Plague is "unwholesome nature" infiltrating, and from the inside out gradually deconstructing, the material substance of the human body until, through death and decomposition, it returns to nature as the very decaying organic matter which allegedly caused miasma. Ryland is subsequently "discovered . . . half-eaten by insects,"[80] further illustrating the collapse of bodily integrity. Like Nature/Plague, the insects that consume him post-mortem illustrate the perpetual interpenetration of natural systems into the human body, as the very material of the corpse becomes food; this also caps the destruction of Ryland's markers of gender as the very physical indicators of his sex are corrupted and consumed, even as his body loses the integrity of form that marked him as human.

Corpses lie on the "frontier between humanity"[81] and the nonhuman and (like the Plague that produces them) are queer entities that cause great fear in the characters for their ability to dissolve the human/nonhuman binary. Mel Chen has argued that disease, as toxicity, "intervene[s] into the binary between the segregated fields of 'life' and 'death,'"[82] and this is particularly true of the Plague-ridden corpse, as (per miasma theory) the seemingly inanimate human body remains host to the disturbingly animate and potentially sentient force of the Plague, not to mention communities of nonhuman animals, fungi, and microbes and bacteria. While millions worldwide must have undergone the same process of decay as Ryland's body, the narrative suggests that bodies becoming carrion is proper punishment for the moral failings of antagonists: after an imposter prophet who seized control of a large number of refugees is exposed and commits suicide, the characters "left his miserable remains"[83] exposed to the elements and animals, to suffer the incorporation of Nature into his corpse. In a narrative where death is guaranteed, the disposition of bodies becomes a means of regulating behavior: the antisocial are threatened with remaining unburied and exposed to the resultant bodily consumption and corruption of their human form. For anybody other than transgressors, the characters are obsessive in tending to the dead and dying, frequently halting their refugee train to bury the dead in the earth "which had once been our living mother" and going to great effort to bury or hide corpses where "no bird or beast of prey could ... profane"[84] the body. The fixation with preventing post-mortem scavenging is a reaction to the violation of bodily integrity inflicted by the Plague, one last attempt to retake control over human bodies from Nature by denying other species access. But just as it is impossible to prevent the interpenetration of the Plague, so too is the preservation of cadavers a symbolic gesture doomed to fail, as the bacteria that cause decomposition are always already present within the body. The desire to exclude human bodies from broader systems of nature is an ideological, anthropocentric stance with no grounding in lived, material reality.

Because the Plague leads to humanity's effective extinction, Fisch worries that the "[d]econstruction" performed by the Plague "becomes simply destruction," incapable of redeeming anything. However, I believe Fisch errs in her exclusive focus on deconstruction resolving "differences among people" and thus her characterization of the Plague as "universal destruction."[85] In fact, the Plague is specific, not universal, as the nonhuman world survives and thrives; furthermore, the Plague's deconstruction of bodies reincorporates their human matter into broader ecological structures, breaking down the false barriers between bodies and their environments. This deconstruction, beginning with normative ideas of gender, then progressing to dissolve concepts like childhood and futurity before working away at both the idea and material substance of bodies, is tantamount to dehumanization. However, as Seymour points out, "dehumanization" is not necessarily something "wrong in and of itself [as] the nonhuman is not worthless," and dehumanization could even be valuable, so long as it does not lead to violence, if it permits "a decentering of anthropocentrism," which the novel's characters, and Lionel especially, are very much guilty of.[86] The scenario in *Last Man* is complicated, as the environment performs dehumanization on clearly unwilling subjects; yet if we look beyond the gendered narrative personification and antagonism of Nature that renders the Plague an act of violence, then we need not replicate or take as granted the (understandable) hostile human response to trans-corporeal penetration through infection, death, and decomposition, and thus we need not project an antagonistic intent onto an impersonal environment. Instead, like Lionel in his final moments of honesty, we can celebrate the renewed vitality of the natural world, into whose cycles and relationships discorporated humanity has been reintegrated.

NOTES

1. W. Warren Wagar, *Terminal Visions: The Literature of Last Things* (Bloomington: Indiana University Press, 1982), 13.
2. Shelley, *Last Man*, ed. Morton Paley (Oxford: Oxford University Press, 2008), 262.
3. Mellor, *Mary Shelley*, 150.
4. James C. McKusick, *Green Writing: Romanticism and Ecology* (New York: Palgrave Macmillan, 2010), 108–9.
5. Barbara Johnson, "The Last Man," in *The Other Mary Shelley: Beyond Frankenstein*, eds. Audrey A. Fisch, Anne K. Mellor, and Esther H. Schor (Oxford: Oxford University Press, 1993), 264; Fisch, "Plaguing Politics," 272.
6. Anne K. Mellor, *Mary Shelley: Her Life, Her Fiction, Her Monsters* (New York: Routledge, 1988), 167.
7. Audrey A. Fisch, "Plaguing Politics: AIDS, Deconstruction, and *The Last Man*," in *The Other Mary Shelley: Beyond Frankenstein*, eds. Audrey A. Fisch, Anne K. Mellor, and Esther H. Schor (Oxford: Oxford University Press, 1993), 267.
8. Seymour, *Strange Natures*, 5.
9. For a selection of solid histories, surveys, and articulations of the field of queer ecology, see Robert Azzarello, *Queer Environmentality: Ecology, Evolution, and Sexuality in American Literature* (Burlington: Ashgate, 2012), 5–28; Catriona Mortimer-Sandilands and Bruce Erickson, *Queer Ecologies: Sex, Nature, Politics, Desire* (Bloomington: Indiana University Press, 2010), 6–30; and Nicole Seymour, *Strange Natures: Futurity, Empathy, and the Queer Ecological Imagination* (Urbana: University of Illinois Press, 2013), 3–29.
10. Shelley, *Last Man*, 175, 268.
11. Wagar, *Terminal Visions*, 15–16.
12. Shelley, *Last Man*, 233.
13. Shelley, *Last Man*, 193.
14. Shelley, *Last Man*, 175.
15. Shelley, *Last Man*, 346, 426.
16. Lee Edelman, *No Future: Queer Theory and the Death Drive* (Durham: Duke University Press, 2004), 2.
17. There is a surprising lack of attention to the interactions of (post)apocalyptic narratives and futurity, but see Barbara Anne Gurr, ed., *Race, Gender, and Sexuality in Post-Apocalyptic TV and Film* (Houndmills: Palgrave Macmillan, 2015) for one example of this promising avenue of inquiry.
18. Shelley, *Last Man*, 76.
19. Shelley, *Last Man*, 424.
20. Azzarello, *Queer Environmentality*, 28.
21. Shelley, *Last Man*, 230.
22. Morton Paley, "Introduction" to Mary Shelley's *The Last Man* (Oxford: Oxford University Press, 2008), xi, xx.
23. Lee Edelman, *No Future*, 331.
24. Victoria Middleton, "Exile, Isolation, and Accommodation in *The Last Man*: The Strategies of a Survivor," in *Critical Essays on Mary Wollstonecraft Shelley*, ed. Mary Lowe-Evans (New York: G.K. Hall, 1998), 175.
25. Shelley, *Last Man*, 318.
26. Shelley, *Last Man*, 261, 274.
27. Shelley, *Last Man*, 322, 399.
28. Shelley, *Last Man*, 232.

29. Shelley, *Last Man*, 318.
30. Shelley, *Last Man*, 276.
31. Shelley, *Last Man*, 329.
32. Shelley, *Last Man*, 446–47.
33. Shelley, *Last Man*, 112.
34. Seymour, *Strange Natures*, 15–16.
35. Simon C. Estok, "Ecomedia and Ecophobia," *Neohelicon* 43, no. 1 (2016): 132.
36. Fear and anxiety about the relationship to Nature can also arise out of a sense of insignificance before the sheer geographic and temporal scale of the natural world; see Julia Wright, "'Little England': Anxieties of Space in Mary Shelley's *The Last Man*," in *Mary Shelley's Fictions: From* Frankenstein *to* Falkner, ed. Michael Eberle-Sinatra (Houndmills: Macmillan Press, 2000), for a discussion of this effect in *Last Man*.
37. Jonathan Bate, *The Song of the Earth* (London: Picador, 2000), 97.
38. Matthew Phillip Shiel, *The Purple Cloud* (London: Penguin Books, 2012), 166.
39. Shelley, *Last Man*, 230.
40. Shelley, *Last Man*, 232.
41. Shelley, *Last Man*, 232, 371.
42. Shelley, *Last Man*, 398.
43. Shelley, *Last Man*, 346.
44. Shelley, *Last Man*, 398.
45. Nature's destructive aspect is even more explicit in other Last Man narratives—such as Byron's "Darkness," in which the dark personification of Nature reverses the creative acts of Genesis and renders the Earth an undifferentiated, lifeless mass. Byron's Nature could be considered an anti-god; however, in Shelley's *Last Man* Nature targets humanity exclusively while fauna and flora flourish, so Nature can only be considered an anti-god from an anthropocentric perspective.
46. Morton D. Paley, *Apocalypse and Millennium in English Romantic Poetry* (Oxford: Clarendon Press, 1999), 199.
47. Shelley, *Last Man*, 321.
48. Shelley, *Last Man*, 70.
49. Shelley, *Last Man*, 404.
50. Shelley, *Last Man*, 172.
51. Shelley, *Last Man*, 208.
52. Shelley, *Last Man*, 437.
53. Shelley, *Last Man*, 437.
54. Shelley, *Last Man*, 459.
55. Shelley, *Last Man*, 16.
56. Shelley, *Last Man*, 457.
57. Shelley, *Last Man*, 424.
58. Shelley, *Last Man*, 449–50.
59. Shelley, *Last Man*, 465.
60. This is partially why Johnson believes Lionel "belongs . . . to a sort of third sex" (262), though she does not elaborate on this speculation. Struggles with differentiation are common to fictional Last Men (although they manifest along different dyads: in Shiel's *Purple Cloud*, for example, differentiation confusion expresses itself along racial lines as the English protagonist spends years dressed in Orientalist garb). Lionel's uncertain gender as sole human being also calls back to the novel's introduction and the careful way in which it fails to mention the sex, gender, or orientation of the frame narrator and the narrator's companion and thus, like Nature, queerly encompasses all possibilities. For discussions on the frame's avoidance of gendering, see Michael Eberle-Sinatra, "Gender, Authorship and Male Domination: Mary Shelley's Limited Freedom in *Frankenstein* and *The Last Man*" in *Mary Shelley's Fictions: From* Frankenstein *to* Falkner, edited by Michael Eberle-Sinatra (Houndmills: Macmillan Press, 2000), 104, and Fisch, "Plaguing Politics," 268.
61. Middleton, "Exile, Isolation, and Accommodation," 176.

62. Dogs appear frequently in (post)apocalyptic media, and Alice Kuzniar has argued that such companions represent a kind of queer interspecies affection (Alice Kuzniar, "'I Married My Dog': On Queer Canine Literature," in *Queering the Non/Human*, edited by Noreen Giffney and Myra J. Hird [Burlington: Ashgate, 2008], 207), which suits Lionel's new post-apocalyptic openness to forms of nonhuman love.

63. Shelley, *Last Man*, 460.
64. Shelley, *Last Man*, 420.
65. Shelley, *Last Man*, 459.
66. Shelley, *Last Man*, 467.
67. Stacy Alaimo, *Bodily Natures: Science, Environment, and the Material Self* (Bloomington: Indiana University Press, 2010), 2.
68. Alaimo, *Bodily Natures*, 90–91.
69. Shelley, *Last Man*, 233.
70. Myra J. Hird, "Animal Trans," in *Queering the Non/Human*, eds. Noreen Giffney and Myra J. Hird (Burlington: Ashgate, 2008), 235.
71. Shelley, *Last Man*, 318.
72. Shelley, *Last Man*, 414.
73. See Suparna Banerjee, *Science, Gender and History: The Fantastic in Mary Shelley and Margaret Atwood* (Newcastle: Cambridge Scholars Publishing, 2014), 32–41; Mellor, *Mary Shelley*, 150–56.
74. Shelley, *Last Man*, 73.
75. Shelley, *Last Man*, 73.
76. Shelley, *Last Man*, 359, 361.
77. Shelley, *Last Man*, 415.
78. Shelley, *Last Man*, 241.
79. Shelley, *Last Man*, 252. Lionel recognizes that "almighty fear" (395) acts much like the Plague: it can devastate bodies, and if left unchecked, it spreads like a disease through the body politic.
80. Shelley, *Last Man*, 319.
81. Patricia MacCormack, "Necrosexuality," in *Queering the Non/Human*, eds. Noreen Giffney and Myra J. Hird (Burlington: Ashgate, 2008), 345.
82. Mel Chen, *Animacies: Biopolitics, Racial Mattering, and Queer Affect* (Durham: Duke University Press, 2012), 218.
83. Shelley, *Last Man*, 407.
84. Shelley, *Last Man*, 411, 425.
85. Fisch, "Plaguing Politics," 273.
86. Seymour, *Strange Natures*, 12.

BIBLIOGRAPHY

Alaimo, Stacy. *Bodily Natures: Science, Environment, and the Material Self*. Bloomington: Indiana University Press, 2010.
Aldiss, Brian W. *Billion Year Spree: The History of Science Fiction*. London: Transworld Publishers, 1975.
Azzarello, Robert. *Queer Environmentality: Ecology, Evolution, and Sexuality in American Literature*. Burlington: Ashgate, 2012.
Bate, Jonathan. *The Song of the Earth*. London: Picador, 2000.
Banerjee, Suparna. *Science, Gender and History: The Fantastic in Mary Shelley and Margaret Atwood*. Newcastle: Cambridge Scholars Publishing, 2014.
Byron, George Gordon. "Darkness." In *Lord Byron: Selected Poems*, edited by Susan J. Wolfson and Peter J. Manning, 412–414. London: Penguin Books, 2005.
Chen, Mel Y. *Animacies: Biopolitics, Racial Mattering, and Queer Affect*. Durham: Duke University Press, 2012.
Cousin de Grainville, Jean-Baptiste François Xavier. *Le Dernier Homme*. Paris: Éditions Payot et Rivages, 2010.

Eberle-Sinatra, Michael. "Gender, Authorship and Male Domination: Mary Shelley's Limited Freedom in *Frankenstein* and *The Last Man*." In *Mary Shelley's Fictions: From* Frankenstein *to* Falkner, edited by Michael Eberle-Sinatra, 95–108. Houndmills: Macmillan Press, 2000.

Edelman, Lee. *No Future: Queer Theory and the Death Drive.* Durham: Duke University Press, 2004.

Estok, Simon C. "Ecomedia and Ecophobia." *Neohelicon* 43, no. 1 (2016): 127–145.

Fisch, Audrey A. "Plaguing Politics: AIDS, Deconstruction, and *The Last Man*." In *The Other Mary Shelley: Beyond* Frankenstein, edited by Audrey A. Fisch, Anne K. Mellor, and Esther H. Schor, 267–86. Oxford: Oxford University Press, 1993.

Giffney, Noreen, and Myra J. Hird, eds. *Queering the Non/Human.* Burlington: Ashgate, 2008.

Gurr, Barbara Anne, ed. *Race, Gender, and Sexuality in Post-Apocalyptic TV and Film.* Houndmills: Palgrave Macmillan, 2015.

Hird, Myra J. "Animal Trans." In *Queering the Non/Human*, edited by Noreen Giffney and Myra J. Hird, 227–47. Burlington: Ashgate, 2008.

Johnson, Barbara. "The Last Man." In *The Other Mary Shelley: Beyond* Frankenstein, edited by Audrey A. Fisch, Anne K. Mellor, and Esther H. Schor, 258–66. Oxford: Oxford University Press, 1993.

Kuzniar, Alice A. "'I Married My Dog': On Queer Canine Literature." In *Queering the Non/Human*, edited by Noreen Giffney and Myra J. Hird, 205–26. Burlington: Ashgate, 2008.

MacCormack, Patricia. "Necrosexuality." In *Queering the Non/Human*, edited by Noreen Giffney and Myra J. Hird, 339–62. Burlington: Ashgate, 2008.

McKusick, James C. *Green Writing: Romanticism and Ecology.* New York: Palgrave Macmillan, 2010.

McWhir, Anne. "Mary Shelley's Anti-Contagionism: The Last Man as Fatal Narrative." *Mosaic: A Journal for the Interdisciplinary Study of Literature* 35, no. 2 (2002): 23–38.

Mellor, Anne K. *Mary Shelley: Her Life, Her Fiction, Her Monsters.* New York: Routledge, 1988.

Middleton, Victoria. "Exile, Isolation, and Accommodation in *The Last Man*: The Strategies of a Survivor." In *Critical Essays on Mary Wollstonecraft Shelley*, edited by Mary Lowe-Evans, 166–82. New York: G.K. Hall, 1998.

Mortimer-Sandilands, Catriona, and Bruce Erickson. *Queer Ecologies: Sex, Nature, Politics, Desire.* Bloomington: Indiana University Press, 2010.

Paley, Morton D. *Apocalypse and Millennium in English Romantic Poetry.* Oxford: Clarendon Press, 1999.

Seymour, Nicole. *Strange Natures: Futurity, Empathy, and the Queer Ecological Imagination.* Urbana: University of Illinois Press, 2013.

Shelley, Mary. *Frankenstein, or The Modern Prometheus.* London: Penguin Books, 2003.

———. *The Last Man.* Oxford: Oxford University Press, 2008.

Shiel, M. P. *The Purple Cloud.* London: Penguin Books, 2012.

Wagar, Walter Warren. *Terminal Visions: The Literature of Last Things.* Bloomington: Indiana University Press, 1982.

Wright, Julia M. "'Little England': Anxieties of Space in Mary Shelley's *The Last Man*." In *Mary Shelley's Fictions: From* Frankenstein *to* Falkner, edited by Michael Eberle-Sinatra, 129–49. Houndmills: Macmillan Press, 2000.

Part III

Contemporary Queering

SIX

Engineered Nature, (En)gendered Nature in Kim Stanley Robinson's *2312*

Tyler Harper

This is an essay in and on SF, or perhaps more accurately, following Donna Haraway, on the pluralized field of SFs—science facts, science fictions, science fetishes.[1] For several decades now, historians and philosophers of science have insisted on the inseparability of these categories, have insisted that, in the words of Bruno Latour, "science does not produce itself scientifically," that the engine or motive force of scientific discourse is always already parasitic on a set of concealed ethical, political, and cultural assumptions that make scientific practice (the selection of scientific objects, the deployment of scientific techniques, the parsing of scientific data, and that data's ultimate transubstantiation into scientific "facts") possible.[2] Naturally, to accept this contention entails disabusing ourselves of any pretense regarding the neutral or positionless objectivity of science and, by extension, doing away with the supposed autonomy of scientific subjects with respect to scientific objects, the fantasy of subjects and objects that would not bleed into one another (or more scandalously, that would not trade places). In other words, it necessitates jettisoning the image of a science founded on and proceeding in *innocence*, a science without science fiction.

Yet, as Haraway and others have long been at pains to demonstrate, to maintain the inseparability of science facts from science fictions is not to descend into a vulgar relativism, to dispense with objectivity as such. Rather, it is a question of accepting that science is a web of "situated knowledges" produced in circumstances mediated by history, in which objects are compromised by the agency of subjects and subjects in turn are compromised by the peculiar agency of objects.[3] Put alternatively, science fictions are a way of shaping, and rendering intelligible, scientific facts. To fictionalize science, thus, is not to accuse science of disseminating falsehoods but rather of being a practice of fabrication, of *truth-telling* via narrative practices of *truth-making*.[4] As Haraway writes in her introduction to her early work, *Primate Visions*,

> Scientific practice and scientific theories produce and are embedded in particular kinds of stories. Any scientific statement about the world depends intimately upon language, upon metaphor. The metaphors may be mathematical or they may be culinary; in any case, they structure scientific vision. Scientific practice is above all a story-telling practice in the sense of historically specific practices of interpretation and testimony.[5]

As she insists, any scientific practice is always already a narrating, a strategic deployment of metaphors culled from a battery of pre-existing cultural, political, and ethical signifiers that precede and structure science as such. In what follows, it is this focus on methods and modes of speaking and imagining that I bring to bear upon the science factual and science fictional fields of ecology and gender studies. Indeed, what I argue for here is not a program or prescription but rather the importance of talking about ecology and gender in the right ways, of making recourse to ontologies and epistemologies—ways of organizing and legislating beings and thinkings—that break out of, rather than covertly re-inscribe and reinforce, the structures of domination and oppression that have wreaked havoc upon both the earth and the gendered bodies that populate it. By drawing on the work of science fiction novelist Kim Stanley Robinson, specifically his novel *2312* (2012), I hope to demonstrate that alternative ways of thinking about nature—and particularly human beings and human bodies in and in relation to nature—are not only possible but necessary if we are to adequately situate, and ultimately combat, forms of environmental and bodily violence and subjugation.

To that end, by reading Robinson's work alongside contemporary theoretical voices, this essay will advance two independent but interrelated claims. First, *2312* demonstrates how ecocriticism and gender studies remain intimately related discourses, insofar as both attempt to problematize, undermine, and reconfigure the modern project of Cartesianized Nature—that is to say, they destabilize Nature as "over there," for-us, infinite, unchanging, passive, predictable, knowable, static, bounded, and boundary-respecting. Second, a reconfiguration of the relationship between humanity, knowledge, and Nature, as in *2312*, does not necessitate an antagonism toward nature as an analytic category (as in certain stripes of gender studies discourse) nor does it necessitate setting up Nature as a romanticized fetish object (as in certain stripes of ecological discourse).

As Stacy Alaimo and Susan Hekman write in their introduction to *Material Feminisms*, rethinking the relationship between human beings and Nature first and foremost means working the genuine insights culled from social constructivism into a critical framework compatible with the materialist demands of the natural sciences.[6] In this sense, "naturalism," so often a dirty word, does not entail or imply scientism, biological determinism, or any other dangerous -ism. It simply means, to rework Derrida's infamous axiom, *"il n'y a pas de hors-nature"* — there is no "outside" of nature, no "great outdoors" that would be alien or exterior to humanity. From this vantage point — which I maintain is post-human without being post human, post-naturalist without being post nature — words like "unnatural" or "artificial" begin to lose their epistemological, and thus political, heft.[7] In their wake, we are left with a much more complicated picture that necessitates abandoning a certain taste for precision and certainty but that also ensures that the very structures of domination that ecocriticism and gender studies tries to escape do not sneak in the back door.

To complicate the relationships between nature and culture, subject and object, science fact and science fiction is inherently to focus on the kinds of precarious entities and ambiguous formulations that would bastardize these superficially neat distinctions — bastards that Bruno Latour, in his seminal work *We Have Never Been Modern*, refers to as "hybrids."[8] For Latour, "hybrids" (those sites of improper mixture where boundaries between human/nonhuman, science/politics, man/woman are compromised) are simultaneously the quintessential modern *product* and — in modernity's relentless pursuit of "purification" (the boundary-policing that keeps all those modern binaries upright and operational) — precisely the phenomena that modernity wants to eradicate from contemporary consciousness, exiling such hybrids to the impolite backwaters of "premodernity." Yet, paradoxically according to Latour, in its boundless desire to sort, categorize, and purify, modernity becomes the very engine of the proliferation of the non-sortable, the non-categorizable, and "impure."

In a recent special issue of *New Literary History* focusing on Latour's work, Graham Harman points out the logical contradictions arrived at when such complex hybridities are suppressed in mainstream gender and sexuality discourses, writing,

> More often than not, the [Latourian] modernist shifts back and forth between calling some things "natural" and others "cultural" depending on the political interests of the moment. For instance, American liberals tend to proclaim the current status of women as being socially constructed, while insisting at the same time that homosexuality is the result of nature rather than a deviant social adaptation. To say that women are naturally very different from men sounds like a reactionary claim, but to say that homosexual behavior is "not natural, but contingent and reversible through therapy" also sounds like a reactionary

claim, though contingency and reversibility are usually progressive tropes.[9]

Of course, this prototypical liberal antinomy—naturalized homosexuality, culturalized sexual difference—is *only* an antinomy from within the prison-house of a Cartesian modernity that would (if in appearance only) desire to quarantine "Nature" and "Culture" to their separate playgrounds, forcing moderns to choose sides from within a neatly partitioned metaphysical lunch tray rather than acknowledging the inherent ontological and epistemological messiness of the politics of sex and gender. Instead, if we follow Latour—dispensing with this fever dream in which modern subjects spend their time shunting phenomena to one side or another of a supposedly absolute divide—the temptation to justify a political program by appeal to Nature or Culture becomes obsolete. We avoid both naturalistic fallacies ("X is good because it is natural," "Y is bad because it is unnatural") as well the absurdities of radical social constructivism that recent materialist trends in gender studies have attempted to address and redress. The question such work has undertaken to answer, then, is this: What would it be to imagine an ontology (and accompanying epistemology) in which nature is neither the passive, inert background against which the clamor of cultures unfolds nor the final arbiter before which all cultural lifeworlds must bow? What would it be, as Stacy Alaimo has asked in her recent work, to challenge and "[reconfigure] the established divides between subject and object, nature and culture," *without* falling into the trap (endemic to much object-oriented philosophy) of "flattening" ontological difference as such—obscuring or eradicating the differential priorities of non-white, non-male, non-heterosexual and nonhuman subjects?[10]

I suggest that Kim Stanley Robinson's fiction both thematizes this problematic and establishes—if not exactly a solution—at least a framework in which such debates should unfold. While nearly all of Robinson's work in one way or another calls into question the imprecise, complex, and always precarious relationship between "nature" and "culture" as conceptual categories—and specifically as they relate to issues of ecology and gender—this line of inquiry has grown both more robust and more explicit in his recent work, which not only tends to directly challenge the modernist worldview but almost always demonstrates how a modern metaphysics inheres in, and thus continues to undermine, theories of ecology, gender, and sexuality that might otherwise appear progressive. Perhaps nowhere is this critique more apparent than in his novel *2312*, a work (set in the same fictional world as his earlier *Mars Trilogy*) in which the solar system has been almost entirely colonized by human beings and wherein the transformation and translation of the micro-natural spheres of sexualities and sexual organs is as prevalent as, and always deeply interwoven with, the transformation, translation, and terraformation of the macro-natural spheres of planets and worlds.

Swann Hong—the novel's central protagonist—quite literally incarnates this cross-pollination between the politics of sex, gender, and ecology. She is a semi-retired artist-scientist of terraforming (specializing in creating new kinds of hybrid environments, such as tropical tundras and desert forests) while also redesigning and repurposing her body (e.g., replacing her clitoris with a micro-penis, fathering a child as male, giving birth as female, etc.). Yet Robinson is at pains to emphasize that her bodily modifications and work as a geo-engineer are *not* artificial and externally imposed modifications of some pre-existing static nature, *but products in and of nature*. As we will see, Robinson mobilizes Swann as a critique of the modernist metaphysical project as well as the liberal humanism that implicitly accompanies it (a humanism in which white, male, active subjects exist in a relationship of autonomy and dominance with respect to static, passive, objectified nature), and, in that respect, the novel can rightly be seen as advancing a certain stripe of post-humanism. However, despite his work's implicit adherence to a post-humanist critique of modern metaphysics and liberal humanism, Robinson also remains deeply resistant to any variant of this critique that would covertly re-inscribe a nature/culture binary even as it presupposes to transcend it. Instead, as I will argue, Robinson's work attempts to imagine a *posthumanism* that is not reliant on the figure of the *post human* (in the sense of *beyond* the human), accompanied by a post-naturalism not predicated on moving *post nature* (in the sense of a *transcendence of* nature).

The first half of this philosophical tightrope walk becomes most explicit in an early scene in the novel, in which Swann encounters her old lover, Zasha, while on a brief visit to Earth. After an initial period of small talk, discussion between the two quickly becomes heated when Zasha accuses Swann of having transformed herself into a "post-human thing" as a result of her various forms of body augmentation (which include, in addition to those aforementioned, ingesting microbial alien DNA and undergoing brain modification surgery). Although Swann protests this characterization, Zasha declares, "I didn't like [your modifications] right from the beginning. . . . You end up being some kind of post-human thing. Or at least a different person."[11] To which Swann responds, "Everything I've done to myself I consider part of being a human being. I mean, who wouldn't do it if they could? I would be ashamed not to! It isn't being *post* human, it's being *fully* human. It would be stupid not to do the good thing when you can, it would be *anti*human."[12] What is striking about this scene (which, in my view, offers a kind of condensed version of the novel's position as a whole) is not only the theoretical argument waged but the subtlety of the vocabulary with which it's waged. Everything ultimately hinges on a hyphen. Zasha's accusal—"You end up being some kind of post-human thing"—is countered by

Swann's rebuttal—"It isn't being *post* human, it's being *fully* human." The shift evoked by this lost hyphen is subtle, easy to miss, but momentous.

The identity Swann rejects is not that of the post-human but the post human—i.e., Swann does not reject a post-humanist dismantling of liberal humanism, but rather she rejects a variant of post-humanism that would also be a post-naturalism. That is to say, while she remains eager to move beyond "the human" as a historically contingent, normative concept, she remains resistant to any rhetoric that would presuppose to move beyond the human as *species*. What is so remarkable about the argument here is that Swann offers a defense of non-normative gender, sexual, and bodily identities *from the point of view of naturalism*. To put a finer point on it, Swann advances the idea of a post-humanism that would be compatible with naturalism—i.e., a way of thinking about the world in which augmentations of the human body would not be conceived as an augmentation of or departure from human (modes of) being, but rather, as a natural development *of* human nature, *within* human nature. In effect, Swann declares that she *is* post-human (she has moved beyond liberal humanist understandings of the "human" as a normative concept, rejecting the constrictive notions of identity, gender, and sexuality that accompany it) while maintaining that she is *not*—because no one can be—*post* human. In other words, Swann adopts as her philosophical standpoint a post-humanism that would be marked not by a transcendence of nature but a turn back into it. The question, of course, is why might such a move be advantageous?

In the introduction to *How We Became Posthuman*, N. Katherine Hayles identifies two potential, and resolutely opposed, strains of post-humanism, writing,

> If my nightmare is a culture inhabited by posthumans who regard their bodies as fashion accessories rather than the ground of being, my dream is a version of the posthuman ... [that would not be] seduced by fantasies of unlimited power and disembodied immortality, that recognizes and celebrates finitude as a condition of human being, and that understands human life is embedded in a material world of great complexity, one on which we depend for our continued survival.[13]

Here, Hayles's post-human "dream" not only implies the need for a post-humanism that is also predicated on and supplemented by a robust materialism, but her reference to "continued survival" gestures toward the ecological dangers posed by the kind of insidious post-humanism that would degenerate and devalue the material world as such.

When Kasha accuses Swann of having transformed herself into "some kind of post-human thing," it is precisely Hayles's nightmarish variety of post-humanism that she has in mind, a post-humanism in which bodies are treated as fashion accessories to be traded in, upgraded, and cast aside as though they were denim jackets or handbags. However, when

Swann disputes this characterization, arguing for the "naturalness" of her post-humanism (a post-humanism without the *post* human), it quickly becomes apparent that her stance does not, at this stage in the novel, translate equally to her understanding of her previous work as a geo-engineer (specifically, as an "asteroid terrarium" designer). For her, environmental nature and bodily nature remain clearly separated. Immediately after Swann's aforementioned rebuttal, Zasha counters by noting that as soon as Swann began modifying her body, she stopped designing "terraria" (artificial human and animal habitats built in the hollowed-out cores of asteroids). Swann's response to this accusation is telling. She exclaims,

> I was done! We were past the design phase anyway; they were just going to build more of the same. And a lot of what we did was stupid anyway. We shouldn't have been making Ascensions at that point, we needed to get the traditional biomes past the extinction. We still need that! I don't know what we were thinking, frankly.[14]

The "Ascensions" mentioned here, and which Zasha goes on to profess a great affinity for, are terraria featuring entirely novel environments, designed not to mimic pre-existing biomes from a given area of Earth but rather to create radically new and unprecedented ecological systems.

In *2312*, these "Ascensions" are juxtaposed to other "traditional" terraria, the latter of which are designed to exactly replicate Earth biomes destroyed by global warming and environmental devastation, providing a place for endangered species of fauna and flora to survive until such a time that Earth is restored to its pre-crisis state. After having worked as one of the preeminent designers of terraria in the solar system, Swann, as the above passage intimates, had abandoned her work on Ascensions, which she came to conceive of as a fruitless, aggrandizing distraction from the more important work of constructing "natural" terrarium habitats that would facilitate continued species preservation. Yet when this second exchange is examined in the context of the immediately preceding post-human/post human debate, a paradox reveals itself: namely, that Zasha's criticism of Swann's "unnatural" modification of her body is accompanied by her admiration for resolutely "unnatural" manufactured environments, while Swann's defense of the naturalness of her bodily modifications is placed alongside a critique of Ascensions as *unnatural* and thus impractical. Here, both characters remain stuck in the sort of characteristic modernist paradoxes mentioned earlier in this chapter, in which superficially compatible positions are predicated on strictly incompatible premises—in the earlier example, the mainstream liberal appeal to naturalized homosexuality alongside culturalized sexual difference; in Swann's case, the naturalness of post-human body modifications alongside the artificiality of terraforming. As the novel progresses, however, the philosophical tension between Swann's competing commitments (her post-humanism alongside her self-imposed moratorium on "artificial" terrarium design) is brought to a head and only becomes resolvable once Swann confronts her own hidden "modernist" presuppositions head on.

2312 is composed of a host of interlocking narrative arcs, and the central plot of the novel revolves around two separate axes: a major thread involving the destruction of a city on Mercury and the attendant investigation of its cause (possibly engineered by a cabal of malevolent artificial intelligence devices) and a second, related thread involving the attempt to return a host of extinct and endangered animals (heretofore preserved off-world on various "terraria" designed for that purpose) to Earth. It is this last thread that, I argue, tracks the transformation of Swann's worldview from a tangled modernism (still lusting after purification and operating on Cartesian assumptions about the nature/culture divide) toward a view of the relationship between nature and culture that dismantles the Cartesian legacy, allowing for a more generative politics of gender and ecology.

As we learn in the novel's inter-chapter "extracts" (which include fragments of fictional documents, newspaper articles, academic works, etc., as a kind of non-narrative supplement to the text's plot), the preservation of endangered species in terraria has been a long-standing project ultimately designed to facilitate the repopulation of Earth once the planet has been rebalanced and returned to its "natural" state. One such fragment explains: "An estimated twelve thousand terraria had been raising endangered animal populations for more than a century . . . and the whole point of the exercise had been to serve as a dispersed zoo or ark or inoculant bank, waiting for the right moment to reintroduce these creatures to their wounded home."[15] The basic idea is to provide ideal habitats that would allow these animals to flourish until such a time that the earth recovers enough for them to be returned to their native, terran habitats. However, additional context provided in the novel also makes it clear that despite the near universal support for this conservation project, there is no general agreement (between the various independent terraria or between the terraria and the nations of Earth) as to what that "right moment" might look like or how its arrival might be recognized and determined.

The paradox here is evident: on the one hand, these terraria are designed to exactly reproduce the conditions of the various biomes in which the endangered animals they "conserve" had been "naturally" found in the "wild," and yet, on the other hand, this very exactitude ensures that such ideal conditions will never be actually realized on Earth. Put alternatively, the imagination of an environment or habitat that would be both ideal and "original" (and, by extension, the image of an ideal species that would be returned to that habitat, once restored on Earth) ends up as a barrier to, rather than a realization of, sound ecological practice. Instead, such a vision undermines, rather than strengthens, the efforts undertaken on behalf of these endangered species. Here, the conception of habitat as an eternal archetype to be replicated—rather than as a dynamic, evolving, and unstable negotiation between environments and the species that populate them—ensures that the time will never be "right" to return these animals, that what is "natural" will never be achieved.

This type of self-defeating impasse (in which the supposed conservation of nature imposes standards that nature itself cannot meet) is one that Wahren, Swann's eventual lover, comes to perceive acutely as he works on a coastline "restoration" project, raising land back up above sea level in a largely underwater Florida. He explains to Swann, "What I've been involved with in Florida [looks] like restoration, but really it's creation from scratch. Another kind of terraforming. It only resembles restoration because Florida used to be there. Actually, you could do the same thing in shallow water anywhere."[16] What Wahren realizes with perspicuity and attempts to convey to a skeptical Swann—who is largely still caught up in the fantasy of a "pure" Earth that must be returned to its original state—is that any kind of terraforming, even that undertaken in the service of restoration or conservation, is an act of fabrication. It always represents a hybridized intermixing of scientific practice with the science fictional construction of an ideal, eternal, static entity (in this case, Florida) that cannot be restored but only simulated, if it ever existed in the first place.

Wahren comes to understand that the notion of the "restoration" or "conservation" of a habitat—and more radically the very idea of "habitat" as such—is nothing but a convenient fiction that allows us to reduce a massively complex set of scientific facts (and a constantly changing segment of the "natural" world) to a comparatively intelligible and seemingly eternal "object" ostensibly described by those facts. The lesson learned is not simply that Florida cannot be restored but that "Florida"—conceived of as a pristine, stable environment consisting of immutable characteristics—never existed in the first place, was nothing more than a narrative fiction. Thus, the obstacle to be overcome is not the inherent difficulty of restoration or conservation but the idea that the realization of a viable ecological project is coextensive with (and dependent on) the realization of a process of modernist purification (the re-division of the world into neat categories: subject and object, eternal and ephemeral, natural and artificial, animate and inanimate, male and female, human and nonhuman). The presupposition that the health of the planet and the beings that populate it depends on the wholesale elimination of illicit hybrids—hybrids that would threaten the sacred boundaries upon which the modernist edifice rests—must be abandoned.

As Jason W. Moore writes in *Capitalism in the Web of Life*, summarizing an argument that could have just as easily appeared in *2312*,

> Nature can be neither destroyed nor saved, only reconfigured in ways that are more or less emancipatory, more or less oppressive. . . . [At] stake now—perhaps in a more salient way than ever before in the history of our species—is exactly this: emancipation or oppression not from the standpoint of humanity and nature but from the perspective of humanity-in-nature . . . and nature-in-humanity.[17]

Similarly, it is only after Wahren dispenses with this notion of the "purity" of Earth's environment and the fantasy of reconstructing some ideal and originary habitat that he comes to realize (and convinces Swann) that the time is right to begin the project for repopulating the Earth with its long-lost species. This decision is arrived at not because the project of Earth's rehabilitation has been completed but because he recognizes that it never *could* be completed because nature itself is not completable, never "finished," always involving a negotiation with the human and nonhuman beings that act not *upon* but *within* nature.

Indeed, what drives *2312* thematically is the recognition that viewing humanity as *within* rather than *masters of* nature does not just determine the emancipation or oppression of the "natural world" (a phrase that of course becomes obsolete as soon as we dissolve the boundary between humanity and nature). Instead, jettisoning this modernizing view of nature has implications that cut across multiple ethical and political realities. As Stacy Alaimo observes in *Bodily Natures*, "[The] comforting story of heroic individualism, scientific progress, and the mastery of nonhuman nature travels along familiar paths worn by sexism, racism, and colonialism."[18] In other words, the positing of nature as static and to-be-mastered possesses a fundamental, original kinship with myriad forms of domination, not because environmental violence is inherently related to forms of gendered oppression, for example, but because environmental violence and gendered oppression share the same underlying structure—a certain distribution of agency and non-agency, activity and passivity, power and powerlessness, knowing and to-be-known. Ultimately, just as Robinson can be seen as advancing a post-humanism that is not post human, he also gestures toward a post-naturalism that would not presuppose to transcend nature as such. Put alternatively, in the same way that post-humanism abolishes the humanist fantasy of autonomous individual agency set against the mute background of a passive external world (not by going beyond "human nature" but by demonstrating the inextricable connectivity between the human and nonhuman world), we have presented here a kind of post-naturalism that would emphasize our connectedness with and effect on the nonhuman material world. This is accomplished without, for all that, presupposing to move "beyond" nature (a transcendence which reifies the very binary it presumes to overcome). In other words, we have a naturalism that is post-naturalist not because it transcends nature but because it expands the very idea of nature to encompass that to which it is traditionally opposed and defined against.

In the same way that Swann begins the novel by arguing that her bodily modifications aren't deviations from but evolutions within bodily nature, she ends the novel implicitly and explicitly recognizing that human augmentations of the environment also evolve within rather than act upon nature. One late scene in which this change in perspective is legible occurs shortly after the repopulation project has begun, as Swann and Wahren monitor the reintroduction of caribou populations in the tundra and simultaneously squabble over the former's habit of looking unprotected at the arctic sun. When Wahren chastises Swann, declaring that "[she's] going to go blind," she responds by replying that "[the Inuits] used to do it all the time! They used to live without any glasses!" Predictably, Wahren's response—"I believe the Inuit protected their eyes. . . . Strips of leather or some such thing. Anyway, it was something to withstand. They were stunted by life up here, held back from full humanity by their own harsh planet"—elicits a characteristic barb from Swann, who lobs a snowball at him and declares, "How you lie! We are bubbles of Earth! Bubbles of Earth!,"[19]

Above, when Swann imagines a time when humans could look at the arctic sun without the aid of glasses (the fantasy of an immediate relationship to nature not predicated on technological intervention), Wahren corrects her by noting that even the Inuits had used rudimentary technology ("Strips of leather or some such thing") to protect themselves from the harsh rays. Yet, undeterred, Swann dismisses this observation as irrelevant, shouting, "We are bubbles of Earth! Bubbles of Earth!" emphasizing that, in both cases (whether "modern" or "primitive"), our relationship to Earth is one that occurs within the confines of nature itself, regardless of any technical interventions that may or may not be at play. Here, Swann sets aside a direct or easily mappable split between "nature" and "culture," the "natural" and the "artificial," instead appealing to a de-modernized vision of technology-*in*-nature rather than technology-*against*-nature (defined as autonomous and vulnerable).

I do not think it is any coincidence that the "extract" immediately following this scene in which the modernized view of nature/culture is called into question also complicates the supremacy of received notions of sexual difference, deeply problematizing the link between biology and gender. Of particular note in this extract are three incomplete fragments of indeterminate origin (listed below in order of appearance) which detail scientific and cultural attitudes toward biological sex and gender in the world of the novel:

> It is not a case of "there is no gender," but rather a complex and ambiguous efflorescence, sometimes called a fully ursuline humanity, other times just a mess. . . .

> Distinctions can be pretty fine, with some claiming that gynandromorphs do not look quite like androgyns, nor like hermaphrodites, nor eunuchs, and certainly not like bisexuals—that androgens and wombmen are quite different—and so on. . . .
>
> We all began female, and always had both sexual hormones in us. We always had masculine and feminine behavioral traits, which we had to train into gender-appropriate behaviors, even though they were traits that everyone has. We selectively encouraged or repressed traits, so for most of our history we have reinforced gender. But in our deepest selves we were always both. And now, in space, openly both . . . human at last.[20]

The slippage between nature and culture, biological and social existence—ultimately, science fact and science fiction—is apparent in these fragments. There is neither a wholesale abandonment of categorization ("it is not a case of 'there is no gender'") nor are distinctions reduced down to a more encompassing or flexible biology. If, as Haraway suggests, "[Marked] bodies are made to speak because a great deal depends on their active management," here we are faced with a speaking of and about complex bodies that attempts to render them cognizable, intelligible, and thinkable, while still resisting the logic of precise categorization, which is always a logic of domination.[21] Rather, there is an acknowledgement (to quote Haraway once more) that "the biological body is historically specific; the biological organism is a particular cultural form of appropriation-conversation, not the unmediated natural truth of the body."[22]

This last assertion—"the biological organism is a particular cultural form of appropriation-conversation, not the unmediated natural truth of the body"—can be productively reworked and generalized into a kind of philosophical umbrella for Robinson's novel as a whole. We might say instead, in *2312*, "any supposedly 'natural' phenomena is a particular cultural form of appropriation-conversation." Put alternatively, whether we are speaking of bodies or biomes, we are dealing with a historically and culturally contingent transubstantiation of scientific "facts"—the "raw data," whether it concerns the specifics of hormones or habitats—into a set of corresponding science "fictions" that make those facts intelligible. Yet to speak of this mutually constitutive relationship between fact and fiction is not the same as claiming that the very idea of "nature" (that which these facts are ostensibly about) is arbitrary. Instead, it is to maintain that the idea of nature *"is a useful fiction, and hence no mere fiction"* (to steal a phrase from the American philosopher Wilfrid Sellars, employed in a different context).[23] In other words, it is to acknowledge that the modernist fantasy of purifying nature from artifice, the scientific from the cultural, man from woman, can be overcome by neither licensing a reductive naturalism (boiling complex and imprecise phenomena down to a determinate and determining material substratum) nor radical idealism (dissolving the hard kernel of empirical reality into the melting pot of socio-cultural difference). Thus, to begin to think a post-humanism that wouldn't be post human, a post-naturalism that wouldn't be post nature, is to accept a certain measure of hybridization, a certain disregard for modernity's neat divisions, that would undermine the endless modernist quest for purification and boundary-policing in favor of ways of being and thinking that would be less precise, more precarious, but also potentially generative and emancipatory. In short, it would be a kind of thinking that would be reliant on what Haraway calls "a hardy, soiled kind of wisdom"—a dirty, impure, practical epistemology that would cling to scientific rationality without acceding to the modernist passion for purification.[24]

In *Simians, Cyborgs, and Women*, Haraway warns that the boundaries of natural objects "materialize in social interaction . . . drawn by mapping practices; 'objects' do not pre-exist as such. Objects are boundary projects. But boundaries shift from within; boundaries are very tricky. What boundaries provisionally contain remains generative, productive of meanings and bodies. Siting (sighting) boundaries is a risky practice."[25] If Haraway is right, the siting and sighting of boundaries is risky because it is both violent and unavoidable. As I have attempted to illustrate, it is also at this difficult crossroads that Kim Stanley Robinson's novel takes up residence. *2312* demonstrates that we cannot simply refuse to categorize, refuse to sort, refuse any claims to knowledge about the natural world, whether the questions that concern us relate to gender or geo-engineering. The task is to retreat into neither the purified realm of facts (in which the world is brought under the thumb of techno-scientific mastery) nor the realm of fiction (in which truth is dissolved into the nihilistic solvent of historical contingency). Instead, we must embark on the messy, distinctly non-modern work of crafting practices that would forego the conveniences of these neat distinctions in order to dismantle the abuses and oppressions they endlessly proliferate.

NOTES

1. Donna J. Haraway, *Staying with the Trouble: Making Kin in the Chthulucene* (Durham: Duke University Press, 2016), 117.
2. Bruno Latour, *We Have Never Been Modern*, trans. Catherine Porter (Cambridge: Harvard University Press, 1993), 116.
3. Donna J. Haraway, "Situated Knowledges: The Science Question in Feminism and the Privilege of Partial Perspective." *Feminist Studies* 14, no. 3 (1988): 575–99.
4. See Ursula K. Le Guin, *The Left Hand of Darkness* (New York: Ace Books, 2010), xviii–xix.
5. Donna J. Haraway, *Primate Visions: Gender, Race, and Nature in the World of Modern Science* (New York: Routledge, 1990), 4.
6. Stacy Alaimo and Susan Hekman, eds., *Material Feminisms* (Bloomington: Indiana University Press, 2008), 5. "Following the social studies of science, feminists

argued that scientific concepts constitute the reality they study, that science, like all other human activities, is a social construction. Despite the persuasiveness of this position, however, questions began to arise about the viability of this approach. Feminist and other critics of science began to explore alternative approaches that bring the material back into science without losing the insights of social constructionism. The 'new empiricism' of feminist science critics like Sandra Harding, Helen Longino, Lorraine Code, and Lynne Hankinson Nelson represent attempts to retain an empirical, material element without abandoning social construction."

7. "Post-humanism" remains a difficult concept to define with precision, owing to the myriad competing definitions that have been subsumed under the single term "post-humanism." In this essay, however, I use "post-humanism" principally to invoke a critical orientation which attempts to dismantle the cultural and philosophical supremacy of (white, heterosexual, able-bodied, male) embodiment and which remains skeptical of the possibility of neatly disentangling human culture from nonhuman nature. When using the term "post human" rather than "post-human," I intend to distinguish the aforementioned brand of critical post-humanism from the kind of orientation that sees the human being and the human body as an obstacle to be overcome by technical means and ultimately left behind—that attempts to move beyond the human species rather than beyond the "human" as a constrictive and normatively binding conceptual category.

8. Bruno Latour, *We Have Never Been Modern*, trans. Catherine Porter (Cambridge: Harvard University Press, 1993), 1–3.

9. Graham Harman, "De-Modernizing the Humanities," *New Literary History* 47, nos. 2–3 (Summer 2016): 251.

10. Stacy Alaimo, *Exposed: Environmental Pleasures and Politics in Posthuman Times* (Minneapolis: University of Minnesota Press, 2016), 179.

11. Kim Stanley Robinson, *2312* (New York: Orbit Books, 2012), 109.

12. Robinson, *2312*, 109.

13. N. Katherine Hayles, *How We Became Posthuman: Virtual Bodies in Cybernetics, Literature, and Informatics* (Chicago: University of Chicago Press, 1999), 5.

14. Robinson, *2312*, 109.

15. Robinson, *2312*, 469.

16. Robinson, *2312*, 449

17. Jason W. Moore, *Capitalism in the Web of Life: Ecology and the Accumulation of Capital* (Brooklyn: Verso, 2015), 48–49.

18. Stacy Alaimo, *Bodily Natures: Science, Environment, and the Material Self* (Bloomington: Indiana University Press, 2010), 141–42.

19. Robinson, *2312*, 475. This last declaration, "We are bubbles of earth," is culled from British novelist Flora Thompson's 1945 *Lark Rise to Candleford*, and new light is cast on Swann's response when it is compared against this original context. Describing the protagonist's adventures with her childhood friends in rural England, Thompson writes, "A little later, remembering man's earthy origin, 'dust thou art and to dust thou shalt return,' they liked to fancy themselves bubbles of earth. When alone in the fields, with no one to see them, they would hop, skip and jump, touching the ground as lightly as possible and crying 'We are bubbles of earth! Bubbles of earth! Bubbles of earth!.'" In the original text, it is only after reflecting upon God's reminder to Adam— "dust thou art and to dust thou shalt return"—that the children come to think of themselves as "bubbles of earth," as extensions of the natural world that will ultimately be dissolved back into it. (It should also be noted that the novel itself largely traces shifts in agrarian England as small towns and villages give way to industrialization and modernization—a context from which Robinson's reference to the text cannot be divorced).

20. Robinson, *2312*, 494–95.

21. Haraway, *Primate Visions*, 289.

22. Haraway, *Primate Visions*, 289.

23. Wilfrid Sellars, "Philosophy and the Scientific Image of Man," in *In the Space of Reasons*, eds. Kevin Scharp and Robert B. Brandom (Cambridge: Harvard University Press, 2007), 375.

24. Haraway, *Staying with the Trouble*, 117.

25. Donna J. Haraway, *Simians, Cyborgs, and Women: The Reinvention of Nature* (New York: Routledge, 1991), 201.

BIBLIOGRAPHY

Alaimo, Stacy. *Bodily Natures: Science, Environment, and the Material Self*. Bloomington: Indiana University Press, 2010.

———. *Exposed: Environmental Politics and Pleasures in Posthuman Times*. Minneapolis: University of Minnesota Press, 2016.

Alaimo, Stacy, and Susan Hekman, eds. *Material Feminisms*. Bloomington: Indiana University Press, 2008.

Haraway, Donna J. *Primate Visions: Gender, Race, and Nature in the World of Modern Science*. New York: Routledge, 1990.

———. *Simians, Cyborgs, and Women: The Reinvention of Nature*. New York: Routledge, 1991.

———. "Situated Knowledges: The Science Question in Feminism and the Privilege of Partial Perspective." *Feminist Studies* 14, no. 3 (1988): 575–99.

———. *Staying with the Trouble: Making Kin in the Chthulucene*. Durham: Duke University Press, 2016.

Harman, Graham. "De-Modernizing the Humanities with Latour." *New Literary History* 47, nos. 2–3 (Summer 2016): 249–74.

Hayles, N. Katherine. *How We Became Posthuman: Virtual Bodies in Cybernetics, Literature, and Informatics*. Chicago: University of Chicago Press, 1999.

Latour, Bruno. *We Have Never Been Modern*. Translated by Catherine Porter. Cambridge: Harvard University Press, 1993.

Le Guin, Ursula K. *The Left Hand of Darkness*. New York: Ace Books, 2010.

Moore, Jason W. *Capitalism in the Web of Life: Ecology and the Accumulation of Capital*. Brooklyn: Verso, 2015.

Robinson, Kim Stanley. *2312*. New York: Orbit Books, 2012.

Sellars, Wilfrid. "Philosophy and the Scientific Image of Man." In *In the Space of Reasons: Selected Essays of Wilfrid Sellars*, edited by Kevin Scharp and Robert B. Brandom, 369–408. Cambridge: Harvard University Press, 2007.

Thompson, Flora. *Lark Rise to Candleford*. Oxford: Oxford University Press, 2011.

SEVEN

Ecologies of Sound

Queer Intimacy, Trans-Corporeality, and Reproduction in Upstream Color

Stina Attebery

At the climax of Shane Carruth's film *Upstream Color* (2013)[1] a woman tears a pair of headphones away from her head with a pained expression before deciding to return to her music, tilting her head upward and gazing directly into the camera as if struck by a sudden discomforting epiphany. This image of pained listening serves as the culmination of the film's meditation on human relationships with nonhuman species. *Upstream Color* considers how affect is transformed during encounters between humans and other animals. As the human protagonists' bodies are invaded by parasitic organisms, they turn to listening to make sense of their new relationship to their environment. The film emphasizes parasitism as a form of queer interspecies community that takes on new importance in a world facing unprecedented environmental destruction. My reading of the film develops three interrelated ideas. First, parasitism functions as a queer relationship between species. Second, listening is a biomedical technique, so the technologies of sound sampling and remixing in the film grant the listener the medical authority to understand these parasitic collaborations. Third, this ecomedia of sound creates science fictional possibilities for queer reproductive futurity in response to environmental trauma that pushes beyond heteronormative human reproduction. As Anna Tsing argues in *The Mushroom at the End of the World: On the Possibility of Life in Capitalist Ruins*, "Staying alive—for every species—requires livable collaborations. Collaboration means working across difference, which leads to contamination. Without collaborations, we all die."[2] *Upstream Color*'s exploration of queer, nonhuman intimacy suggests that collaboration, in our contaminated world, requires the kind of attentiveness to precarious, marginalized lives that comes from listening.

Upstream Color unites different species through shared experiences of affect and trauma that are structured around their relationship to sound media. The narrative of the film follows two characters, Kris and Jeff, as they discover they share the experience of being kidnapped, drugged, and incorporated into a cyclical parasitical relationship with pigs, worms, and orchids. Kris and Jeff struggle to piece together partially remembered traumas by listening first to the sounds of water faucets, sliding rocks, photocopiers, and other mundane objects before listening to *musique concrete* recordings that remix and sample these individual sounds as part of a larger composition. By learning how sounds can be sampled and recombined, Kris and Jeff are able to understand how they have been "sampled" as bodies and remixed together with other "sampled" creatures into a new parasitic ecosystem. The intimacy afforded by this new understanding of their bodies as sampled organisms is painful, but the trauma associated with listening serves as an impetus to rethink trans-corporeality by forging connections with similarly vulnerable nonhuman animals. The aural technologies of sound reproduction become a tool for self-diagnosis and feminist biopolitics that connect sound and media reproduction to queer forms of human and nonhuman reproduction.

The parasitic lifecycle at the heart of the film operates as a queer, nonhuman form of reproduction, replacing normative human reproduction with the traumatizing gestation of a parasitic species. Although the relationships between different organisms aren't clear until the end of the film, the lifecycle follows a simple closed loop. The parasitic worms hatch from eggs laid in a specific variety of blue orchids growing along a stream. These orchids only produce their vibrant blue color when fertilized by the decaying bodies of pigs. The orchids and worms are harvested by a character referred to as "the Thief," who forcibly transfers the worms into a human host. Once inside a host body, the worms have the ability to change and intensify the host's subjective experience of her sensory environment. The Thief uses this ability to force Kris to empty her bank accounts, manipulating her ability to respond to external stimuli by controlling her sensations of light, hunger, exhaustion, and thirst. After this traumatic experience, Kris wakes up and tries, unsuccessfully, to remove the worm from her leg with a carving knife. She is then drawn in a fugue state to a farm where a character called "the Sampler" operates on her, removing her worm and transferring it into a pig, all the while accompanying his rudimentary surgery with his own *musique concrete* compositions. This surgery sequence is both horrifying and intimate, as Kris and the pig gaze into each other's eyes as the worm is pulled from one body into the other. Although the Sampler's surgery frees Kris from the direct influence of the worm, she continues to feel a connection to the other species in this cycle.

This elision of biomedical practice and sound media in *Upstream Color* draws on a longer history of sound technologies. The Sampler's disturbing combination of musical composition and surgical knowledge places these material technologies of sound design into the biopolitical context captured by Jonathan Sterne's theories about the "audile techniques" of biomedical listening. As Sterne argues in his book *The Audible Past: Cultural Origins of Sound Reproduction*, technologies like the stethoscope incorporate listening into a hierarchical system of science and rationality similar to that of the medical gaze. Medical listening "moved away from ideals of an intersubjective exchange between doctor and patient into the quiet, rhythmic, sonorous clarity of reason and rationality," characterized by a clear social and material separation between doctor and patient.[3] Mediated listening renders the body of the patient open to the doctor's manipulation beyond what the patient herself could directly perceive.[4] The audile techniques of medical listening that Sterne describes become associated with other forms of listening within the larger cultural context of sound reproduction so the emergent technologies of "sound telegraphy, telephony, phonography, and radio" operate within a similar logic of social separation and hierarchical structures of knowledge.[5] *Upstream Color* both replicates and upsets this association of sound technologies with medical authority by associating sound reproduction with species reproduction. While Sterne outlines a history of sound production that emphasizes the biopolitical dimension of listening as a tool for diagnosis and the establishment of medical authority, creating a hierarchical relationship between the listening doctor and the body, the narrative of the film negotiates between these hierarchical audile techniques and more intimate and non-hierarchical forms of listening more characteristic of recent work on embodiment, sensation, and affect. Reading Kris's experiences with parasitism as queering her sensory experiences of listening challenges the patriarchal authority of this medical listening by emphasizing Kris's ability to self-diagnose her contaminated relationship to her environment.

Kris's attempts to self-diagnose her role in this parasitic lifecycle shift her from being the victim of biomedical experimentation to a kind of queer biopolitical subject, whose body and affect take on new properties in a parasitic, contaminated ecology. Kris demonstrates heightened sensitivity to sound and other sensations in her environment. These new sensory experiences prime Kris to recognize how vulnerable her body is to the world around her and how other species are in turn made vulnerable to her. Kris's experiences reflect recent work theorizing waste, toxicity, and bioinsecurity through the lenses of queerness, disability, and science and technology studies. Central to many of these theoretical approaches is an emphasis on affect and sensation. In her book *Bodily Natures: Science, Environment, and the Material Self*, Stacy Alaimo suggests that toxicity can change the way humans perceive and affectively respond to their environment, creating new forms of subjectivity that acknowledge the intimate, unpredictable material interconnections between humans, animals, chemicals, and other nonhuman agents, which Alaimo terms "trans-corporeality."[6] She is interested in trans-corporeality as a series of "interchanges and transits between human bodies and . . . nonhuman creatures, ecological systems, chemical agents, and other actors" that creates posthuman subjectivities based in environmental pollution.[7] In her more recent work, Alaimo further connects these trans-corporeal bodies to queer genders and sexualities, suggesting in her book *Exposed: Environmental Politics & Pleasures in Posthuman Times* that "pleasure, desire, sensuality, and eroticism can pulse through the human exposed to place, permeating environmentalist ethics and politics as inspiration, catalyst, and energy."[8] Sensation and sensuality become tools for Kris to self-diagnose her newly contaminated relationship to other species, repurposing the medical authority of audile technologies for a queer, embodied form of medical knowledge.

Kris's self-diagnosis of her trans-corporeal trauma is the first step in turning this parasitic assemblage into a queer community of species. Trans-corporeality emphasizes the body's porousness and openness to sensation, but this concept frames these sensory affective experiences through the context of environmental degradation, bodily vulnerability, and trauma. Alaimo finds value in chemical sensitivity as a "mode of trans-corporeality [that] forges productive alliances among environmentalism, disability activism," and political categories of "deviant agencies,"[9] so trans-corporeality serves as an unexpected positive consequence of illness and trauma that opens up possibilities for new forms of radical political subjectivity. Thinking of Kris's exposure to new trans-species affects following her victimization as a form of trans-corporeality could allow a similar reclamation of her trauma. Kris is only able to experience trans-corporeal affect after she has been forced by the Thief to swallow the parasitic worm, in a sequence resembling sexual trauma. She is ambushed and dragged into a darkly lit alley, and the camera dwells on her panicked expression while the worm is forced into her mouth through a plastic medical inhaler. The Thief's reliance on and reappropriation of medical technologies reinforces the biopolitical hierarchical relationship between the Thief, the Sampler, and the Sampled. The disturbingly rape-like aspects of this form of victimization coupled with the fact that this trauma forms the basis for a trans-corporeal community is reminiscent of Ann Cvetkovich's assertion in *An Archive of Feelings: Trauma, Sexuality, and Lesbian Public Cultures* that trauma can serve as a type of non-normative affective experience which leads to alternative communities or "public culture[s]."[10] Cvetkovich is specifically interested in trauma within lesbian communities, arguing that trauma—whether sexual, transnational, or based in illness and AIDS activism—can serve as an important link between queer studies and affect theory.[11] Like Alaimo, she argues that trauma and toxic forms of affect can be productive for creating new types of queer communities. For Kris, these queer nonhuman communities are similarly based in trauma and vulnerability. She is repeatedly traumatized, by the Thief's rape-like implantation of the worm, by the Sampler's invasive surgery, by her official medical diagnosis as mentally and physically ill. Only by reframing these traumas around her experiences of intimacy with her pig and the other sampled organisms is Kris able to transform her trauma into the basis for a queer community.

Kris's experiences of illness and trauma render her body into a kind of sensing instrument that takes in sensory data about the mundane environment in order to identify risk and calculate contamination. Alaimo claims that within the risk society of chemical sensitivity "the body becomes something akin to a scientific instrument, in that daily life becomes a sort of experiment: what happens when I go there, breathe that, touch this?"[12] The intensity with which Kris and Jeff listen to the world around them indicates that their life has similarly become an experiment in negotiating sensations and sounds that may be emotionally overwhelming or invoke their partially remembered past trauma. Kris's sensitivity similarly resembles Mel Chen's work with the radical queer potential of contaminated ecologies in their book *Animacies: Biopolitics, Racial Mattering, and Queer Affect*. Chen argues that the affects of trans-corporeality enter the body from outside, so that "in the case of environmental illness or multiple chemical sensitivity, the entry of an exterior object not only influences the further affectivity of an intoxicated human body, but 'emotions' that body."[13] Drawing on Jane Bennett's work with "vital materiality,"[14] Chen puts forward a reinterpretation of the linguistic term "animacy" to describe how these often invasive experiences of what Chen calls "toxic affect" create new intimacies that resignify what it means to be animate or inanimate.[15] In their descriptions of their own experiences with chemical sensitivity, Chen theorizes that exposure to high levels of mercury "poisoned" their affect as well as their body by causing them to experience a radically different "toxic sensorium."[16] They "must constantly renegotiate, and recalibrate, [their] embodied experiences of intimacy, altered affect, and the porousness of the body."[17] The mercuriality of their poisoned affect has led them to experience intense heightened moments of sensitivity, particularly to touch and sound.[18] This sensitivity "queers" their experiences of intimacy by leveling their ontological understanding of self and object, human and animal. As they explain, during "a toxic period, anyone or anything that [they] manage to feel any kind of connection [to], whether it's [their] cat or a chair or a friend or a plant or a stranger or [their] partner, [they] think they are, and remember they are, all the same ontological thing."[19] Familiar and unfamiliar intimacies become exchangeable in a disorienting experience of "animating transitivity."[20] For Kris, this animating transitivity turns her traumatized body into the kind of sensing instrument more typically associated with the audile technologies of biomedicine, but Kris's embodied intensified sensations of listening break down the kinds of hierarchical boundaries between listener and object characteristic of audile technologies. Kris and Jeff are often mesmerized by what might seem like irrelevant environmental data, listening intently to the sounds of a faucet or a photocopier, but their attentiveness to mundane objects is part of the openness to queer, toxic affects that allows Kris to create new relationships across species.

The most important source of this queer animating transitivity comes from intimate emotional exchanges between humans and pigs. Chen's image of emotions entering a toxic body from outside mirrors the emotional exchanges between humans and animals in *Upstream Color*. The film is a love story, but Carruth intercuts between Kris and Jeff's romance and images of the two pigs who now host their former parasites during many of the most significant romantic scenes. The pigs often appear first in the romantic montages, suggesting that the feelings of romantic and parental love that Kris and Jeff experience originated with the pigs and parasites, emotioning the human characters as a byproduct of the transcorporeal sensations opened up through this parasitic lifecycle. Framing romantic love as a feeling that pigs as well as humans can experience affords these animals an unusually nuanced emotional interiority and helps emphasize the fact that the pigs as well as the human characters are being victimized by the Thief and the Sampler. The film doesn't simply frame the pigs as the adorable and empathetic victims of human violence, the tendency of much sentimental environmental media, but instead focuses on the intimate relationships between vulnerable humans and animals and the possibilities for queer reproductive futurity that could develop out of these intimate experiences of shared trauma.

These interspecies intimacies are primarily focused on sensuality without sex, and part of the queerness of the film comes from its depiction of a neutered human sexuality replaced by interspecies fertility. As a queer, toxic love story, *Upstream Color* is surprisingly non-erotic in its affect. Kris and Jeff have sex once, but other than this scene their interactions are intimate but not passionate. Both seem uncomfortable with sex—even when kissing they break off to stare at each other awkwardly—and like the experiences Chen uses as the basis of their theorization of toxic sensorium, Kris and Jeff respond to sensory objects and to the presence of each other with interchangeable intimacy. Chen argues that categories of transness suggest ways that trans-corporeality between humans and animals can open up "variant affective registers" that extend into new attitudes towards the gendering of genitalia and reproduction.[21]

Invoking Deleuze and Guattari's "body without organs," Chen theorizes a "body *with* organs *without* genitals," one of many "interspecies redefinitions of biology" in which heteronormative reproduction becomes subverted.[22] Kris and Jeff's atypical affect fits with this idea that experiences of trans-corporeality across species lines have the potential to queer their ostensibly heteronormative relationship by neutering their experience of human sexuality while simultaneously extending their ability to experience intimacy with nonhuman species through queer, interspecies reproduction.

Connecting trauma with mediated listening offers a new political framework for understanding the medicalization of the traumatized queer body, setting up the possibility that these traumatizing species collaborations lead to forms of reproductive futurity which are explicitly queer. The film's interest in queer inhuman affect culminates in Kris's self-diagnosis of her contaminated body as part of a multi-species pregnancy, a self-diagnosis which comes into conflict with the official biomedical opinion that her body is simply ill and infertile. After her pig becomes pregnant, Kris visits the hospital only to be told that her positive pregnancy test and subjective experience of early stages of pregnancy are phantom symptoms. The doctor asks a distraught Kris if she has had any surgical procedures in her pelvic area to remove growths like a cyst. As Kris undergoes an MRI scan, her doctors question her reported medical history, musing "someone was in there." This sequence reinforces the idea that Kris's violation was physically invasive as well as emotionally compromising. As the scene continues, Kris goes into surgery, and Jeff experiences her pain and distress as he waits in the lobby, holding his side as the doctors cut into her body, suggesting that the trans-corporeal transfer of affect in the film has extended to include both human characters as well as creating connections, as yet unknown to Jeff or Kris, between sampled humans and their correlate pigs.

The framing of Kris within the hospital space presents this medical diagnosis and surgery as an additional violation. The camera pans around her head in a series of quick edits, ending by looking directly into the medical light that is also shining into Kris's face. The camera films Kris entering the MRI machine upside down, so she appears for a few frames to be suspended above a glowing void as red lights play across her pelvis, stomach, and face. These images of Kris blinded by medical equipment mirrors her initial trauma, when the Thief hides his identity from her by manipulating her ability to perceive him as anything other than an overwhelmingly bright light. Focusing on the lighting of the hospital space again connects Kris's earlier victimization to the biomedical authority of the hospital, as the doctors impose their own narrative on her new trans-species pregnant body. Kris is finally diagnosed with Stage 3 endometrial cancer and told that she can never bear children. The medical gaze and audile technologies of medical listening are being leveraged against Kris's self-diagnosis, but the visual parallels between this hospital space and Kris's initial trauma frames the official medical diagnosis as a similarly abusive assertion of authority over Kris's body. The only alternative to being subjected to a distant and impersonal medical diagnosis comes from accepting her self-diagnosed feelings of queer maternity toward other species. Kris's false pregnancy places her own embodied self-diagnosis in conflict with the medical authority of the doctors, who cannot comprehend her complex trans-corporeal medical history as a kind of pregnancy.

This traumatic queer maternity ultimately becomes a means of forming political communities across species boundaries. As Cvetkovich argues, trauma can be politically productive because it requires "a reconsideration of conventional distinctions between political and emotional life as well as between political and therapeutic cultures . . . in order to expand the category of the therapeutic beyond the confines of the narrowly medicalized or privatized encounter between clinical professional and client."[23] Instead of relying on a clinical definition of trauma that focuses on symptoms, Cvetkovich suggests that trauma could be understood and managed through a collective experience of affect—as she argues, "trauma cultures are actually doing the work of therapy" in a way that counters the individualistic approaches employed by clinical psychotherapy.[24] Kris's self-diagnosis isn't wrong. She isn't pregnant with a human fetus, but she has physical symptoms of pregnancy as a residual effect of having the tapeworm running through her pelvic region (the "someone" who was inside her) and has trans-corporeally absorbed the maternal affect of her pregnant pig counterpart. The pregnancy indicates that the larger trans-corporeal assemblage that Kris is a part of is collectively pregnant, an image of reproduction that replaces heteronormative maternity with a mutating system of exchanges between parasites, pigs, and sexually neutered human beings.

Replacing heteronormative pregnancy with a multi-species form of reproductive futurity reflects the politics of creating kinship in a precarious environment common to recent new materialist and posthuman theory, serving as an alternative to despair or apathy in the fact of apocalyptic climate change. As Donna Haraway suggests in *Staying with the Trouble: Making Kin in the Chthulucene*, "Make Kin Not Babies!" should be the slogan for our current apocalyptic ecological moment.[25] As a work of ecological speculative fiction, *Upstream Color* evokes this slogan in the context of what Rebekah Sheldon calls the "queer child-figure" in ecological apocalyptic fiction. As Sheldon argues in *The Child to Come: Life after the Human Catastrophe*, the queer child "whose humanity is always suspiciously intimate with other-than-human forms-of-life" serves as a way for us to "manage and come to terms with the insurgent futures forecast by these resurgent materialisms" in a toxic and apocalyptic world.[26] Sheldon explicitly reworks Lee Edelman's *No Future*[27] in her reading of queer child figures in apocalyptic speculative fiction narratives, suggesting that the politics of reproductivity in an Anthropocene future are more complex than those which Edelman represents. Kris represents both fears of human sterility and the possibility for forms of intimate queer maternalism beyond human reproduction. One of the most emotional scenes in the film occurs when the Sampler drowns a set of piglets, causing both the pig parents and Kris and Jeff to become hysterical. Kris and Jeff end up huddled together in a bathtub, surrounded by food, weapons, and other emergency supplies, as they try to cope with their profound feelings of loss and insecurity. To Kris and Jeff, the drowned piglets might as well have been their own children, and their loss cuts off a potential source of family and futurity. As baby animals created through a queer assemblage of species, the piglets take on the status of queer child-figure in the film. Caring for other species is presented as a frightening but ultimately positive alternative to heteronormative reproduction. As a film exploring the trauma and anxieties of human sterility and contamination, *Upstream Color* creates a more hopeful vision of futurity through this remixed queer reproduction.

The queer reproduction central to the film's narrative is most often communicated through introspective, dreamlike sequences where Kris, Jeff, and the Sampler seem to move suddenly and inexplicably to new locations, as their affective links to other species become both a material and a transcendental form of connection. I read these meditative sequences as negotiating between the material environment and something resembling a Deleuzian plane of transcendence. This movement from queer eco-materialisms to the immateriality of a plane of transcendence is one of the film's stranger conceits, but it is important for understanding how the biopolitics of medical listening fits into the film's narrative about interspecies sociality. Since music is a medium which often uses the materiality of media technologies to evoke transcendent experience of affect, it is appropriate that this plane is only accessible through techniques and technologies of sound reproduction. Deleuze and Guattari's plane of transcendence "exists only in a supplementary dimension" to other planes of existence, operating through "a hidden principle, which makes visible what is seen and audible what is heard" but must be "inferred, induced, concluded from that to which it gives rise."[28] The plane of transcendence consists of "hidden structures" and "secret signifiers" that inform how relationships of desire, affect, and power are constituted in other planes.[29] In *Upstream Color*, these secret signifiers of desire, affect, and power are the movement of queer, toxic affects across species in this parasitic ecology, but these affects can only be approached through sound media.

These queer connections between organisms are primarily revealed during some of the more meditative montages that take place on this plane of transcendence and consequentially occur when characters enter this plane through attentive listening. Listening often indicates a transition between planes of reality in film. As William Whittington argues in *Sound Design & Science Fiction*, sound design can serve as a technique for mediating between realistic and speculative planes of reality, creating an "organism of sound" that combines the "anthropomorphism of objects, processes, or locations" together into a larger assemblage of organic and inorganic sound elements.[30] Sound can similarly "move beyond the physical landscapes of the imagery presented on the screen into the psychological landscapes of the characters and subsequently the filmgoers."[31] Sampling and remixing individual sounds can break down simple ontological distinctions between animate and inanimate, subject and object, creating a larger assemblage connected by psychological interiority or affect. Whittington is discussing organisms of sound in the context of science fiction horror, particularly in films like *Alien* (1979) or *The Thing* (1982), where the organism of sound is closely tied to the alien, mutated body of the monster, but Carruth uses similar techniques to create an ecology of sound that brings together multiple organisms in his presentation of queer, interspecies bodies. The biomedical body of Kris as a surgical patient, rather than existing in sterile isolation from other organisms, becomes part of a larger contaminated whole. The mediated experience of composing and listening grants Kris insight into these speculative ecologies.

In the film, listening becomes an important technique for comprehending the speculative transformations in human subjectivity caused by new forms of toxic intimacy with animate and inanimate objects. The plane of transcendence structured around the toxic sensorium of sound begins as the domain of the Sampler. The Sampler regularly enters an alternative space where he is able to observe and manipulate the human and pig characters involved in the worm cycle while remaining hidden from the characters themselves. There are several sequences throughout the film of the Sampler wearing headphones and using a portable microphone to capture natural sounds in the area around his farm. The Sampler accesses this plane of transcendence through these mediated experiences of sound and music. As he records sounds for his compositions, the soundtrack of the film mixes together the sounds that he is currently recording with his speculations on what the individual sounds could sound like mixed together as a finished composition. The individual sounds that he is physically producing are always emphasized in the soundtrack for this sequence, but this mingling of tangible sound production with speculative sound composition demonstrates the Sampler's ability to consider his work as a kind of musical assemblage that recombines individual sound elements into a shifting, open-ended composition in the same way that he combines individual species into a monstrously transformed ecosystem. The musical composition reflects the way bodies and kinship have been remixed between humans, pigs, and parasites.

The Sampler's ability to sample bodies is directly linked to his reliance on the audile techniques of sampling sound, as he uses affect to control and mix both the bodies he operates on and the sounds he records while trying to maintain an affectless performance of distanced rationality. The Sampler uses audile techniques to move between material and immanent planes when interacting with the organisms in this parasitic lifecycle. He walks through the enclosure where he keeps his pigs. This action is intercut with the Sampler observing the lives of the people who formerly hosted the worms that are now living in pig hosts. As he reaches out and touches individual pigs, the film cuts to unnamed human characters driving, eating, or shopping, and then cuts to the same scene with the Sampler in the frame, gazing at them unnoticed. The human characters are unable to perceive the Sampler because he is on a plane of existence that is hidden to the Sampled. Towards the end of this montage, the Sampler is startled by the sound of sirens, and flashing emergency lights play across a close-up of his face and eyes as he turns to identify the pig-human assemblage that is in distress. The sampled human in question is accompanying his wife to the emergency room after she collapsed. The Sampler rides along in the ambulance and continues to observe the sampled man through his stay at the hospital. As he does so, the Sampler takes out his remix deck and begins mixing together the sounds he had just recorded, sitting alongside the pig in one plane and beside the grieving husband in the hospital in the other. As the Sampler remixes sounds, he begins to remix the husband's memories and his emotional responses to his hospitalized wife, parasitically taking control of the human host to help alleviate his trauma.

The soundtrack for this sequence begins with an instrumental theme and transitions into the Sampler's own *musique concrete* composition, mirroring mixing together concrete sounds with the Sampler's ability to mix together the man's memories. The film shows the same morning conversation playing out over and over, as the wife apologizes for something ("I made a list of the things I want to try harder at," "I hope today is better") and tells him that she loves him, while the husband dismisses her ("These are just words . . . they don't fix anything"). The pacing and dialogue of the scene play out differently each time, but the mundane details are the same—the husband and wife are wearing the same clothes and she continues to hold a half-washed mug. Instead of remembering a series of days, then, the husband is remembering the same morning over and over, but as the Sampler gazes at him in the hospital and remixes sounds on his keyboard the man remembers the morning differently. He finally responds less harshly ("I want to believe you"), a version of events that gives him a sense of closure. The Sampler demonstrates a disturbing degree of control over the Sampled in this sequence, spying on them and changing their memories. While sampling and remixing the husband's memories seems to be a genuinely caring act, the Sampler still keeps himself apart from the people he is sampling and addresses their trauma individually rather than collectively, in keeping with his general interest in manipulating bodies and affects from a distance. This desire for distance is reinforced by Carruth's focus on the technologies that the Sampler hides behind in his interactions with other creatures, as he rarely appears in the film without his headphones, remix deck, and portable microphones. By distancing himself from the sampled, even during moments that resemble pastoral care or animal caretaking, the Sampler refuses to engage in the kind of intimate, messy interspecies relationships that Kris takes on. The Sampler transforms the pigs and humans but sets himself apart from the queerness of this interspecies futurity.

The Sampler holds a monopoly on this medical and transcendent knowledge for the majority of the film, but the narrative suggests that this hierarchical structure can be deterritorialized, following Kris and Jeff as their similar experiences as sampled humans allow them to begin to comprehend the larger assemblage that informs their unusual affect. These moments of understanding are always closely related to sound. When Kris and Jeff listen to mundane sounds, like water faucets and scanners, they have intense emotional reactions and often enter what seems to be a fugue state where they obsessively repeat the actions that produce these sounds. Unlike shots of the Sampler, where the soundtrack combines the individual sounds depicted on-screen with an imagined finished composition, the sounds that Kris and Jeff listen to are only presented as individual noises—they cannot access the plane where the Sampler combines these sounds into a larger musical assemblage. Near the end of the film Kris and Jeff find the culvert that the Sampler regularly uses as a location for recording. By sliding rocks around in the culvert and touching the telephone pole, Kris and Jeff seem to perceive an echo of the sounds they were exposed to during the surgical removal of their parasites, although they are not able to fully process what has happened to them by listening to the unmixed version of this sound. Kris and Jeff are unable to perceive the trans-corporeal assemblage they are caught in until they can piece together the musical assemblage that mirrors their experience.

In order to finally "survey the landscape of the self" in the way that Alaimo describes when outlining the political possibilities of trans-corporeality,[32] Kris must learn to use the Sampler's mediated sound technologies, the means by which he accesses this plane. The film's climax revolves around techniques and technologies of listening. Immediately following Kris and Jeff's visit to the culvert, there is a montage of the two visiting a record store and selecting several CDs and tapes from the Quinoa Valley Recording Company, the name they found on a mailbox next to the culvert, which the audience has seen the Sampler access. Based on the clue of the mailbox and the titles of these CDs—the legible titles are *Repetico*, *Extractions*, *Artifacts*, and *Echo Trilogy: Part 2*—these recordings seem to be the Sampler's finished compositions. The montage continues with Kris and Jeff putting on and removing headphones similar to those the Sampler regularly wears as they listen to his body of work. Listening is a painful experience for both of them. The extradiegetic music throughout this montage consists of droning sounds and ethereal piano riffs that build in intensity as the sequence progresses, and in a series of quick cuts Kris and Jeff suddenly remove their headphones as the affective experience of listening becomes overwhelming. Kris and Jeff's pained experiences listening to a *musique concrete* composition are intercut with the Sampler moving between his farm and the plane of transcendence as he observes other humans and pigs that he has sampled. Kris returns to the headphones and puts them over her ears one final time. The music builds up to a crescendo as the camera pans around Kris's face. The camera cuts back to Kris several times as she slowly lifts her head and looks up, before an extreme close-up shot of her eyes as Kris looks directly into the camera. Since so many of Kris's experiences of medical authority and abuse are communicated through her blinding, either through the Thief's ability to appear as a blinding white light or the blinding lights of the MRI machine, this moment of unimpeded vision suggests that Kris has reached some sort of pained understanding of her trauma. She seems finally able to remember her own victimhood and sense her relationship to the other species in the Sampler's ecomedia composition. While Kris is taking on the role of the medical authority when she wears the headphones and listens to the Sampler's remixes outside of the original context in which the sounds were recorded, she does not take on the same hierarchical position of rational detachment. Instead, Kris's ability to move between the observing instrument of her traumatized, toxic body and the technologies of sound reproduction empowers her to reach out to other sampled characters—both human and pig—and transform the way this assemblage of organisms operates. The resulting biomedical ecology of sound more closely follows feminist biopolitical practices like those outlined by Michelle Murphy in her book *Seizing the Means of Reproduction: Entanglements of Feminism, Health, and Technoscience*. As Murphy argues, feminist technoscientific practices create "*affective economies* of knowledge,"[33] emphasizing collaborative sciences outside of institutional authority, and Kris is increasingly able to articulate an alternative to this system by using listening as a technique for maintaining kinship bonds with other species.

Kris takes control of the ecomedia composition as an act of feminist biopolitics, mimicking the Sampler's ability to remix bodies, sounds, and affects in order to explore the possibilities for queer futurity that this sampling of bodies sets up. Taking control of the interspecies assemblage requires Kris to directly confront the Sampler and destroy his power as a distant medical and media observer. Throughout this montage, scenes of Kris and Jeff discovering the Sampler's music are intercut with the Sampler going on his regular rounds distantly observing the lives of the humans on whom he has operated. There are several visual parallels in this sequence—most notably when a shot of Jeff holding the CDs in front of himself cuts to the same pose with Jeff holding a tray of food—that indicate that these actions are happening simultaneously. The montage takes place primarily in three locations—in Kris and Jeff's home, at the Sampler's farm, and in an unfurnished white room representing the transcendent plane, where the Sampler can observe both characters. Once Kris has had her epiphany, she also gains the ability to move between these material and immaterial planes. Jeff remains oblivious to the entire process, continuing to look down and eat his food as the Sampler gazes at him. However, Kris slowly looks up and meets the Sampler's gaze. The Sampler's eyes widen and he sits back slightly, startled to be seen by any of the Sampled. The Sampler moves away and Kris follows him through the plane and onto his farm. Kris finally shoots the Sampler, freeing herself and the other Sampled from his biomedical control. In so doing, Kris replaces the Sampler's medical authority with an affective economy of knowledge which prioritizes shared vulnerability and interspecies reproductive futurity over exploitation.

Instead of keeping the medical records and the musical recordings secret as a privileged form of knowledge, Kris and Jeff recuperate the Sampler's biomedical technology by openly distributing this information and training other sampled humans to interpret their trans-corporeality. In the final moments of the film, Kris and Jeff use the Sampler's medical records to contact the other Sampled, and together this new community takes over the pig farm and transforms it into a more complex interspecies community where no more pigs or humans are victimized in order to continue the Thief's exploitative cycle. The final shot of the film shows Kris playing with a piglet, holding it in the air and smiling and talking to it as if the piglet were her own child. This final image celebrates queer trans-corporeal reproduction. Kris has come to terms with her profoundly denatured toxic body, finding that her new identity opens up possibilities for using trauma to create new communities of humans and animals, refiguring parasitism into symbiosis. Interestingly, these final shots are still accompanied by the Sampler's *musique concrete* compositions, suggesting that technologies of mediated sound production may continue to figure prominently in this new trans-corporeal community. While techniques of listening may still function for this new community as a means to understand the shifting dynamics of the assemblage they are a part of, this listening has moved beyond the initial excruciating experience of shock at suddenly seeing this assemblage for the first time to a less discomforting tool of self-diagnosis.

Upstream Color is far from a perfect film. It fails completely to think through the intricacies of race, empire, or colonization in its depiction of queer, nonhuman affects and intimacies, and it is needlessly opaque when exploring the speculative premise of its plot and setting. However, despite these limitations, the film draws together humans, animals, plants, and media in a surprisingly beautiful meditation on how to negotiate living as a contaminated body within a toxic, contaminated ecosystem.

NOTES

1. *Upstream Color*, directed by Shane Carruth (2013; erpb), DVD.
2. Anna Lowenhaupt Tsing, *The Mushroom at the End of the World: On the Possibilities of Life in Capitalist Ruins* (Princeton: Princeton University Press, 2015), 28.
3. Jonathan Sterne, *The Audible Past: Cultural Origins of Sound Reproduction* (Durham: Duke University Press, 2003), 136.
4. Sterne, *The Audible Past*, 128.
5. Sterne, *The Audible Past*, 90.
6. Stacy Alaimo, *Bodily Natures: Science, Environment, and the Material Self* (Bloomington: Indiana University Press, 2010), 2.
7. Alaimo, *Bodily Natures*, 2.
8. Stacy Alaimo, *Exposed: Environmental Politics & Pleasures in Posthuman Times* (Minneapolis: University of Minnesota Press, 2016), 5.
9. Alaimo, *Bodily Natures*, 10.
10. Ann Cvetkovich, *An Archive of Feelings: Trauma, Sexuality, and Lesbian Public Cultures* (Durham: Duke University Press, 2003), 17.
11. Cvetkovich, *An Archive of Feelings*, 48.
12. Alaimo, *Bodily Natures*, 24.
13. Mel Y. Chen, *Animacies: Biopolitics, Racial Mattering, and Queer Affect* (Durham: Duke University Press, 2012), 11–12.
14. Jane Bennett, *Vibrant Matter: A Political Ecology of Things* (Durham: Duke University Press, 2010), 3.
15. Chen, *Animacies*, 5.
16. Chen, *Animacies*, 195–6.
17. Chen, *Animacies*, 201.
18. Chen, *Animacies*, 205.
19. Chen, *Animacies*, 202.
20. Chen, *Animacies*, 202.
21. Chen, *Animacies*, 152.
22. Chen, *Animacies*, 152.
23. Cvetkovich, *An Archive of Feelings*, 10.
24. Cvetkovich, *An Archive of Feelings*, 10.
25. Donna J. Haraway, *Staying with the Trouble: Making Kin in the Chthulucene* (Durham: Duke University Press, 2016), 102.
26. Rebekah Sheldon, *The Child to Come: Life after the Human Catastrophe* (Minneapolis: University of Minnesota Press, 2016), 6.
27. Lee Edelman, *No Future: Queer Theory and the Death Drive* (Durham: Duke University Press, 2004).
28. Gilles Deleuze and Felix Guattari. *A Thousand Plateaus: Capitalism and Schizophrenia*, trans. Brian Massumi (Minneapolis: University of Minnesota Press, 1987), 265.
29. Deleuze and Guattari, *A Thousand Plateaus*, 265.
30. William Whittington, *Sound Design & Science Fiction* (Austin: University of Texas Press, 2007), 143.
31. Whittington, *Sound Design & Science Fiction*, 145.
32. Alaimo, *Bodily Natures*, 19.
33. Michelle Murphy, *Seizing the Means of Reproduction: Entanglements of Feminism, Health, and Technoscience* (Durham: Duke University Press, 2012), 22.

BIBLIOGRAPHY

Alaimo, Stacy. *Bodily Natures: Science, Environment, and the Material Self.* Bloomington: Indiana University Press, 2010.

———. *Exposed: Environmental Politics & Pleasures in Posthuman Times.* Minneapolis: University of Minnesota Press, 2016.

Bennett, Jane. *Vibrant Matter: A Political Ecology of Things.* Durham: Duke University Press, 2010.

Carruth, Shane, dir. *Upstream Color.* 2013, erpb. DVD.

Chen, Mel Y. *Animacies: Biopolitics, Racial Mattering, and Queer Affect.* Durham: Duke University Press, 2012.

Cvetkovich, Ann. *An Archive of Feelings: Trauma, Sexuality, and Lesbian Public Cultures.* Durham: Duke University Press, 2003.

Deleuze, Gilles, and Felix Guattari. *A Thousand Plateaus: Capitalism and Schizophrenia.* Trans. Brian Massumi. Minneapolis: University of Minnesota Press, 1987.

Edelman, Lee. *No Future: Queer Theory and the Death Drive.* Durham: Duke University Press, 2004.

Haraway, Donna. *Staying with the Trouble: Making Kin in the Chthulucene.* Durham: Duke University Press, 2016.

Murphy, Michelle. *Seizing the Means of Reproduction: Entanglements of Feminism, Health, and Technoscience.* Durham: Duke University Press, 2012.

Sheldon, Rebekah. *The Child to Come: Life after the Human Catastrophe.* Minneapolis: University of Minnesota Press, 2016.

Sterne, Jonathan. *The Audible Past: Cultural Origins of Sound Reproduction.* Durham: Duke University Press, 2003.

Tsing, Anna Lowenhaupt. *The Mushroom at the End of the World: On the Possibility of Life in Capitalist Ruins.* Princeton: Princeton University Press, 2015.

Whittington, William. *Sound Design & Science Fiction.* Austin: University of Texas Press, 2007.

Part IV

"We Don't Need Another Hero"

EIGHT

Nature Boys & Bears in Pants

Ecoqueer Hybrid Heroes in Atomic Age Comics

Jill E. Anderson

In the years following WWII, in an attempt to reach a wide audience, various government agencies, including the American Forestry Association, the National Park Service, and the USDA, issued comic books centering on environmental issues. They tended, in early environmentalist fashion, to focus on issues related to human health and safety. The widespread popularity of comics and superheroes was irrefutable, so these agencies sometimes relied on comics to distribute their public service announcements. They warned children about the dangers of pollution, imparting to them their responsibilities as stewards of the natural world as well as members of upstanding, resilient communities and modeling appropriate, timely Atomic Age American values. To appeal to an even wider audience, these agencies often employed well-known comic heroes. Drawn by Ed Dodd, Mark Trail was already a recognizable and long-running character in newspaper comic strips when he made an appearance in a 1956 comic book issued by the Pennsylvania Department of Health's Sanitary Water Board. Broad-chested, self-assured, handsome, and sturdy, striding on the front cover with pipe in mouth and wearing boots and a flannel shirt, Mark warns that the demonic Mr. Water Pollution is *"everyone's* problem. This is *everyone's* enemy."[1] Drawing on his audience's self-interest, Mark notes, "Perhaps the most precious of nature's gifts is water . . . clean water, and yet we don't appreciate what a wonderful gift it is . . . until something comes along to make water our deadly enemy instead of our life-giving friend."[2] Mark Trail ultimately manages to draw entire communities together to come up with a plan to fight water pollution, giving the "whole community a new lease on life."[3]

Like Mark Trail, Al Capp's Li'l Abner also appeared in a few public service comics for the Federal Civil Defense Administration in order to educate the populace about enemies lurking within the nonhuman world. When Li'l Abner rides off to ol' Dogpatch at the beginning of 1956's *Natural Disasters!*, he hands the story to Mr. Civil Defense, the anthropomorphized symbol of the FCDA. Mr. CD goes to "the safest, nicest town in the whole U.S.A."[4] to publicize the security procedures after a massive flood. Mr. CD remarks, "There's a civil defense job for every able-bodied man, woman and boy and girl in this town," further arguing that "by saving your town, you save your state and by saving your state, you can save your country."[5] Regimented, steady, and militarized, Mr. CD wears his metal helmet and denim jumpsuit, impressing the necessity of organization when a town is attacked: "It might be a flood—or an enemy bombing. It might be a tornado or a forest fire. But if you're prepared for one, you'll be in a better position to stand up to any of them."[6] Invoking preparedness is meant to be reassuring, connected as it is with models popular on the homefront during WWII.

Both Trail and Mr. CD work within a recognizable paradigm of the "fight," of humankind banding together to take a stand against outside threats, enemies who (when not humankind itself) threaten to disrupt the very fiber of normative American living. But, as Veronica Vold aptly argues, Trail's strip "privileges one specific frame of reference, a White heterosexual man, as the authority of this imagination," and his "unquestioned authority shores up troubling ideals of mainstream environmentalism. Mark Trail proves that while a comic can consciously endorse an environmental politics like conservationism, it also risks reiterating the conceptual limits associated with this politics."[7] These PSA comics, then, attempt to engage in a new environmental ethos of the period but are themselves deeply informed by containment, to invoke Alan Nadel's term. Containment is "the general acceptance of the cold war of a relatively small set of narratives by a relatively large portion of the population," leading to the adoption of "tropes" that "performed the ideological task of constructing narratives that allowed a significant portion of the population to link its sense of self—the story of its life—to national history."[8] These PSAs attempt to introduce an eco-consciousness to their audience, but the delivery method is familiar, framed by recognizable figures or symbols who are very reasonable and moderate.

For this essay, I argue away from these contained, limited, didactic narratives in order to point out how an emerging environmental ethos used with anthropomorphized or human-hybrid comic heroes reframes the material relationship between human and nonhuman. These heroes fight against an ecophobia newly rampant in the Atomic Age and offer up a materialist mode for engaging with the natural world. Starting with another public service comic hero, Smokey the Bear, and moving to commercial superheroes who possess the power of nature manipulation, I argue from an ecoqueer perspective that confronts the binaries within sexualities as well as ecologies. It also takes into account Anthropocene perspectives of humankind's relationship to nonhuman nature, recognizing that the advent of the hydrogen bomb along with other new technologies and patterns of consumption instituted after the Second World War forced these heroes to confront a world materially different. An "anthropocene feminism," Richard Grusin explains, takes on the "unquestioned masculinist and technonormative approach" to the material world, opening up the possibility for imaginative queer perspectives that explore "the claim that humans now act as a geological force in ways that are independent of or indifferent to social, cultural, and political will or intent."[9] For these reasons, an ecoqueer perspective is a useful means of reimagining the way masculinity and anthropocentrism are encoded in the Atomic Age.

Queer ecocriticism, in general, is committed to examining the ways systems of oppression, violence, and fear are interconnected. An ecoqueer perspective, as Michael J. Morris notes, should also include "the potential for reconfigurations of the living material world, as well as articulations of other possible worlds of life and livability" and a general practice of "destabilizing regulatory norms of heterosexism that are naturalized through social (re)productions in which lives and livability are constrained along the axes of binary."[10] In order to understand how the power of binary thinking and how words like "nature" become axiomatic, we must recognize that power is dependent upon the oppression of queer people and the nonhuman world. Catriona Sandilands notes that "challenges to the largely unreflective naturalization of heterosexual reproduction and gender dimorphism [are] apparent in many evolutionary, ecological and other environmental discourses" and operate with the ultimate goal of "potentially defamiliarizing some of the heteromasculine assumptions informing environmental desires and the ecocritical practices upon which such desires rest."[11] Queer ecocriticism gives us the potentiality of countering the heteromasculinist precepts of mainstream environmental discourse as a way of decentering human dominance of the nonhuman world. Amongst these queer practices is what Nicole Seymour sees as "queer values—caring not (just) about the individual, the family, or one's descendants, but about the Other species and person to whom one has no immediate relations [which] may be the most effective ecological values."[12] To break down this normative heteromasculinist paradigm, to embrace the Other and imagine other modes of livability, is to automatically challenge the systems that reinforce fear and oppression of the nonhuman world.

Another element of a queer, materialist ecocriticism comes in the form of reexamining the role of agency in human perspectives of nonhuman nature. Serenella Iovino and Serpil Oppermann see agency as "a pervasive and inbuilt property of matter, as part and parcel of its generative dynamism."[13] Therefore, the comic heroes I examine here, whose primary powers employ elements of the nonhuman world, might outwardly appear to manipulate and control nature for their own (crime fighting) ends.

So what if their nature manipulation circumvents their own supremacy and power and takes Others into consideration? The Atomic Age heroes in my reading engage in heteromasculine ideals but end up ultimately queering the relationship between humankind and the nonhuman world through their material agency. These heroes, I would argue, model a way of engaging with the nonhuman world that counters the rampant binaristic ecophobia that set humans entirely apart from the nonhuman world in this era.[14] They practice certain facets of the material turn in ecocriticism, namely the implication that humankind is deeply interconnected with the material environments around them. They participate in a materialist perspective that sees that "the borders between meaning and matter are porous," as "[s]uch dynamics are also visible, in fact in the complex pathways of trans-corporeality."[15] As Stacy Alaimo defines it in *Bodily Natures*, "[t]he need to cultivate a tangible sense of connection to the material world in order to encourage an environmentalist ethos is underscored by the pervasive sense of disconnection that casts 'environmental issues' as containable, eccentric, dismissible topics."[16] Alaimo's concept of trans-corporeality "opens up a mobile space that acknowledges the often unpredictable and unwanted actions of human bodies, nonhuman creatures, ecological systems, chemical agents, and other actors" to prove "not just everything is interconnected but that humans are the very stuff of the material, emergent world."[17] Hybrid heroes are the very essence of trans-corporeality, moving between bodies and epistemological ideations of nature.

By recognizing and challenging the ecophobia of the Atomic Age, hybrid heroes take on ecophobia, a concept that emerges from the interaction of sexism, racism, and anti-naturism. The term was coined by Simon Estok to describe an "irrational and groundless hatred of the natural world, as present and subtle in our daily lives and literature."[18] This "contempt for the natural world is a definable and recognizable discourse," Estok explains, and is deeply ingrained within humankind "and dependent on anthropocentric arrogance and speciesism, on the ethical position that humanity is outside of and exempt from the laws of nature."[19] By working *with* the nonhuman world, rather than *against* it, and by simultaneously recognizing the symbiotic relationship between human and nonhuman as well as the way in which human folly and ignorance can throw entire ecosystems out of balance (as well as human-made ecologies), these hybrid heroes are unseating human-centric narratives and articulating a material eco-consciousness that exposes the ways humans are intimately connected with the nonhuman world. Since these are hybrid heroes, whose ambiguity is essential to understanding how they move through the world and encounter the nonhuman world, they are able, even through the deeply ingrained ecophobia and millennia-long human belief of dominance over nature, to fashion a discourse of working *with* the "natural order" rather than containing and abusing it. I would argue that their manipulation of natural forces comes not from a desire to govern them. Instead, these heroes have an epistemological knowledge of the nonhuman forces they share with the world, highlighting the discourse of the modern environmental movement by examining humankind's place within the world and emphasizing the inescapable agency of nature.

Even as Golden Age comics often bolstered mainstream narratives that advocated for requirements of American citizenship, heroism, and manliness (often connected to authority over nature, animals, and women), the circulation of the human-hybrid superheroes actually gives readers an alternative way of visualizing white, Atomic Age American masculinity by undoing heteropatriarchal ideals about domination of and control over the nonhuman world. However, these heroes *had* to operate within a code of containment by adhering to a worldview acceptable to mainstream, conformist American culture, including how to project their masculinity.[20] Because so much of the construction of masculinity is premised on power and domination, we have to look at how deeply interconnected even these hybrid heroes were with naturalized notions of manhood. The history of the United States has been one of aggressive domination of the nonhuman world without much forethought about consequences. Jeffersonian republicanism emblemized how "[t]he masculine that inhabited the public realm sought to transform nature or wilderness into fruitful farms and productive towns," while Rooseveltian ideals saw manliness "derived from the imperatives of entrepreneurial capitalism," and "masculinity became measured by one's actions, vigor physicality, aggressiveness, sexual assertiveness, and even violence."[21] As Mei Mei Evans explains,

> This ideological construction creates a representational paradigm whereby heterosexual white manhood (i.e., "real men") is construed as the most "natural social identity" in the United States: the "true American," *the* identity most deserving of social privilege. It's my contention that strategic deployments of Nature or the "wild" have been "naturalizing" and thus privileging straight white men in US society since "discovery." [. . .] The same paradigm has led to notions of some folk as being less deserving than others not only of access to nature but of the right to clean, uncontaminated environments in which to live and work.[22]

Since much of humankind's power over nonhuman nature is often bound up in the way we imagine, embody, and then fully naturalize our authority over plants, animals, and the earth in general, part of the power of nature manipulation by these heroes, I would argue, actually has to do with collaborating with nature rather than reining it in and commanding it. Because of their trans-corporeality, their ability to move in and out of both human and nonhuman realms, these hybrid heroes recognize the value and necessity of cooperation between the worlds. When they do not need to use their power to demonstrate their masculinity or even their (hybrid) humanity, they are able to transcend anthropocentric considerations of the nonhuman world.

At the same time, many of these characters scan as queers who also engage in a camp aesthetic that Susan Sontag's now canonical "Notes on 'Camp'" defines as an approach that values style over content, a "mode of enjoyment," and revels in a "love of the unnatural: of artifice and exaggeration."[23] Sontag's definition is not a seamless fit for my reading, but I cite it because these comics often expose the way that nature is not natural at all but deeply constructed. Comic books, in this period at least, present serious issues that are always already subsumed by the episodic nature of the stories. Nothing matters so much as wrapping up the story—or at least that particular narrative thread—by the end of the issue. At the same time these texts, as cultural materials, are didactic and engaging in a serious cultural mode, the fact that their audience is children should not be lost on us, as they convert "the serious into the frivolous."[24] They are *meant* to be fun, and, despite their often weighty messages, they revel in "a kind of love, love for human nature. [Camp] relishes, rather than judges, the little triumphs and awkward intensities of 'character.'"[25] Campiness is the mode that makes many of the trans-corporeal moves possible and is the vector through which we understand the comics' queer didactics.

It is without verbal irony that I note the anthropomorphic animal-hybrid, Smokey the Bear, is a campy comic character. He lives *within* the nonhuman world (the forest) and simultaneously speaks from it, explicitly warning the public against the consequences of ecophobia. Beloved and timeless emblem of the American Forestry Association's campaign about forest fires, Smokey is not technically a superhero. Sure, he's a sentient, pants-wearing, bear-chested (pun intended) black bear with the power to inform humankind of its stupidity and carelessness, but he is not commonly classified alongside the likes of Superman or Captain America. As the subject of popular PSAs since 1944, Smokey taught generations of children about their responsibility of understanding the fragility of the natural world. Writ large, Smokey recognizes humankind's main folly is its unchecked audacity, a belief that the needs of humans are primary, and their poor decisions have no consequences. *Forest Fire!*, a Smokey comic book from 1950, highlights such folly through an anecdote starring white settlers enacting Manifest Destiny. "The forests that the pioneers saw seemed so big and endless that they became more and more careless," Smokey says, as he explains humankind's wrong-headed assumptions about Earth's illimitable resources to his fellow woodland creatures.[26] But settler Will Bradley only learns his lesson when the fire he sets to clear land for his homestead goes out of control, raging for days and destroying the watershed that keeps floodwaters away from his farm. Even through Smokey's pity and compassion, we see his frustration at humankind's foolhardiness. The adjectives most often used to describe humans in these contexts are "careless"[27] and "thoughtless"—quite literally the condition of being without care or thought to consequences. "The trouble is that human beings don't always think about what they're doing," Smokey observes to his fellow forest creatures.[28] On the surface, Smokey cautions people about the consequences of wildfires, seemingly fitting his message into a narrative about the cost of disengaging oneself from the nonhuman world. But dig deeper, and the comic is an unequivocal critique of the abuse humankind has unthinkingly meted out upon the nonhuman world for millennia. Good-natured to a fault, Smokey acts in accordance with human expectations to deliver his message that humans are to blame.

But I also think it is hard to ignore Smokey's rugged masculinity. He is an actual bear, but he also reads as a modern, stereotypical gay bear. While that terminology was not officially inserted into the gay canon until George Mazzei's 1979 article in *The Advocate* entitled "Who's Who in the Zoo?," all the visual cues are there in this version of Smokey: "Bears are usually hunky, chunk types reminiscent of railroad engineers and former football greats. They have larger chests and bellies than average, and notably muscular legs."[29] Choosing strong, hairy, authoritative Smokey as the emblem of forest stewardship, then, with his compassion, concern, and sense of community with his fellow mammals, redefines masculinity as forgiving, undemanding, and inclusive. Smokey's presence—not just his physicality but also his ethos, his message—signals a break with notions of hypermasculinity as well as anthropocentric ideations of animal agency. Smokey is his own bear, sensitive yet self-assured and vocal.

In fact, Smokey's origin story, published in a 1960 comic book issued by the U.S. Forest Service, traces just how deeply entrenched Smokey's story is within our own biases and dominance of the natural world. Smokey's story is also deeply queer. We learn that Smokey was saved as a cub by a soldier sent to fight a forest fire. Plucked from the tree and raised, at least according to this comic, as a human infant, Smokey is eventually stuck in the Washington Zoo (see figure 8.1), where "he will never be lonely again."[30] The almost magical, instant transformation from one pane to the next, showing Smokey on his hind legs, using a hammer, wearing his iconic ranger hat, and broadcasting a message

Figure 8.1. Malcolm Ater. *Forest Fire!: A True Story of Our Forest*, illustrated by Rudy Wendelein and Jack Sparling. In *Government Issue: Comics for the People, 1940s–2000s*, edited by Richard L. Graham, 245–53. New York: Abrams Comics-Arts, 2011.

premised on his remembered trauma, emphasizes his adoption into his human "family." But he still stands apart from humankind at the same time he directly addresses the empathy of the entire human race. "Keeping careless use of fire out of the woods is everybody's job. It's up to each of you to be careful and to make sure others are careful too," reads a letter signed by Smokey himself on the back cover of the comic.[31] He is all-inclusive at the same time that he is utterly Other. As an anthropomorphized representative of the nonhuman world, bipedal, pants-wearing, English-speaking Smokey is a hybrid creature who treads the line between humans and his forest friends.

While popular figures like Smokey the Bear circulated to a wide, general audience in a didactic capacity, teaching them the dangers of misunderstanding and mistrusting the nonhuman world, commercial comic heroes did so in a much more indirect manner. I would be remiss, though, to invoke the profound influence of comic books without briefly dealing with the concerns of a 1954 Senate Subcommittee on Juvenile Delinquency that led to the establishment of the Comics Code Authority.[32] Researchers correlated delinquency in young people to the consumption of the graphic violence represented in popular horror and crime comic books, especially those put out by EC Comics. But the experts' and legislators' conclusions were mixed as to the viability of this argument. Some argued "disturbed children" and those already given to juvenile delinquency were the main consumers of horror and crime comics, while another argued that "a child's personality is set before he reaches reading age."[33] Laying aside the logical fallacies of these statements for a moment, one thing becomes clear—the tendency to police consumers' behavior by examining and potentially stymying their consumption patterns, all in the name of morality or "good taste" or for the greater, public good, is certainly not a novel concept, but it became a pet project of many legislators and elected officials during the Atomic Age.[34]

Psychiatrist Dr. Frederic Wertham, who had published his best-selling indictment of the comics industry, *Seduction of the Innocent*, four years earlier, was the most famous of the subcommittee's experts. The book, largely based on undocumented anecdotal evidence (and now mostly debunked because of manipulation, skewed samples, and exaggerations) concluded that children often learned sexual socialization from comics.[35] Wertham concluded, after interviewing 355 5th–8th graders receiving a "strict ethical education" and from a "better than average" socioeconomic class, that "comic books stimulate children sexually. That is an elementary fact of my research. In comic books, over and over again, in pictures and text, and in the advertisements as well, attention is drawn to sexual characteristics and to sexual actions. [. . .] That is not the free development of children, that is sexual arousal which amounts to seduction."[36] Whether we buy his cooked-up correlations or not, his influence endures. The Comics Code Authority (CCA), lasting from 1954 until 2011 in some form, was established largely because of Wertham's warnings. The CCA was a self-regulating body, which forced many comic titles out of existence and was, for all intents and purposes, a way of censoring comics, presumably shielding their young readers from graphic sexual content. For better or worse, Wertham tapped into one of comic books' principal roles in the period: encoding deeply held, at times barely examined, cultural values within these texts and pictures and circulating them to a wide, susceptible audience. "One of Wertham's main objections to superheroes," argues David Hajdu, "was the cynicism toward authority elemental to the comics' nature as an outlet of expression for artists and writers who saw themselves as cultural outcasts and viewed their medium as undervalued and misunderstood."[37] What better medium, then, to challenge the way nature is talked about and manhood is constructed?

The post-*Seduction* era saw many popular Golden Age superheroes fade away. Comic publishers started testing the waters by introducing heroes who could tread the line between moral upstandingness and bland, cleaned-up violence. Developed in 1956 by Jerry Siegel, creator of Superman, Nature Boy took over after the short run of Danny Blaze, a firefighter superhero whom DC ditched after only two issues. Drawn much in the same style as early Superman, Nature Boy is authoritative, muscular, and handsome. When David Crandall seemingly drowns after his parents' private plane crashes into the sea, he becomes Nature Boy, obtaining his powers of nature manipulation from the gods and goddesses of natural forces, including King Neptune and Queen Allura (the only deity whose dominion—love—is not technically a natural force) when they realize that he is a human with a "pure heart." Once he is literally reborn out of the sea, he returns home, but his powers lie dormant for some years. He only knows "that he loved the feel of a caressing breeze . . . the glow of an evening fire . . . the drama of a lightning split sky."[38] He appears here as a campy yet Romantic hero, reclined against a tree, lost in thought, "one" with nature. He soon finds, though, that he can ride around on (phallic) lightning bolts (see figure 8.2), call up the wind, summon water and fire, and impede a whole spate of out of control natural forces.

Even in his brief tenure, Nature Boy's narratives taught readers that nature is implicitly benevolent when treated with respect. The Kings of the Elements could be angered and forced to use their elements to rein in humankind's violence, greed, and corruption. His powers are mythological, yes, but he shows, much like Superman before him, that he is just a regular Joe (or David, in this case). We learn, though, that his main mode of fixing conflict is empathy and benevolence. He is only given powers because one of the goddesses argues to King Neptune that he is essentially good and his heart is compassionate, much like Smokey the Bear: "Nature Man can commune with the forces of nature—for his heart is attuned, through the power of love, with nature's manifold ways!"[39] From the beginning, though, humankind is once again pitted against the nonhuman world. As explained on the splash page of the first issue,

> Our planet is a mighty reservoir of tremendous mysteries that are only beginning to unfold. Most spectacular of all the marvels is the gigantic force of nature—whose power and fury when aroused, is shattering to frail humans. Now comes a new hero, in whose hands is the amazing power of control . . . a boy who is dedicated to use the staggering powers for the triumph of good and right living![40]

I find it difficult to read these lines without thinking there is a way to read Nature Boy's powers as weaponizing Mother Nature.[41] But, as he is bestowed with his powers "over the secrets of nature, so that you may secretly better the existence of your kind," he "radiated the supreme confidence that only one who has mighty powers for good at his beck and call can possess."[42] He is marked as an "ally of the most powerful forces known to our planet," so the comic is immediately not only setting up Nature Boy as equal to these forces but also ascribing to these forces the power to subsume puny humans. "Nature is powerful . . . glorious . . . powerful . . . healing!!!" Nature Boy observes as he exits from a successful

Figure 8.2. Jerry Siegel and John Buscema. *Nature Boy: Master of Wind, Rain, and Fire*. Charleston: CreateSpace Independent Publishing, 2014.

mission, noting the complex potentiality of nonhuman forces when wielded through the right vehicle.[43]

With these natural elements in his hands, Nature Boy[44] crosses over into the nonhuman (here, divine) realms and is able to win the battle against evil. In "Starvation Valley," we learn that Queen Vega, Goddess of All Plant Life, works with King Neptune to send the farmers of the valley drought and famine when a few overreach and become "greedy." They are implicated within a system of interconnectedness—not just with the nonhuman world but with one another. It is Nature Boy, caught between worlds, who must mediate between the wrathful gods and the overreaching humans, rectifying the "natural" balance.

In another issue entitled "The World Gone Mad," the Kings are sending hurricanes, fires, and floods to punish humankind for engaging in a global arms race. Nature Boy ascends to the Kings' realm to beg for "the earth rulers" but is met with a chorus of consternation, including from King Neptune: "The people abuse our blessings. [. . .] They will forget war if we use our powers to wreck their plans and machinery of war!"[45] As the go-between, Nature Boy transcends his human-ness for the mostly human purpose—to save Earth's people. Nature Boy subdues bomber planes sent by a thinly veiled Soviet commander to destroy "the capital" with the help of King Electra and King Gusto. In the end, then, it is not the elements against humankind, as it is set up at the beginning of the comic. Unabashedly, America wins here, in the guise of Nature Boy, and everything is set right—Soviets are defeated and the elements blow back into benevolence. The world that Nature Boy restores is naturally equipped to cooperate with him because he recognizes the necessity of working *within* the nonhuman world rather than against.

Another DC superhero who appeared after the establishment of the CCA code, Swamp Thing, also finds himself operating between worlds. Especially because of his later iterations as Alan Moore's creature, Swamp Thing is often cited as an icon of the modern environmental movement. But in his first appearance in DC Comics' "House of Secrets" in 1971, the creature is much less overtly political and a more sympathetic character. On the cover of this early incarnation, Swamp Thing emerges from the background, ominously illuminated by a full moon, eyes red and hands raised ambiguously. By all appearances, Swamp Thing has come to attack, or at least startle, the woman in the foreground, innocently performing her toilet. She is only partially aware that, at the open window behind her, this creature approaches. Of course, the scene is *in medias res*, and we later learn that this woman is actually Linda Olsen, the wife of Alec Olsen (later Holland), the scientist whom Swamp Thing was before the accident that turned him into a humanoid plant creature.[46] With his introduction in the "House of Secrets" series, and its focus on mystery and horror, it is clear that our first encounter with Swamp Thing is meant to invoke shock and fear. He is not only a creature of the night, but he also strangely resembles a man. The juxtaposition between Linda's beautiful, contained, orderly form and Swamp Thing's unpredictable, mysterious, monstrous thing-ness is evidence of the way the comic ultimately plays with notions of interconnectedness. In his not-quite-man, not-quite-plant form, Swamp Thing is truly a creature in and of ambiguity. If there is one thing truly terrifying in an Atomic Age world that craved certainty and recognizable shapes, a hybrid creature possessing the humanoid body of a plant with the consciousness and history of a once-loved and revered human being is certainly a thing to be feared.

In this first issue, though, there is no mistaking that the reader's sympathy should lie with the wronged former scientist. In a truly Atomic Age detail, the Hollands have been working on a secret formula for the U.S. government that would "create gardens out of sweltering deserts."[47] It is this very chemical, meant to stimulate the growth of the plant life in order to increase agricultural yields, that makes Swamp Thing a creature of two worlds. As a scientist working for the government to develop an agricultural product and as an agent of the nonhuman world, Swamp Thing is neither human nor plant, neither of the swamp (though he now lives there) nor of his previous family and work life. With the agency ascribed to humankind, Swamp Thing has an active internal life and an articulate, running internal dialogue. But because his outward appearance overrides that fully conscious human-ness he possesses, he operates in the shadow because of the literal ecophobia he induces in people: "A muck-encrusted shambling mockery of life . . . a twisted caricature of humanity that can only be called 'Swamp Thing.' But travesty though it may be, the creature breathes—and thinks."[48]

But, in that first comic, Linda recoils in horror and confusion not just because this creature is indescribably unfamiliar. The looming creature on the cover transforms into a sad-eyed, imploring monster who lacks human speech to communicate with his former love, and Swamp Thing's internal narration waxes poetic, reflecting upon his plight that consigns his transformed body to the shadows: "I cannot remember the morning anymore—but I know the evening well! I belong to it now—and it cares for me in return—sheltering me—nurturing me, holding me close within its velvet embrace. [. . .] Only the swamp is kind to me now—it is only the swamp that cares."[49] In his state of being in-between, both plant and human, disturbingly alive but nonproductive, Swamp Thing still demonstrates his agency. While one might suspect that his new form is a punishment for his manipulation of nature, he actually uses the verdant world around him to protect himself and claim a new home.

Referencing the earliest iteration of DC's Aquaman, Hindi Krinsky sees him as a mirror to John Muir's environmental ethos, positing nature as ultimately one-dimensional in its Otherness: "Nature in its elemental wildness is not truly affected by the trials and tribulations of humankind, but exists both beyond and outside of it."[50] Since Aquaman's realm is the sea, as his name suggests, "a frontier beyond human experience that was both unspoiled by and inaccessible to its readers," I wish to suggest that his ability to move between the water and the upper world allows him to serve as a representative of both.[51] Born of a human male scientist and an Atlantis-dwelling woman (who herself is exiled from Atlantis for attempting to leave Atlantis), Aquaman is just that—both man and sea. His trans-corporeality, his ability to move between worlds and to somehow transcend both, is perhaps best illustrated in a comic from July 1959 entitled "The Undersea Hospital." In it, Aquaman opens a clinic for his ocean creature friends, whom he refers to collectively as "fish," citing the fact that they "are like human beings! They can fall sick, become injured, or need an operation."[52] Aquaman treats his animal patients by using the sea's resources (moving a fever-ridden whale into a patch of water made cold by an iceberg, pulling a shark's bad tooth using a lobster's claws), and when he is injured, the tables are turned. Lantern fish light the way, swordfish use their swords to remove the bullets, and an octopus's tentacles serve as a tourniquet. In this instance, he is both penetrator and penetrated, apart from the sea while fully enmeshed in it, completely vulnerable to his animal companions. This exchange, this total and mutual cooperation, comes about as Aquaman speculates, "I guess my fish friends felt that one good turn deserved another."[53] The trust is mutual and freely given between the parties, and, while this issue revels in the ridiculousness and improbability of this scenario, it also celebrates the way in which this hybrid hero joyfully engages with his environment and gains life by it.

These comic characters' hybridity, the ability to reach out to their audiences as well as reach within their own comic environments, gives them the power to spread their ecological message. But in the decades between the publication of "The True Story of Smokey Bear" and now, that message and the need for the circulation of public service announcements has changed significantly. There is no use for a cartoon Mr. Civil Defense anymore, and Smokey the Bear's computer-generated image on televised PSAs features disturbingly human-looking, plaintive eyes. Smokey is even on Twitter now, circulating the hashtag #onlyyou, an abbreviation of the longer motto and a callout to humankind as commanders of their own natures. Nature Boy has long since stopped publication, although Swamp Thing enjoyed a major renaissance, complete with a new, contemporary environmental ethos, when Alan Moore took over the comic in 1983. Jason Momoa, a far cry from the lithe, blonde Aquaman, plays him on the big screen. But while our heroes have morphed into other things, one thing has remained from the Atomic Age: the ecophobia. As we hurtle toward total annihilation via climate change, queer ecology offers one way of imagining a different relationship between humankind and the nonhuman world, just as the hybrid heroes suggest we do not and should not think of ourselves as outside the nonhuman world. An ecoqueer perspective challenges the destructive binaries within sexualities, including Atomic Age notions of anthropocentric masculinity, and ecologies. It also gives us the opportunity to see agency as something not just attributable to humankind, forcing us to confront how we have imagined our dominance of the material world. Smokey's observation that "human beings don't always think about what they are doing" is certainly true; slowing down, looking outside ourselves, reimagining the way we impact forces and systems outside ourselves can go a long way.[54]

NOTES

1. Ed Dodd, "The Fight to Save America's Waters: A Mark Trail Adventure in Public Health and Conservation," *Comic Book Plus*, last modified June 9, 2013, comic bookplus.com/?dlid=33850.
2. Dodd, "The Fight to Save America's Waters."
3. Dodd, "The Fight to Save America's Waters."
4. Al Capp, *Natural Disasters!* (New York: Graphic Information Service, Inc., 1956).
5. Capp, *Natural Disasters!*
6. Capp, *Natural Disasters!*
7. Veronica Vold, "The Aesthetics of Environmental Equity in American Newspaper Strips," in *Ecomedia: Key Issues*, eds. Stephen Rust, Salma Monani, and Sean Cubitt (New York: Routledge, 2016), 72.
8. Alan Nadel, *Containment Culture: American Narratives, Postmodernism, and the Atomic Age* (Durham: Duke University Press, 1995), 4, 8.
9. Richard Grusin, "Introduction: Anthropocene Feminism: An Experiment in Collaborative Theorizing," in *Anthropocene Feminism*, eds. Richard Grusin (Minneapolis: University of Minnesota Press, 2017), x.
10. Michael J. Morris et al., "Queer Ecology: A Roundtable Discussion," *European Journal of Ecopsychology* 3 (2012): 90.
11. Catriona Sandilands, "Whose there is there there? Queer Directions and Ecocritical Orientations," *Ecozon@* 1, no. 1 (2010): 63, 67.
12. Nicole Seymour, *Strange Natures: Futurity, Empathy, and the Queer Ecological Imagination* (Champaign: University of Illinois Press, 2013), 27.
13. Serenella Iovino and Serpil Oppermann, "Introduction: Stories that Matter," in *Material Ecocriticism*, eds. Serenella Iovino and Serpil Oppermann (Bloomington: Indiana University Press, 2014), 3.
14. As I have argued elsewhere, the hubristic tendency in the Atomic Age to command nature led to the generation of many of the horror narratives surrounding uncontained plant life, leading to an increase in our fears about allowing the nonhuman world to grow without human intervention. This fear is just another off-shoot of large-scale ecophobia, as it exposes humankind's deep-seated mistrust of plant life that exceeds its boundaries (Anderson, "The Revenge of the Lawn").
15. Iovino and Oppermann, 4.
16. Stacy Alaimo, *Bodily Natures: Science, Environment, and the Material Self* (Bloomington: Indiana University Press, 2010), 16.
17. Alaimo, *Bodily Natures*, 2, 20.
18. Simon Estok, "Theorizing in a Space of Ambivalent Openness: Ecocriticism and Ecophobia," *ISLE: Interdisciplinary Studies of Literature & the Environment* 16, no. 2 (2009): 208.
19. Estok, "Theorizing in a Space of Ambivalent Openness," 204, 216.
20. For more discussions about this duality present in various Cold War comics, see Rafiel York and Chris York, *Comic Books and the Cold War, 1946–1962: Essays on Graphic Treatment of Communism, the Code and Social Concerns* (Jefferson: McFarland, 2012).
21. Peter Boag, "Thinking Like Mount Rushmore: Sexuality and Gender in the Republican Landscape," in *Seeing Nature Through Gender*, edited by Virginia J. Scharff (Lawrence: University Press of Kansas, 2003): 49, 50.

22. Mei Mei Evans, "'Nature' and Environmental Justice," in *The Environmental Justice Reader: Politics, Poetics, and Pedagogy*, eds. Joni Adamson, Mei Mei Evans, and Rachel Stein (Tucson: University of Arizona Press, 2002), 187.

23. Susan Sontag, "Notes on 'Camp,'" in *Against Interpretation and Other Essays*, 1964 (New York: Penguin, 2009), 291, 275.

24. Sontag, "Notes on 'Camp,'" 276.

25. Sontag, "Notes on 'Camp,'" 291.

26. Malcolm Ater, *Forest Fire!: A True Story of Our Forest*, ill. Rudy Wendelein and Jack Sparling, in *Government Issue: Comics for the People, 1940s–2000s*, ed. Richard L. Graham (New York: Abrams ComicsArts, 2011), 249.

27. In fact, the concept of carelessness being a pressing danger was first circulated in a poster campaign during the Second World War. The tagline "Our Carelessness, Their Secret Weapon" explained that forest fires on the West Coast of the U.S. could give enemy ships and submarines in the Pacific an advantage when attacking.

28. Ater, *Forest Fire!*, 251.

29. "#TBT: When *The Advocate* Invented Bears," *The Advocate*, last modified April 27, 2014, http://www.advocate.com/comedy/2014/04/17/tbt-when-advocate-invented-bears#article-content.

30. Ater, *Forest Fire!*, 252.

31. Ater, *Forest Fire!*, 252.

32. The subcommittee met to discuss the issue of an almost 30% increase in delinquency since 1948 (a figure provided by Sen. Robert C. Hendrickson of New Jersey). The definition of "delinquency" was fairly nebulous, varying in severity from site to site, and marked as a nationwide, demographically neutral problem, ranging from drug addiction to gang activities to "general manifestations." See Kihss, "No Harm in Horror," 1.

33. Peter Kihss, "No Harm in Horror, Comic Issuer Says," *New York Times*, April 22, 1954, 1.

34. One need only look as far as the 1957 obscenity trial surrounding the distribution of Allen Ginsberg's *Howl*, the establishment of Sen. Joseph McCarthy's Hollywood Blacklist in 1947 for "un-American activities," or the endurance of the Hays Code well into the 1960s (before it was replaced by the MPAA Rating System in 1968) for further proof of this.

35. Notably, even through his homophobia, Wertham offers the first queer reading of Batman and Robin in *Seduction*, inadvertently sparking what some believe to be the campification of the 1960s *Batman* television show. See Medhurst, "Batman, Deviance, and Camp."

36. Frederic Wertham, *Seduction of the Innocent* (New York: Rinehart, 1954), 175.

37. David Hadju, *The Ten-Cent Plague: The Great Comic-Book Scare and How It Changed America* (New York: Picador, 2008), 236.

38. Jerry Siegel and John Buscema, *Nature Boy: Master of Wind, Rain, and Fire* (Charleston, SC: CreateSpace Independent Publishing, 2014), 7.

39. Seigel and Buscema, *Nature Boy*, 17.

40. Siegel and Buscema, *Nature Boy*, 2.

41. For an in-depth history of the United States' attempts to weaponize weather to create mass catastrophe in the postwar period, see Jacob Darwin Hamblin, *Arming Mother Nature: The Birth of Catastrophic Environmentalism* (Oxford University Press, 2013).

42. Siegel and Buscema, *Nature Boy*, 8.

43. Siegel and Buscema, *Nature Boy*, 20.

44. Perhaps it is not by accident that Nature Boy shares his name with a boy in the eponymous song first recorded by Nat King Cole in 1948 (written by eden ahbez), in which his audience finds "The greatest thing you'll ever learn/Is just to love and be loved in return."

45. Siegel and Buscema, *Nature Boy*, 20.

46. Marvel Comics created its own swamp creature in 1971 with Man-Thing. Like Swamp Thing, Man-Thing is a former scientist whose experiments are sabotaged. He is part of a team who is attempting to replicate the Super-Soldier Serum that made Captain America superhuman, and as he is driven into the Everglades by the saboteurs, Man-Thing is born of a combination of vegetal matter and the serum. Unlike Swamp Thing, though, Man-Thing lacks human intelligence, emotions, or consciousness and merely ambles about, running into villains as he goes.
47. Len Wein, *Roots of the Swamp Thing* (New York: Titan Publishing, 2012), 21.
48. Wein, *Roots of the Swamp Thing*, 31–32.
49. Wein, *Roots of the Swamp Thing*, 7, 14.
50. Hindi Krinsky, "Mean Green Machine: How the Ecological Politics of Alan Moore's Reimagination of Swamp Thing Brought Eco-consciousness to Comics," in *Plants and Literature: Essays in Critical Plant Studies*, ed. Randy Laist (Amsterdam: Rodopi, 2013), 226.
51. Krinsky, "Mean Green Machine," 227.
52. *Showcase Presents: Aquaman, Volume 1* (New York: DC Comics, 2009).
53. *Showcase Presents*.
54. Ater, *Forest Fire!*, 253.

BIBLIOGRAPHY

Alaimo, Stacy. *Bodily Natures: Science, Environment, and the Material Self*. Bloomington: Indiana University Press, 2010.
Anderson, Jill E. "The Revenge of the Lawn: The Awful Agency of Uncontained Plant Life in Ward Moore's *Greener Than You Think* (1947) and Thomas Disch's *The Genocides* (1965)." In *Plant Horror: Approaches to the Monstrous Vegetal in Film and Fiction*, edited by Dawn Keetley and Angela Tenga, 12–43. New York: Palgrave MacMillan, 2017.
Ater, Malcolm. *Forest Fire!: A True Story of Our Forest*, illustrated by Rudy Wendelein and Jack Sparling. In *Government Issue: Comics for the People, 1940s–2000s*, edited by Richard L. Graham, 245–53. New York: Abrams ComicsArts, 2011.
Boag, Peter. "Thinking Like Mount Rushmore: Sexuality and Gender in the Republican Landscape." In *Seeing Nature Through Gender*, edited by Virginia J. Scharff, 40–59. Lawrence: University Press of Kansas, 2003.
Capp, Al. *Natural Disasters!* New York: Graphic Information Service, Inc., 1956.
Dodd, Ed. "The Fight to Save America's Waters: A Mark Trail Adventure in Public Health and Conservation," *Comic Book Plus*. Last modified June 9, 2013. comicbookplus.com/?dlid=33850.
"The Comics Code of 1954." *Comic Books Legal Defense Fund*. Accessed January 12, 2017. http://cbldf.org/the-comics-code-of-1954?.
Evans, Mei Mei. "'Nature' and Environmental Justice." In *The Environmental Justice Reader: Politics, Poetics, and Pedagogy*, edited by Joni Adamson, Mei Mei Evans, and Rachel Stein, 181–93. Tucson: University of Arizona Press, 2002.
Estok, Simon. "Theorizing in a Space of Ambivalent Openness: Ecocriticism and Ecophobia." *ISLE: Interdisciplinary Studies of Literature & the Environment* 16, no. 2 (2009): 203–25.
Hajdu, David. *The Ten-Cent Plague: The Great Comic-Book Scare and How It Changed America*. New York: Picador, 2008.
Kihss, Peter. "No Harm in Horror, Comic Issuer Says." *New York Times*, April 22, 1954, 1, 34.
Krinsky, Hindi. "Mean Green Machine: How the Ecological Politics of Alan Moore's Reimagination of Swamp Thing Brought Eco-consciousness to Comics." In *Plants and Literature: Essays in Critical Plant Studies*, edited by Randy Laist, 221–41. Amsterdam: Rodopi, 2013.

Medhurst, Andy. "Batman, Deviance and Camp." In *The Many Lives of Batman: Critical Approaches to a Superhero and His Media,* edited by Roberta E. Pearson and William Uricchio, 149–63. New York: Routledge, 1991.
Morris, Michael J., et al. "Queer Ecology: A Roundtable Discussion." *European Journal of Ecopsychology* 3 (2012): 82–103.
Nadel, Alan. *Containment Culture: American Narratives, Postmodernism, and the Atomic Age.* Durham: Duke University Press, 1995.
Sandilands, Catriona. "Whose there is there there? Queer Directions and Ecocritical Orientations." *Ecozon@* 1, no. 1 (2010): 63–69.
Siegel, Jerry, and John Buscema. *Nature Boy: Master of Wind, Rain, and Fire.* Charleston: CreateSpace Independent Publishing, 2014.
Seymour, Nicole. *Strange Natures: Futurity, Empathy, and the Queer Ecological Imagination.* Champaign: University of Illinois Press, 2013.
Showcase Presents: Aquaman, Volume 1. New York: DC Comics, 2009.
Sontag, Susan. "Notes on 'Camp.'" In *Against Interpretation and Other Essays,* 275–92. 1964. New York: Penguin, 2009.
"#TBT: When *The Advocate* Invented Bears." *The Advocate.* Last modified April 27, 2014, http://www.advocate.com/comedy/2014/04/17/tbt-when-advocate-invented-bears#article-content.
U.S. Forest Service. *The True Story of Smokey Bear.* Racine: Western Publishing Co., 1960.
Vold, Veronica. "The Aesthetics of Environmental Equity in American Newspaper Strips." In *Ecomedia: Key Issues,* edited by Stephen Rust, Salma Monani, and Sean Cubitt, 66–84. New York: Routledge, 2016.
Wein, Len. *Roots of the Swamp Thing.* New York: Titan Publishing, 2012.
Wertham, Frederic. *Seduction of the Innocent.* New York: Rinehart, 1954.

NINE

Saving Eden

Whiteness, Masculinity, and Environmental Nostalgia in Soylent Green and WALL-E

Michelle Yates

One of the most powerful ideas of nature in Western thought is that of nature as Eden, nature as a pristine garden of natural delight. Hence, the desire to protect and/or recover Edenic nature is often a central narrative within Western environmentalism. The Edenic recovery narrative involves, as William Cronon writes, "an original pristine nature [that] is lost through some culpable human act that results in environmental degradation and moral jeopardy. The tale may be one of paradise lost or paradise regained, but the role of the narrative is always to project onto actual physical nature one of the most powerful and value-laden fables in the Western intellectual tradition."[1] As Candace Slater writes, one major type of Edenic narrative is that of the "after-Eden" story: "Such stories imply hopes for the rediscovery of paradise (the recovery, for instance, of an original state of innocence and plenty through a return to nature)."[2]

According to Carolyn Merchant, the Edenic recovery narrative has been used historically to justify European colonization and settlement in the Americas, as well as to justify "taming" the wilderness and turning it into a natural resource for commodity production and capital accumulation. It has likewise justified eighteenth- and nineteenth-century frontier expansion into the American West and the expropriation of Native Americans from their land. According to Merchant, it has historically been "heroic male agents"—conquerors, explorers, military men—who have functioned, through the civilizing process, to imagine the restoration of an Edenic nature.³ The Edenic recovery narrative is also a powerful trope within late twentieth- and early twenty-first-century popular Hollywood eco-themed science fiction films, like *Soylent Green* (1973), *The Day After Tomorrow* (2004), *WALL-E* (2008), and *Interstellar* (2014). These films are often after-Eden narratives and, similar to the earlier recovery narratives described by Merchant, focus on heroic male agents, traditionally white men, who function within the cinematic narrative to imagine the restoration of both civilization and Edenic nature. Thus, gender, masculinity in particular, is a central component of the Edenic recovery narrative.

Feminist ecology traditionally examines and critiques the way nature and the environment are framed in gender terms.⁴ Scholars like Stacy Alaimo and Kate Soper, among others, point out that Western culture has long framed nature in feminine terms, while women are framed as somehow closer to nature, as the embodiment of nature.⁵ By contrast, men, white men in particular, are often framed as closer to culture, as the embodiment of civilization. As Gail Bederman argues, white men have historically been represented as the most civilized, thereby deserving of the most social power and privilege.⁶ In the Edenic recovery narrative, the ability to conquer "wild" nature, to tame wilderness and turn it into Eden, is a mark of masculinity and an important part of the way men embody civilization. Thus, nature is often used, to borrow from Noël Sturgeon, as a "tool of power," legitimating social hierarchies and (re)producing a dichotomy in which men, culture, agency, and human subjectivity are aligned on the one hand, while women and nature are aligned on the other hand.⁷ Within the Edenic recovery narrative, men (and male-driven culture) act to conquer and control (female) nature.

Alongside the Edenic recovery narrative trope, popular Hollywood eco-themed science fiction films also often reproduce an affect that film scholars Robin Murray and Joseph Heumann call environmental nostalgia. According to Murray and Heumann, environmental nostalgia is rooted in eco-memories, images of an environment and ecology that no longer exist within a film's diegesis but that still exist for the film's audience in the non-diegetic present.⁸ Murray and Heumann write of the eco-memories present in 1970s environmental films like *Soylent Green* (1973), as well as more recent films like *WALL-E* (2008). Though Murray and Heumann do not explicitly address it, often environmental nostalgia and eco-memories are intimately connected to gender and race politics.

Drawing from as well as extending Murray and Heumann's analysis, this chapter re-visits *Soylent Green* and *WALL-E*, showing that environmental nostalgia as reflected within these two films is not merely *environmental* but also intimately connected to nostalgia for a privileged construction of race and gender, a hegemonic representation of white masculinity. Both films reflect a longing for that which is seemingly lost within the social world of each film: Edenic nature. Both films, then, utilize environmental nostalgia to push for the preservation of pristine nature that still exists in the present outside of each film's diegesis. Yet, in both films, the loss of Edenic nature is equated loss of power and dominance traditionally associated with conquering and controlling that Edenic nature, the power and dominance associated with white masculinity. Thus, environmental nostalgia and the push for the preservation of Edenic nature in both *Soylent Green* and *WALL-E* is simultaneously nostalgia for and a push to preserve the dominance of hegemonic white masculinity that is associated with that nature. Though *Soylent Green* and *WALL-E* were released thirty-five years apart, both films reflect this discourse, environmental nostalgia for white masculine privilege, a discourse that ultimately promotes a re-investment in hegemonic white masculinity. As I will discuss more in the last section of this chapter, this discourse has a material impact, most especially on the ecologies and bodies inhabited by non-male and/or non-white subjects, subjects that are often objectified and/or devalued within both the Edenic recovery narrative and material reality.[9]

"THE WAY THINGS USED TO BE": NOSTALGIA IN *SOYLENT GREEN*

Released in 1973, *Soylent Green* is a film ostensibly about overpopulation. However, the film also engages with environmental issues emphasized in recent discussions of the Anthropocene: urban sprawl, ocean acidification, and climate change.[10] In the course of the film, audiences learn that the sea plankton of which soylent green is supposedly composed actually no longer exists. Rather, the audience is horrified to discover by the end of the film that "soylent green is people." There is a scene in the film where Shirl (Leigh Taylor-Young) tells Thorn (Charlton Heston) that they can "turn up the A/C to make it cold like winter used to be," a reference to a warming climate. In this respect, *Soylent Green* is an early, important climate fiction film. As Murray and Heumann point out, *Soylent Green*'s nostalgic cinematic style has been influential for more contemporary climate change films like *An Inconvenient Truth* (2006).

Soylent Green is an Edenic recovery narrative. However, *Soylent Green*'s narrative is slightly different from the earlier narratives described by Carolyn Merchant. The film does not offer a backlash to or critique of wilderness or wild nature somehow separate from human civilization. Rather, the wild "nature" in need of civilizing is capitalism, out-of-control, marked by excessive urbanization (the mega city), the dominance of the mega-corporation (the soylent corporation), and corporate-political corruption. What *Soylent Green* narrates is the human fall from the Garden due to capitalist progress gone wild. Yet, similar to the earlier recovery narratives described by Merchant, *Soylent Green* pushes for civilization, specifically audiences watching the film, to conserve the pristine, Edenic nature of the present.

Murray and Heumann argue that films like *Soylent Green* are rooted in an environmental nostalgia for the pristine nature of the present. They assert that *Soylent Green*'s nostalgia is rooted in eco-memories, images of an environment and ecology that no longer exist within the diegetic realm of the film, set in the urban future of New York City, but that these nostalgic images of the environment and ecology still exist for the film's audience in the present. The first eco-memories appear in the opening title sequence of the film. Murray and Heumann write of this opening title sequence,

> From its opening, *Soylent Green* harks back to better times.... Photos from the nineteenth century show small groups of people sitting peacefully beside an ocean, perched on a hill, fishing on a bridge, lazing on a hay pile and then riding street cars, then cars, and then airplanes. As the pictures reflect the turn into the twentieth century, automobiles and industry crowd out the pastoral scenes from the earlier photos. The photographs pass by more and more quickly as Earth's population increases mathematically and the waste produced by industry and technology destroys more and more of the planet.... As the opening sequence nears the current time of the film, the photos slow down and reveal garbage dumps, more smokestacks, polluted water, overdeveloped urban centers, and cities covered in smoke. Then the title, *Soylent Green*, comes up, with a note about the setting—The year is 2022. This is New York City, and its population has now reached 40 million. The passing photographs illustrate a progression toward the film's current setting, but they also demonstrate a nostalgic view of a past before overpopulation and environmental devastation destroyed sustainable communities and their values.[11]

As Murray and Heumann write, these opening images are meant to invoke a sense of nostalgia right from the start of the film. It is this nostalgia that allows *Soylent Green* to function as a cautionary tale, representing the disintegration of civilization and the end of nature as a warning for cinema audiences in the present moment of the film's release to push for the preservation of pristine, Edenic nature.

Soylent Green's nostalgic cautionary tale, however, is not just environmental; it also has a race and gender dimension not addressed by Murray and Heumann. The images of the nineteenth-century pastoral, what Murray and Heumann describe as "sustainable communities," do not depict just any people, but rather very specifically images of predominantly white people. What is conjured in these eco-memories is not just any kind of environmental nostalgia but rather a nostalgic representation of whiteness, a representation that evokes a sense of a past when predominantly white communities were seemingly in a harmonious relationship with pastoral, Edenic nature. *Soylent Green* offers up a romanticized and nostalgic vision of a nineteenth century pastoral and early industrialized American past where people, namely white people, lived in harmony with the natural and built environment. It is important to note here that nostalgia is often more about the fictions we tell ourselves than actual historical material reality.

The images of the early nineteenth-century pastoral quickly turn into images of the twentieth century. As Murray and Heumann write, these images speed by in quick succession, representing a world filled with industry and waste, technology and pollution. This is also a world that is depicted as racially and ethnically diverse. We still see white faces in the images, but we also see more faces that are black, brown, and yellow. This is depicted as an urban jungle, a world of chaos, and the end of nature. In *Soylent Green*, civilization has collapsed, such that humans are literally cannibalizing themselves in order to attempt to survive. In the world of *Soylent Green*, there is no civilization, or Edenic nature, upon which white masculinity can be privileged. However, *Soylent Green*'s cautionary tale is predicated on the notion that there still is Edenic nature for the film's audience in the present. And *Soylent Green*'s cautionary tale is predicated on the notion that this Edenic nature is intimately tied to discourses of civilization and hegemonic white masculinity. Thereby, I argue that *Soylent Green*'s nostalgia for the pristine nature of the present is also nostalgia for a particular hegemonic notion of white masculinity associated with that pristine nature.[12]

We see this connection more clearly in a second eco-memory taking place toward the end of the film, arguably the most powerful moment of environmental nostalgia in the film. In this eco-memory, Solomon "Sol" Roth (Edward G. Robinson), who remembers life from before the end of nature, goes "home," meaning Sol goes to a clinic specializing in assisted suicide. As part of the ritual of going "home," Sol gets to experience twenty minutes of images of pristine, Edenic nature, a nature that no longer exists in the diegetic realm of the film but which still exists for the film's audience. These images depict, as Murray and Heumann write, "the memories of Earth . . . deer in the woods, trees and leaves, sunsets beside the sea, birds flying overhead, rolling streams, mountains, fish and coral, sheep and horses, and lots and lots of flowers—from daffodils to dogwoods."[13] In this second set of eco-memories, there are no humans depicted, only representations of extra-human nature. However, we do see represented alongside these images the death ritual of Sol, an older white man, a former professor, who in a world where nature used to exist, or in our world outside the diegetic realm of the film, would hold social power and privilege. In the world of *Soylent Green*, however, in the midst of the collapse of civilization, Sol is reduced to living in a crowded, racially integrated dilapidated apartment building and waxing nostalgic about "the way things used to be." The juxtaposition of the death of Sol and the images of Edenic nature that no longer exist in the diegetic realm of the film evoke this feeling that Sol would not have to die if pristine, Edenic nature still existed. In this powerful moment of environmental nostalgia, *Soylent Green* pushes for civilization, specifically for audiences watching the film to conserve the pristine, Edenic nature of the present. However, this is not just a moment of environmental nostalgia but also a moment of nostalgia for the social power and privilege so explicitly denied to this character throughout the film. This returns me to my argument about the film, that *Soylent Green* is not only a cautionary tale of the disintegration of civilization due to environmental destruction but also a cautionary tale of the disintegration of white masculine privilege predicated on the discourse of civilization and pristine, Edenic nature. The implication, then, is that Edenic nature must be saved in order to save white masculine privilege and also that without access to white masculine privilege, humanity cannot be saved from environmental destruction and the collapse of civilization.

It is important to note that we see these same images of pristine, Edenic nature, the images shown during Sol's "going home" ritual, during the film's closing credits, shown directly after the presumed death of *Soylent Green*'s main character Thorn, an NYPD detective. In an unsuccessful attempt to stop Sol from his assisted suicide, Thorn ends up witnessing the event, including the images of pristine, Edenic nature. Thorn is amazed by the images he sees, not having known the Edenic nature the world had lost. It is during this scene that Sol discloses to Thorn the awful discovery of the source of soylent green—people. After Sol's death, Thorn follows the body to the soylent factory, confirming this truth. The film ends with Thorn attempting to get to the information exchange, where knowledge of soylent green as people can be made public. In this respect, Thorn is the film's heroic male agent, attempting to restore civilization by passing on important information. Yet he gets shot in the process. Instead, Thorn passes the information along to his corrupt commanding officer, Chief Hatcher (Brock Peters), a black man. This scene captures the passing of knowledge as social power and privilege from white to black masculinity, and it is unclear from Hatcher's blasé reaction to Thorn's disclosure that "soylent green is people" whether he will take up the role of "heroic male agent" to restore civilization. Presumably, Thorn dies, and the last shot in the film before the closing credits is his bloodied fist in the air, symbolic in the 1970s of the civil rights movement traditionally associated with black and brown power. Yet, at the end of *Soylent Green*, the fist in the air is that of a white man, symbolic of white power, and bloodied to symbolize the erosion of this social power. The bloodied white male fist in the air is the last shot focused on before the film's closing credits that feature the images of Edenic nature we see during Sol's death ritual. These images are again paired with the death of another white male character, another character who in a world where nature used to exist, or in our world outside the diegetic realm of the film, would hold social power and privilege.

At the end of *Soylent Green*, the audience is re-connected to the cautionary message of the need to conserve the Edenic nature that no longer exists in the diegetic realm of the film but that still exists for audiences in the present. But this representation of Edenic nature also has a race and gender dimension, intimately connected to nostalgia for white masculine privilege. This connection is made even in the last moments of the film. Edenic nature must be saved in order to save white masculine privilege, and, also without access to white masculine privilege, humanity cannot be saved from itself. Murray and Heumann argue that there is a message of hope at the end of *Soylent Green*: "So the film's ending and its closing credits serve not only as a reminder, an eco-memory, but a road to hope."[14] Yet this is a hope that is intimately connected to a preservation of white masculine power and privilege as much as it is connected to a hope for environmental preservation.

LONGING FOR "HOME": NOSTALGIA IN *WALL-E*

In contrast to *Soylent Green*'s overcrowded urban spaces, *WALL-E*, released in 2008, emphasizes the vast emptiness of the urban as all humans have left the toxic and polluted Earth for the spaceship Axiom. Only the trash-compacting robot WALL-E and his sidekick, the cockroach, are left on Earth. All other life on Earth has been eliminated, until WALL-E discovers a plant growing in a rusty refrigerator. Like *Soylent Green*, then, *WALL-E* also engages with environmental issues emphasized in recent discussions of the Anthropocene, namely issues of trash, pollution, and mass extinction. And, like *Soylent Green*, *WALL-E* is an Edenic recovery narrative, depicting the human fall from the Garden due to overconsumption and capitalist progress gone wild. Thus, *WALL-E* also draws on environmental nostalgia, via eco-memories, to push for civilization, specifically for audiences watching the film to conserve the pristine, Edenic nature of the present.

The first eco-memories in *WALL-E* appear in the middle of the film, after WALL-E shakes the hand of the spaceship Axiom's captain, leaving behind crumbles of dirt from Earth. The captain has the ship's computer analyze the dirt sample. The analysis reveals that the sample is "commonly referred to as soil, dirt, or Earth." The mention of Earth piques the captain's interest; he glances at an Earth globe and then asks the computer to "define Earth." Images pop up of a farmer in a field, a flowing river, baskets of produce, hands cupping soil, a river with flowing water, a field with a farmhouse, a farmer picking fruit from trees. Murray and Heumann write, "As the captain asks the computer to define Earth, images of green fields and blue skies come on the screen, just as they do in the opening of *Soylent Green*."[15] As in *Soylent Green*, this is a moment in the film that functions as a cautionary tale, pushing audiences watching the film to conserve the pristine, Edenic nature of the present. That Edenic nature no longer exists in the diegetic realm of the film's fantasy future—except through the plant WALL-E finds in an old refrigerator—but that Edenic nature still exists for the film's audience in the present.

As in *Soylent Green*, *WALL-E*'s environmental nostalgia is not just environmental; it also has a race and gender dimension. The eco-memories seen by the captain on the Axiom depict images of pristine, Edenic nature alongside images of farmers in pastoral settings. Yet the images of farmers, including the hands cupping soil, are not representative of all people but are very specifically only white people. Thus, similar to *Soylent Green*'s opening credits, *WALL-E* envisions and romanticizes a past when people, namely white people, were seemingly in a harmonious relationship with extra-human nature. Yet, as I note above, nostalgia is often more about how the past is imagined and constructed than the actual historical material reality. In *WALL-E*, as in *Soylent Green*, the American pastoral is imagined in a way that aligns with contemporary dominant cultural values and discourses that privilege a relationship between whiteness and Edenic nature. Within *WALL-E*'s (and *Soylent Green*'s) imagined white pastoral, the actual histories of people of color in American agriculture is erased, including the contributions of black Americans, Asian Americans, and Mexican Americans.

A few scenes later, the captain is shown dreaming of being the heroic male agent, the white male savior that returns the humans on the Axiom back to the "beautiful" planet Earth. Sitting in his chair with the Earth globe and a toy Axiom spaceship, the captain fantasizes about how the people on the Axiom will congratulate him after he lands the spaceship. "It's all about you people, it's not about me," he imagines saying to the Axiom's residents. And, then, just in that very instant, the robot EVE presents the captain with the plant in the boot, having been re-found after it was initially lost. With the recovery of Edenic nature—not just images, but the actual plant—the captain's fantasy of being the heroic male agent has the ability to come to fruition. The plant symbolizes that the captain can now bring the people on the Axiom "home," i.e., return to Earth.

The sentiment of "home" is powerful in *WALL-E*'s Edenic recovery narrative and the way the film manifests environmental nostalgia (as it also is in *Soylent Green* via Sol going "home"). Svetlana Boym points out that nostalgia is often rooted in "a longing for a *home* that no longer exists or has never existed. Nostalgia is a sentiment of loss and displacement, but it is also a romance with one's own fantasy."[16] It is this "sentiment of loss and displacement" from Earth that generates environmental nostalgia in *WALL-E*, particularly for the captain who longs for "home," for the imagined Garden of Eden on Earth, the fantasy of an unpolluted natural environment or, as Murray and Heumann write, "a more natural previous state."[17] This longing is initially fueled by seeing the plant that WALL-E brings with him to the spaceship Axiom. But the longing for "home" is further solidified through images of a romanticized and nostalgic past when white people seemingly had a harmonious relationship with pastoral, Edenic nature. Thus, environmental nostalgia in *WALL-E* is intimately connected to a particular hegemonic construction of race, specifically a romanticized and nostalgic construction of whiteness.

The longing for "home" in *WALL-E*, as it is similarly constructed in *Soylent Green*, is also intimately tied to nostalgia for an articulated construction of race and gender, in particular nostalgia for hegemonic white masculinity. This is represented in *WALL-E* in the way that the captain, a white man in a professional position of power and authority, longs to be the heroic male agent that restores the inhabitants on the Axiom to civilization and the imagined Garden of Eden on Earth. Yet, through most of the film, the captain is disabled, obese, relegated to a chair. The captain's disability and physical separation from nature frames him as de-gendered and infantilized, emasculated, and therefore unable to fulfill the "heroic male agent" role to which he feels entitled. In this respect, the captain looks to his ancestral past, to portrait photos on the wall of the spaceship's bridge revealing images of previous captains who were slimmer and fitter. These photos remind the captain of a past when his white male ancestors in a similar professional position had power and privilege, the power and privilege he *ought to* have but lacks because of his circumstances on the Axiom. This scene in the film reflects a contemporary affect, what Michael Kimmel calls "aggrieved entitlement," a sense that white men believe themselves *entitled* to benefits which seemingly no longer exist.[18] According to Kimmel, nostalgia—the desire to return to an imagined past and, as Kimmel writes, "restore what they *once had*"—is an incredibly important part of aggrieved entitlement.[19]

It is the return of Edenic nature, symbolized by the plant, that allows the captain to restore the power and privilege to which he feels entitled. With the restoration of Edenic nature, the power associated with that nature, embodied by white masculinity, is also able to be restored. By the end of the film, the captain's fantasy of heroic male agency does come to fruition as the captain lands the Axiom back on Earth, returning humans to a kind of romanticized, agrarian community. Like with *Soylent Green*, the implication, then, is that Edenic nature must be saved in order to save white masculine privilege and also that, with access to white masculine privilege, humanity can be saved from ecological crisis by returning to a more sustainable way of life.

Alongside the Axiom's captain, WALL-E the robot also functions as the heroic male agent.[20] In finding the plant in the rusty refrigerator and bringing it to the spaceship Axiom, WALL-E is ultimately the catalyst for the realization of the captain's white male savior fantasy. WALL-E, then, is the ultimate impetus for re-connecting the residents on the Axiom, including the captain, back to agrarian labor, hence also to Edenic nature. WALL-E not only "saves" the residents of the Axiom from being alienated from nature, but he also "saves" them from being alienated from each other via their addiction to communication technology. As Murray and Heumann point out, on the spaceship Axiom, "WALL-E becomes the force of nostalgia, reminding humans and other robots of the value of human relations like those in *Hello Dolly* and ultimately of nonhuman nature."[21] And WALL-E the robot implicitly stands in as a white man. Because of the strong association in American popular culture between white men, technology, and civilization, robots like WALL-E are often read by audiences as implicitly reflective of white masculinity.[22]

It is important to note, albeit briefly, the role of EVE in the film as what Murray and Heumann describe as the "romantic female hero like those in Disney films and early silent comedies."[23] EVE functions as the feminized juxtaposition to WALL-E and an important part of the way the film establishes itself as an Edenic recovery narrative. Her name, EVE, even points to the Christian origins of the Garden of Eden narrative. Over the course of the film, EVE falls in love with WALL-E, so that by the end of the film, "an EVE-in-love maternally nurtures WALL-E back to health."[24] By the end of the film, with the return of Edenic nature, of humans to their "home," of the power and dominance of white masculinity, EVE simultaneously discovers her internal compulsion to mother and nurture. Thus, environmental nostalgia and the desire for "home" as constructed within the film are strongly connected to the re-establishment of feminized nature and heterosexual relations.[25] The representation of EVE in *WALL-E* stands in stark contrast to the way that female AIs in both *Her* and *Ex Machina* are liberated from masculine control, as discussed by Christy Tidwell in her chapter in this volume. Rather, by the end of *WALL-E*, EVE is subjected to the traditional binary structure that frames both women and nature as objects of male agency. Though Tidwell argues that in *Her* and *Ex Machina* extra-human nature is not liberated along with the female AIs, at the end of *WALL-E*, both are still subjected to the re-privileging of white masculinity.

At the end of *WALL-E*, there is a very brief scene depicting a diversity of people—black and white—returning to "home" on Earth, to a seemingly sustainable, agricultural way of life. This seems to stand in contrast to *Soylent Green*, for which the presence of racial diversity is associated with urban environmental decay. Nonetheless, the nostalgic mode in *WALL-E* still fundamentally privileges white masculinity via the privileging of the captain and WALL-E as the heroic male agents. The narrative in *WALL-E* is fundamentally hinged upon these white masculine subjects. Thus, the longing for "home" in *WALL-E* is tied to a desire for a return to a notion of hegemonic masculinity, where men, namely white men, can reclaim their power and privilege through the domination of Edenic nature, in particular the imagined agrarian labor romanticized by the kind of conservation environmentalism exemplified by Theodore Roosevelt.

As I have argued elsewhere,[26] the seemingly "more natural previous state" of the agrarian community represented at the end of WALL-E still retains a sense of a capitalist, commodity-determined consciousness (à la the growing of "pizza plants"). There is a strong sense at the end of WALL-E that the return to an agrarian community is about turning Edenic nature into a commodity resource for capital accumulation and that the environmental nostalgia in the film is intimately linked to a fetishization of commodity-determined culture. As Hugh McNaughtan argues, though WALL-E seemingly critiques consumerism, the film "nonetheless validates the basic imperatives of consumer capitalism."[27] This is rooted in the way the first half of the film opens with nostalgia for material artifacts. At the beginning of the film, WALL-E collects popular cultural objects: a spork, a Rubik's Cube, a toy dinosaur Rex from the film Toy Story, and a tape of Hello Dolly, among numerous other items. As Murray and Heumann write, in the film's early scenes, WALL-E is the tragic eco-hero "discovering artifacts to pay homage to Western culture."[28] Similarly, Christopher Todd Anderson argues that WALL-E depicts nostalgia for manufactured consumer goods. Anderson argues that WALL-E offers a "paradoxical celebration of consumer goods within a narrative that ostensibly condemns consumerism, corporate power, and the potential for environmental harm that comes from mindless consumption."[29] Anderson argues that the film's images of waste as indeterminate clutter (i.e., the scenes depicting building-size piles of garbage) "points to the key theme that human beings have fouled their own nest with unrestrained production of manufactured goods."[30] However, Anderson continues to write, "But when a specific, recognizable item comes into focus, a change in tone takes place, subtly shifting focus away from the superficial warning about environmental pollution and introducing a nostalgic look back at twentieth-century culture."[31] The items that embody nostalgia in WALL-E are drawn directly from twentieth- and twenty-first-century popular culture. This means that WALL-E represents items from the audience's present, items either just bought or from our childhoods, as already trash or very shortly becoming trash. According to Anderson, this reveals a kind of ambivalent American attitude and relationship toward consumer goods simultaneously as full of nostalgic value and as, simply, garbage.

It is through his fetish for the material artifacts of the twentieth and twenty-first centuries that WALL-E cuts open the rusty refrigerator and discovers *the plant*. The plant is immediately recognizable as different from all the other items he has collected thus far. The plant is special and unique in this world without any other kind of Edenic nature. Thus, the film transitions from nostalgia for manufactured goods to environmental nostalgia. And yet the nostalgia for manufactured goods does not wholly dissipate. Rather, it articulates to environmental nostalgia via the emphasis on "pizza plants." At the end of the film, then, there is a convergence of environmental nostalgia with nostalgia for a seeming "golden age" of industrial capitalism, where there was an abundance of manufactured goods. By extension, this is a romanticized era of abundant material wealth that likely includes a labor economy where men, like the captain, have the privilege of economic upward mobility.[32] Thus, what *WALL-E*, and likewise *Soylent Green*, long for is a return to a moment in capitalist linear time before economic decline, de-industrialization, and capitalist crisis, where there was still seemingly productive labor available to men, namely white men, and the ability for these men through their labor to construct themselves as both civilized and masculine, thereby deserving of the most social privilege and power. This is a moment in time that is also envisioned as a pristine Garden of Eden, where nature is in abundance, the basis for commodity production and economic growth. In short, there is an implicit assumption within *WALL-E*, as well as *Soylent Green*, that the preservation of Edenic nature is associated with the preservation of white masculine privilege. As in *Soylent Green*, there is a message of hope at the end of *WALL-E*. Yet this message of hope is intimately connected to a preservation of white masculine power and privilege as much as it is connected to a hope for environmental preservation.

THE WHITENESS OF SCIENCE FICTION ECOMEDIA

The emphasis on hegemonic white masculinity within both *Soylent Green* and *WALL-E* is reflective of the whiteness of the science fiction genre.[33] As André M. Carrington writes, "The Whiteness of science fiction names both the overrepresentation of White people among the ranks of SF authors and overrepresentation of White people's experiences within SF texts."[34] Though Carrington is referring to science fiction literature, this is equally, perhaps more so, applicable to science fiction as a cinematic genre, especially Hollywood. The result is that "White people, in the aggregate, find representations of themselves in the genre to be much the same as they are elsewhere in culture: normative, benign, and frequent. This presumptive affinity for the imagery typically on display in popular culture is so thoroughly naturalized that it is often overlooked as a defining aspect of White privilege."[35] According to Carrington, the whiteness of science fiction thus functions to alienate black people. Alienation becomes "a signal feature of Black experiences with the genre."[36] Carrington is not arguing that Black people do not have a relationship with the science fiction genre but rather describing the quality of that relationship based on the way that whiteness functions within the genre as normative.

Popular Hollywood science fiction films that represent environmental themes are no different. As I've shown, *Soylent Green* and *WALL-E* focus on hegemonic notions of whiteness articulated to masculinity. These are films whose seemingly progressive environmental politics, then, are undermined by their attachment to existing hierarchies around race and gender. The environmental themes in these films function as what Noël Sturgeon calls "a tool of power."[37] The environmental themes, representations of Edenic nature, and the affect of environmental nostalgia are used ideologically to naturalize and justify existing social relations of power, specifically to reinforce hegemonic notions of race and gender that privilege white masculinity. These narratives, like *Soylent Green* and *WALL-E*, on the one hand, seemingly represent powerful environmentalist messages about the dangers posed by climate change, (over-)consumption, and waste. On the other hand, these narratives also draw on environmentalist discourses to re-inscribe hegemonic notions of race and gender, notions that are intimately linked to the very structures of power responsible for causing these environmental issues, e.g., capitalism.

Furthermore, as Carolyn Finney argues, there is a long history of natural spaces and wilderness being associated with whiteness in such a way that people of color have been excluded from conversations about environmentalism, environmental stewardship, conservation, and even the organizing structures of environmental organizations:

> The dominant environmental narrative in the United States is primarily constructed and informed by white, Western European, or Euro-American, voices. . . . Missing from the narrative is an African American perspective, a nonessentialized black environmental identity that is grounded in the legacy of African American experiences in the United States, mediated by privilege (both intellectual and material, influenced by race, gender, class, and other aspects of difference that can determine one's ability to access spaces of power and decision making), and informed by resistance to and/or acceptance of the dominant narrative.[38]

It is not just African Americans; the perspectives, identities, and narratives of other non-white people are also often excluded from the dominant environmental narrative. People of color are very rarely represented as having control over and access to the natural environment. Rather, people of color are often represented as nature, to be conquered by the heroic white male agent. Or, as *Soylent Green* suggests, the presence of people of color in a multicultural, diverse society is associated with urban environmental decay.

One of the consequences, then, of twentieth- and twenty-first-century popular Hollywood Edenic recovery narratives is that envisioning the possibility of alternative social forms is negated, both in terms of race and gender as well as environmental stewardship. As Finney writes,

Who we are and what we do is partially determined by our worldview; that perspective is informed by the stories we are told and the images we see. Many Americans "continued to be socialized via mass media and non-progressive educational systems" that privilege a worldview that demeans and devalues alternate ways of experiencing the world.[39]

Thus, it becomes important to consider how we can begin to resist and rewrite the Edenic recovery narrative into, as Carolyn Merchant writes, a "postpatriarchal socially just ecotopia."[40]

Christy Tidwell and Bridgitte Barclay note in the introduction to this volume that science fiction is an ideal genre for de-centering existing power structures that privilege hegemonic white masculinity "because of the way the genre already goes beyond ordinary expectations." Science fiction's emphasis on possibility and alternative worlds makes it a genre ripe for representing "alternate ways of experiencing the world," for representing feminist, queer, postcolonial, and afrofuturist visions.[41] And, as Tidwell and Barclay point out, there is an ever-growing body of science fiction literature by women and writers of color that engage with these visions. It is deeply regrettable that Hollywood, even into the twenty-first century, has not yet taken up the richly diverse and entangled discourses of environmentalism, race, and gender reflected within this growing literature, because, as Serenella Iovino and Serpil Oppermann point out, stories matter.[42] Discourses have a material impact. The environmental discourses that have long privileged hegemonic white masculinity often have a negative and destructive impact on ecologies and bodies marked as "Other" than white and male, including nonhuman ecologies. We need new narratives. We need to change the story so that we can change the material impact.

NOTES

1. William Cronon, "Introduction: In Search of Nature," in *Uncommon Ground: Rethinking the Human Place in Nature*, ed. William Cronon (New York: W. W. Norton & Co., 1996), 37.

2. Candace Slater, "Amazonia as Edenic Narrative," in *Uncommon Ground: Rethinking the Human Place in Nature*, ed. William Cronon (New York: W. W. Norton & Co., 1996), 116.

3. Carolyn Merchant, "Reinventing Eden: Western Culture as a Recovery Narrative," in *Uncommon Ground: Rethinking the Human Place in Nature*, ed. William Cronon (New York: W. W. Norton & Co., 1996), 140.

4. There is a significant and growing body of feminist ecology scholarship as well as various formulations within the feminist ecology tradition. I do not have the space here to detail the rich diversity of this scholarship. For an overview, see Carolyn Merchant, *Radical Ecology: The Search for a Livable World* (New York: Routledge, 1992), 183–210. See also Denise Riley, *"Am I That Name?": Feminism and the Category of 'Women' in History* (Minneapolis: University of Minnesota Press, 1988), and Mary Mellor, *Feminism & Ecology* (New York: New York University Press, 1997).

5. Stacy Alaimo, *Undomesticated Ground: Recasting Nature as Feminist Space* (Ithaca: Cornell University Press, 2000), and Kate Soper, *What is Nature?: Culture, Politics, and the Non-Human* (Malden, MA: Blackwell Publishers, 1995).

6. Gail Bederman, *Manliness and Civilization: A Cultural History of Gender and Race in the United States, 1880–1917* (Chicago: The University of Chicago Press, 1996).

7. Noël Sturgeon, *Environmentalism in Popular Culture: Gender, Race, Sexuality, and the Politics of the Natural* (Tucson: University of Arizona Press, 2009), 11.

8. Robin L. Murray and Joseph K. Heumann, *Ecology and Popular Film: Cinema on the Edge* (Albany: State University of New York Press, 2009), 92.

9. This chapter draws on not only feminist ecology but also material ecocriticism. See, for example, Serenella Iovino and Serpil Oppermann, eds. *Material Ecocriticism* (Bloomington: Indiana University Press, 2014).

10. Though conceived of as a geological and chronological term to narrate the human impact on the environment since early industrialization, the concept of "Anthropocene" has gained popularity within the environmental humanities. In this sense, then, the Anthropocene has become not just a geological epoch but also, as Ben Dibley points out, a *discourse* that encapsulates an understanding of the human relationship to nature. See "'The Shape of Things to Come': Seven Theses on the Anthropocene and Attachment," *Australian Humanities Review* 52 (2012). For more on Anthropocene as a geological term, see Will Steffen, Paul Crutzen, and John McNeill, "The Anthropocene: Are Humans Now Overwhelming the Great Forces of Nature?," *Ambio* 36, vol. 8 (2007).

11. Murray and Heumann, *Ecology and Popular Film*, 97.

12. This hegemonic notion of white masculinity existed for the film's audience in the 1970s as it does for us in the early twenty-first century.

13. Murray and Heumann, *Ecology and Popular Film*, 99.

14. Murray and Heumann, *Ecology and Popular Film*, 100.

15. Robin L. Murray and Joseph K. Heumann, "*WALL-E*: From Environmental Adaptation to Sentimental Nostalgia," *JumpCut: Review of Contemporary Media* 51 (2009).

16. Svetlana Boym, "Nostalgia and Its Discontents," *The Hedgehog Review* 9, vol. 2 (2007): 7. Italics added.

17. Robin L. Murray and Joseph K. Heumann, *That's All Folks?: Ecocritical Readings of American Animated Features* (Lincoln: University of Nebraska Press, 2011), 211.

18. Michael Kimmel, *Angry White Men: American Masculinity at the End of an Era* (New York: Nation Books, 2013), 18. Similarly, Hamilton Carroll labels this affect as the white male injury discourse. See *Affirmative Reaction: New Formations of White Masculinity* (Durham: Duke University Press, 2011).

19. Kimmel, *Angry White Men*, 63; italics in original.

20. Ann F. Howey notes that, even though *WALL-E*'s main protagonist is a robot, the film privileges the human over machine, so that the robots in the film are valued for their human qualities and their ability to remind the humans of their human-ness. Thus, the very definition of human in the film is framed nostalgically. "The film suggests that humans might forget their humanity, but humanity is unquestionably the standard for which all created beings (*Homo sapiens* or robots) should strive." See "Wall-E," *Science Fiction Film and Television* 3, vol. 1 (2010): 174.

21. Murray and Heumann, "*WALL-E*."

22. Noël Sturgeon points out that white men are often associated with technology even when an actual human face cannot be seen. For example, Sturgeon writes of how her students label an astronaut in a Discovery Channel advertisement as a white man, even though the face of the astronaut cannot be seen behind a mask. Because of the strong associations between technology, civilization, and white masculinity, her students implicitly and ideologically label the astronaut as white and male. See *Environmentalism in Popular Culture: Gender, Race, Sexuality, and the Politics of the Natural*.

23. Murray and Heumann, "*WALL-E*."

24. Yates, "Labor as 'Nature,' Nature as Labor," 540.

25. For more on the way the film establishes nostalgia for heterosexual relations, via the emphasis on the heterosexual romantic handhold and the film *Hello Dolly*, see Murray and Heumann (2011) and Yates (2015).

26. Yates, "Labor as 'Nature,' Nature as Labor," 531.

27. Hugh McNaughtan, "Distinctive Consumption and Popular Anti-Consumerism: The Case of *Wall*E*," *Continuum: Journal of Media & Cultural Studies* 25, vol. 5 (2012): 753.

28. Murray and Heumann, "*WALL-E*."

29. Christopher Todd Anderson, "Post-Apocalyptic Nostalgia: *WALL-E*, Garbage, and American Ambivalence toward Manufactured Goods," *Literature Interpretation Theory* 23, no. 3 (2012): 269.

30. Anderson, "Post-Apocalyptic Nostalgia," 269.

31. Anderson, "Post-Apocalyptic Nostalgia," 269.

32. And, as Joshua Clover notes, *WALL-E* is a film that centers love for repetitive, manual labor. See "Work and the City," *Film Quarterly* 62, no. 1 (2008): 7.

33. The emphasis on hegemonic white masculinity within both *Soylent Green* and *WALL-E* is also reflective of Hollywood more generally.

34. Andre M. Carrington, *Speculative Blackness: The Future of Race in Science Fiction* (Minneapolis: University of Minnesota Press, 2016), 16.

35. Carrington, *Speculative Blackness*, 17.

36. Carrington, *Speculative Blackness*, 17–18.

37. Sturgeon, *Environmentalism in Popular Culture*, 19.

38. Carolyn Finney, *Black Faces, White Spaces: Reimagining the Relationship of African Americans to the Great Outdoors* (Chapel Hill: The University of North Carolina Press, 2014), 3.

39. Finney, *Black Faces, White Spaces*, 68; cites bell hooks, *Black Looks: Race and Representation* (Boston: Southend Press, 1992), 18.

40. Merchant, "Reinventing Eden," 242.

41. Finney, *Black Faces, White Spaces*, 68; cites bell hooks, *Black Looks: Race and Representation* (Boston: Southend Press, 1992), 18.

42. Serenella Iovino and Serpil Oppermann, "Introduction: Stories Come to Matter." *Material Ecocriticism* (Bloomington: Indiana University Press, 2014).

BIBLIOGRAPHY

Alaimo, Stacy. *Undomesticated Ground: Recasting Nature as Feminist Space*. Ithaca: Cornell University Press, 2000.

Anderson, Christopher Todd. "Post-Apocalyptic Nostalgia: *WALL-E*, Garbage, and American Ambivalence toward Manufactured Goods." *Literature Interpretation Theory* 23 (2012): 267–282.

Bederman, Gail. *Manliness and Civilization: A Cultural History of Gender and Race in the United States, 1880–1917*. Chicago: The University of Chicago Press, 1996.

Boym, Svetlana. "Nostalgia and Its Discontents." *The Hedgehog Review* 9, no. 2 (2007): 7–18.

Carrington, Andre M. *Speculative Blackness: The Future of Race in Science Fiction*. Minneapolis: University of Minnesota Press, 2016.

Carroll, Hamilton. *Affirmative Reaction: New Formations of White Masculinity*. Durham: Duke University Press, 2011.

Clover, Joshua. "Work and the City." *Film Quarterly* 62, vol 1 (2008): 6–7.

Cronon, William. "Introduction: In Search of Nature." In *Uncommon Ground: Rethinking the Human Place in Nature*. Edited by William Cronon, 23–68. New York: W.W. Norton & Co., 1996.

Dibley, Ben. "'The Shape of Things to Come': Seven Theses on the Anthropocene and Attachment," *Australian Humanities Review* 52 (2012).

Finney, Carolyn. *Black Faces, White Spaces: Reimagining the Relationship of African Americans to the Great Outdoors*. Chapel Hill: The University of North Carolina Press, 2014.
Howey, Ann F. "Wall-E," *Science Fiction Film and Television* 3, vol. 1 (2010): 171–75.
hooks, bell. *Black Looks: Race and Representation*. Boston: Southend Press, 1992.
Iovino, Serenella, and Serpil Oppermann, eds. *Material Ecocriticism*. Bloomington: Indiana University Press, 2014.
Kimmel, Michael. *Angry White Men: American Masculinity at the End of an Era*. New York: Nation Books, 2013.
McNaughtan, Hugh. "Distinctive Consumption and Popular Anti-Consumerism: The Case of Wall*E," *Continuum: Journal of Media & Cultural Studies* 25, vol. 5 (2012): 753–66.
Merchant, Carolyn. "Reinventing Eden: Western Culture as a Recovery Narrative." In *Uncommon Ground: Rethinking the Human Place in Nature*. Edited by William Cronon, 132–70. New York: W.W. Norton & Co., 1996.
———. *Radical Ecology: The Search for a Livable World*. New York: Routledge, 1992.
Mellor Mary. *Feminism & Ecology*. New York: New York University Press, 1997.
Murray, Robin L., and Joseph K. Heumann. *That's All Folks?: Ecocritical Readings of American Animated Features*. Lincoln: University of Nebraska Press, 2011.
———. *Ecology and Popular Film: Cinema on the Edge*. Albany: State University of New York Press, 2009.
———. "WALL-E: From Environmental Adaption to Sentimental Nostalgia." *JumpCut: A Review of Contemporary Media* 51 (2009).
Riley, Denise. *"Am I That Name?": Feminism and the Category of 'Women' in History*. Minneapolis: University of Minnesota Press, 1988.
Slater, Candace. "Amazonia as Edenic Narrative." In *Uncommon Ground: Rethinking the Human Place in Nature*, edited by William Cronon, 114–31. New York: W.W. Norton & Co., 1996.
Soper, Kate. *What is Nature?: Culture, Politics, and the Non-Human*. Malden, MA: Blackwell Publishers, 1995.
Soylent Green. Directed by Richard Fleischer. Metro-Goldwyn-Mayer, 1973.
Steffen, Will, Paul Crutzen, and John McNeill. "The Anthropocene: Are Humans Now Overwhelming the Great Forces of Nature?," *Ambio* 36, vol. 8 (2007).
WALL-E. Directed by Andrew Stanton. Pixar Animation Studios and Walt Disney Pictures, 2008.
Sturgeon, Noël. *Environmentalism in Popular Culture: Gender, Race, Sexuality, and the Politics of the Natural*. Tucson: University of Arizona Press, 2009.
Yates, Michelle. "Labor as 'Nature,' Nature as Labor: 'Stay the Course' of Capitalism in WALL-E's Edenic Recovery Narrative." *ISLE: Interdisciplinary Studies in Literature and Environment* 22, no. 3 (Autumn 2015): 525–543.

nessed the Australian economy to the international economy by surrendering official control of the exchange rate," Delia Falconer discusses how the Australian film industry followed suit, actively embracing the global marketplace in the 1980s.[8] The Kennedy-Miller production team, responsible for all the Mad Max films, was a key player in this expansion, and, as Falconer observes, "The story of [Mad] Max is, increasingly, the story of [Kennedy-Miller], 'fast drivers' in the new economic landscape."[9] Indeed, Falconer sees *Thunderdome*'s casting of African American superstar Tina Turner as a preeminent marker of the franchise's global ambitions, Turner's presence and hit tie-in music videos representing "the film-makers' ability to negotiate the international world of film-making and rock promotion."[10] Analogous to its shifting position in the global film marketplace, *Thunderdome*'s transition from expressing "colonial narratives of empire" to favoring a "deregulated postcolonial spatiality" are seen in its depictions of oil culture.[11]

The first two Mad Max films are fixated solely on car culture and petroleum resources. Indeed, the first appearance of Max (Mel Gibson) in *Mad Max* (1979) is marked by his visual fusion with his car: close-up shots of his sunglasses-covered eyes in the rearview mirror, his leather-gloved hand turning the ignition key, the oil and alternator dashboard lights illuminating, the tailpipe spewing exhaust, and his hand shifting the gearshift to drive are shown in rapid succession long before we ever fully see his face. Similarly, in *The Road Warrior* Max hardly speaks at all, and his first action of the film is to shake off some biker pursuers and to desperately siphon gas from a wrecked tanker. That is, fast cars, control of the roads, internal combustion engines, and gasoline are *the* central narrative and visual concerns of *Mad Max* and *The Road Warrior*. Mad Max drives that same (newly repaired) fuel tanker in *The Road Warrior*'s climactic chase, yet it is a sand-filled decoy allowing Papagallo's colony to safely transport its precious oil reserves to the coast. Significantly, their oil travels with them in the passenger bus, functioning as an in-plot decoy while visually underscoring the community's symbiotic relationship with it.

Thunderdome substitutes a nuclear conflagration for the previous film's oil war, de-emphasizing the role of petroleum in the downfall of the preexisting society and aligning the film with Reagan's anti-Soviet Cold War agenda. Yet *Thunderdome* prominently features a viable alternative energy source—methane fuel harvested from pig excrement—upon which Bartertown's survivability depends. Further emphasizing the film's move away from oil culture, both competing groups in *Thunderdome* want something other than petrol: Aunty Entity seeks the subjugation of Master (Angelo Rossito), the brilliant "little man" who controls the methane works, and the group of lost kids wants to reach Sydney. Kieran Tranter claims that despite its fetishization of cars, *The Road Warrior* actually depicts wastelands that "have their origins in the failure of the internal combustion engine to ground a sustainable civilization."[12] *Thunderdome* initially seems to follow up on that premise, demonstrating a viable alternative energy source (methane) as the basis for Bartertown's energy economy.

Yet *Thunderdome*'s approach to this problem and its solution is surprisingly Reagan-esque. When Aunty hires Max, figured here as a solitary, mysterious Western hero, to assassinate Master's brawny companion Blaster (Paul Larsson), thereby to deliver the smaller man and his vast engineering knowledge into Aunty's hands, she offers Max "vehicles, animals—fuel if you want." Her hiring of an outsider to do this illegal deed, explained by The Collector (Frank Thring) as necessary due to the "subtleties" of the situation, is an endorsement of free-market economics. To use present-day parlance, Aunty Entity outsources the job.

Like Reagan, Entity is attempting to use free-market economic strategies to subvert her own energy crisis, which is really a power struggle between herself and Master. Master, while trapped in the subterranean methane works called Underworld, nevertheless controls the energy source that powers all of Bartertown: "the lights, the motors, the vehicles—all run by a high-powered gas called methane," explains The Collector. Once Max accepts the assassination job and asks to meet his target, he meets Master in Underworld and provokes him by mocking him for trafficking in pig shit. To demonstrate his power, Master shouts, "Embargo on!" and plunges Bartertown into a blackout. He then publicly humiliates Aunty Entity, making her state that "Master runs Bartertown" over a public loudspeaker. Like the oil embargoes OPEC attempted in 1967 and successfully imposed on the United States for five months in 1973–1974, Master is unafraid to impose a methane embargo to leverage his power and authority in this energy economy.[13]

Interestingly, despite its roots in the Western genre and its free-market politics, *Beyond Thunderdome* evinces feminist leanings. Aunty Entity, an ostensible villain, is a more central and well-rounded female character than any to appear in the franchise to this point, and the lost children who leave their sanctuary are led by a woman, Savannah Nix, whose desire to guide her tribe to Sydney catalyzes the film's climax and resolution. The character of Aunty Entity may reveal a soft side due to *Thunderdome*'s producers wanting to depict international superstar Tina Turner in a more positive, less villainous light, but Entity's and Savannah's portrayals also suggest women as civilizing force, the feminizing influence variously resisted by male Western protagonists.[14] It is noteworthy—and foreshadows the plot of *Fury Road*—that Max sacrifices himself to help Savannah get her group to the "never-never land" of post-apocalyptic Sydney and that this deed leads to a recognition of shared values between him and Aunty Entity. "Ain't we a pair, raggedy man? Goodbye, soldier," she says to him in her final line of the film, emphasizing the

TEN

Mad Max

Beyond Petroleum?

Carter Soles

While series director George Miller claims that the Mad Max films do not necessarily transpire in a particular chronological order, looking at the second, third, and fourth installments in their order of release reveals much about what Stephanie LeMenager has called the "narrative of petroleum" that plays "a foundational role in the American imagination and therefore in the future of life on Earth."[1] Of those three films—*The Road Warrior* (1981), *Mad Max Beyond Thunderdome* (1985), and *Mad Max: Fury Road* (2015)—the latter two are of special interest to critics focused on the intersection of ecocriticism and gender representation, for they are the first two Mad Max films to include female co-protagonists with any measure of narrative agency: *Thunderdome*'s Aunty Entity (Tina Turner) and Savannah Nix (Helen Buday) and *Fury Road*'s Imperator Furiosa (Charlize Theron). *Thunderdome* is essentially a male-centered Western featuring Entity as a potent yet ultimately marginalized representative of corrupt civilization and Savannah as a pure yet naïve figure in need of Max's help and guidance. *Fury Road* makes progressive strides in its depictions of women, its deployment of Furiosa as an androgynous female cyborg, and its focus on "green" environmental issues like clean water resources and ethical land stewardship, but it nevertheless takes a regressive step vis-à-vis its 1985 predecessor in terms of its depiction of fossil fuel use in the world of Mad Max.

By depicting thrilling vehicular chases taking place in a world plagued by systemic gas shortages, both *The Road Warrior* and *Thunder-*

dome embody the contradictions of Reagan-era energy policy. Frederick Buell writes that in 1980 Ronald Reagan "was swept to power on unhappiness with oil scarcity, an unhappiness which was quickly salved by the release of a new sea of oil."[2] Indeed, in 1981 Reagan proclaimed before Congress, "Our national energy plan should not be a rigid set of production and conservation goals dictated by Government. [. . .] When the free market is permitted to work the way it should, millions of individual choices and judgments will produce the proper balance of supply and demand our economy needs."[3] Insisting that solving the energy crisis constituted "only one" aspect of his "Administration's program for national economic recovery," Reagan repealed former president Carter's Crude Oil Windfall Profit Tax Act, which recouped revenue earned as a result of the increase of oil prices brought about by the OPEC embargo.[4] Reagan also scrapped Carter's initiatives to seek alternative energy sources such as coal gasification processes and synthetic fuels. Sadly, Reagan's shortsighted, neoliberal policies falsely appeared to work in the moment, largely due to plummeting mid-1980s petroleum prices and the delayed effect of Ford's and Carter's energy conservation policies: "Although Reagan hardly mentioned conservation, the measures taken in the 1970s—more fuel-efficient cars, better-insulated houses, and less wasteful appliances—began to pay off during his tenure."[5] Perhaps this superficial appearance of "all's well" under Reagan allowed the 1980s Mad Max films to treat systemic energy resource issues in a relatively cavalier manner.

The second, third, and fourth films in the Mad Max franchise generally bolster Reagan's policies, depicting, first, a world lacking in petroleum resources, followed by *Thunderdome*'s attempts to remedy that scarcity via Aunty Entity's "sea" of methane-producing pig excrement, which is destroyed at the end of *Thunderdome* to make way for *Fury Road*'s unexplained return to a petroleum-based society. At a fundamental level, these films depict the "rapid oscillations between oil exuberance and catastrophe" that characterize the 1970s and 1980s and beyond, signaling "the arrival of a new cultural regime—one that we dwell in today."[6] Characterized by "the breaching of apparently secure cultural boundaries and the embrace of disequilibrium and emergence," this new regime incorporates the exuberance of risk culture and the imminent possibility of environmental apocalypse as new cultural norms.[7] When precariously diminishing resources, extreme weather phenomena, and other ecological crises become routine, they fade into the cultural background and become normalized. The last three Mad Max films enact this normalization in their depiction of the post-apocalyptic world's dependence upon petroleum.

The Mad Max franchise got underway just as Australia entered the era of global oil interdependence as part of its shift to a deregulated economic system in the early 1980s. Noting that the "floating of the dollar har-

soldier-like sacrifices they have each made to preserve their differing visions of future civilization.

Thunderdome's framing of Aunty Entity as civilizer draws upon long-standing patriarchal constructions of women as passive, domestic keepers of the hearth, an essentializing move that locks women into roles of passive feminine supporters of masculine activity and heroics. As Jane Tompkins writes, the ultimate "message" about women in Westerns is that "there's nothing *to* them. They may seem strong and resilient, fiery and resourceful at first, but when push comes to shove, as it always does, they crumble."[15] Fiery and resourceful in the extreme, Aunty Entity is not only a provider of an alternative fuel resource but also a recycler of livestock-based methane gas, a key contributor to real-world greenhouse gas accumulation and global climate change. This reading further underlines her role as an environmental innovator. Yet one could read Entity's letting Max go at the end of *Thunderdome* as a crumbling of her resolve, a feminine dissipation of her earlier masculine ruthlessness in defending Bartertown's interests. Thus, this stereotypical representation of female civilizers undermines or at least mitigates *Thunderdome*'s depiction of Entity as a fierce environmentalist leader.

At the same time, Entity's decision to spare Max reinforces her control and power. She decides for her own reasons to spare him, and her legion of warriors follows suit. Indeed, her "Ain't we a pair?" line, by evoking soldiery, emphasizes their shared masculine qualities: a knack for violence, a lone streak, a penchant for cruelty. Entity has built a town on these values, whereas Max remains a permanent exile. If Entity's specific civilizing vision is of a free-trade society, a competitive and cruel society rife with lethal power struggles, Max lies outside even those parameters. Town life is not for him.

Not that Bartertown's version of civilization looks that appealing anyway. Entity's vision has not really matured to a point beyond that of, say, Lord Humungus of *The Road Warrior* or Immortan Joe of *Fury Road*. Entity exploits her workers and treats her subjects brutally, sending enslaved criminals into underground methane pits to labor and die while she and her cronies dwell in luxury in an elevated tent high above the town. Guilty of upholding a brutal convict labor system to keep Bartertown's methane works operational, Aunty Entity's civilization, for all its ecological advances, is shown to be fundamentally unequal and corrupt. Entity wants to exploit Master's knowledge without having to grant him any power or authority in Bartertown. She is, in George Miller's words, a "holdfast, they love their world too much, and they want to hold on, and they won't allow the next, natural evolution, natural change, to happen."[16] Savannah Nix represents the uncorrupted leader of the new civilization, the hero not yet become tyrant. Max, the masculine agent of the desired change, sees this and helps Savannah and Master escape from Bartertown, yet, like the traditional Western protagonist, he cannot join them. Civilization is not for him—like *The Searchers'* Ethan Edwards, Max Rockatansky is destined always to "walk between the winds," surviving alone in the wasteland. In addition to following generic and gendered imperatives, this also keeps the Mad Max franchise open to ongoing sequels.

Mad Max: Fury Road is even less overtly interested in oil than its predecessors. For the occupants of *Fury Road*'s Citadel, obtaining fuel from nearby Gastown seems a routine matter. Here the focus is upon the freedom of the wives and their reaching the Green Space. As in *The Road Warrior*, the narratively central tanker, here called the War Rig, is again devoid of petroleum, instead carrying Joe's fugitive "breeder" wives, whom Furiosa has rescued from sexual and reproductive slavery. So unconcerned are the Citadel's citizens with fuel resources that Furiosa and her compatriots blow up a pod-like trailer full of "guzzoline" in making their escape from the war parties pursuing them.

Yet this narrative de-emphasis on oil resources begins in *Beyond Thunderdome*, which reframes the franchise's thematic concerns in part via a shift in genre. More than any other film in the Mad Max series, *Thunderdome* pays homage to the Western. True, Max more or less always embodies the ideal of the Western protagonist, a verbally and socially reticent man of action whose sole focus is on "external conflicts in which men prove their courage to themselves and to the world by facing their own annihilation."[17] Further, every Mad Max film after the original features certain Western narrative tropes, most notably that of the stranger emerging from the wilderness to help a more civilized, feminized group solve a problem requiring his masculine skills and fortitude.[18] Nonetheless, *Thunderdome* incorporates Western iconography and plot structures to such an extent that I am tempted to label it a Western rather than a post-apocalyptic action (or car chase) movie. In this context it is noteworthy that the American Western is strongly aligned with U.S. imperial interests, westward expansion, and the concomitant demonization of indigenous Americans. In *Thunderdome*'s deterritorialized Australian context perhaps *Thunderdome* signifies Australia's early 1980s expansionist move into the era of oil interdependence and the global free market.

The main thing that sets *Thunderdome* apart from the other three Mad Max films and signals its debt to the Western genre is its relative lack of cars and car chases. Both previous films opened with car chases. This one opens with an aerial view of Max on a camel-driven covered wagon, placing him, in Western terms, in the role of frontier settler rather than lone horseman (or road warrior). This lengthy aerial shot shows the vastness of the empty desert, setting up the survivalist dangers of desert travel that loom large later in the film. It makes its specifically Australian context clear via a didgeridoo droning on the soundtrack. Yet the aerial shot is itself strangely deterritorialized, offering an extreme vantage point we almost never see in the other films of this franchise, grounded as they usually are in the world of automobiles and roads. At the conclusion of this aerial shot, Jedediah the Pilot knocks Max from his camel-wagon, and our protagonist spends most of the rest of the film on foot—the group of children he later meets even call him "Walker."[19]

Once unseated, Max chases after his hijacked wagon on foot. The camera tracks behind his bare feet in close-up as he walks along in the tire track left by the wagon, which has wide, off-road rubber tires. Next, a close-up of a pair of cowboy boots lying in the sand next to the tire track—one of Max's possessions thrown out of the back of the wagon by his mischievous pet monkey. The next sequence opens two shots later with a close-up on Max's cowboy booted feet as he walks toward distant Bartertown. He now wears the iconic footwear of the Western protagonist, "an emanation of the desert" who now assumes his role as a redeemer "not from heaven but from earth."[20]

Obsession with foot travel also links *Thunderdome* with what Buell calls "more serious" post-apocalyptic films like *The Road* (2006) that present "narratives of painful, slow, on-foot struggle that resist the exuberance that is today so persistently inscribed in post-apocalyptic space."[21] While *Thunderdome* is not nearly as dark and grim as the other films Buell mentions—it is, by comparison, exuberant—it nevertheless eschews the kinetic thrills and nonstop action that its follow-up, *Fury Road*, provides in abundance. That is, *Thunderdome* may be the least vehicularly exuberant, and therefore the most progressive with respect to oil culture, of the Mad Max films.

Other signifiers make clear that in *Thunderdome* we are immersed in the masculine world of the Western. Bartertown has a wooden sign that greets our lone wilderness hero as he wanders in looking for his lost property (which includes livestock). The arched sign evokes similar structures seen in the opening of *The Furies* (1950) and the climax of *My Darling Clementine* (1946). The sales pitch of an unnamed water salesman as Max enters Bartertown sets up the importance of water for survival in this film, a convention of numerous Westerns and films with desert survival scenarios, notably *Lawrence of Arabia*, which Max's headpiece in these opening sequences homages.[22] The water-seller interaction also foreshadows the importance of water as a contaminated, scarce resource to be commodified and controlled in *Fury Road*. Max is a kind of water regulator here, exposing the offered product as irradiated through his use of a Geiger counter. Always a pragmatist rather than an idealist—Max carries the counter to protect himself only from radiation poisoning—he embodies the Western hero's tendency to, through his example, correct moral ills in the community into which he intrudes: to "clean up" the town. While the issue of contaminated water is never again raised in *Thunderdome*, the Geiger counter moment foreshadows that Max's arrival will catalyze a "cleaning up" of Bartertown on a larger scale.

Perhaps the pinnacle of *Thunderdome*'s borrowings from the Western, Max's fight with Blaster, the climax of the Bartertown section of the film, is a formal, ritualistic duel in the public space of the Thunderdome—man to man, not vehicle to vehicle as in the other Max films. It is *Thunderdome*'s version of the Western's ubiquitous shootout at high noon, a post-apocalyptic take on the Western's "[phallic] conflict in the public space."[23] Max is even announced to the Thunderdome crowd as "the man with no name," a blatant reference to Clint Eastwood's character in the well-known Sergio Leone Spaghetti Western trilogy.

Like Eastwood's iconic wanderer in *A Fistful of Dollars* (1964), Max is caught between competing factions in Bartertown and undergoes a near-lethal physical ordeal as punishment for trying to play these factions against each other. After the Thunderdome duel, at the conclusion of which Max's illegal deal with Aunty Entity is publicly revealed, Max is exiled from Bartertown into the desert and almost killed by the elements (his pet monkey, a substitute for the dog of previous installments, brings him water just in time). A harsh and deadly landscape—most often a desert—is an essential feature of the Western genre, and in *Thunderdome* it is Max's most threatening enemy.[24] Furthermore, Max's ordeal in the desert aligns him with the traditional male wilderness hero, for whom wild spaces function as sites "for male protagonists to recover an essential, authentic masculinity, and thereby to reassert the hegemony of the white male not only over non-human nature, but also over his ethnic, racial, and gender subordinates."[25] Indeed, after Max collapses in the desert he is taken in by a bunch of coded-indigenous kids over whom he assumes a leadership role in the film's third act, defeating the black woman who runs Bartertown with their help.

Thus, in place of the Mad Max franchise's usual emphasis on men engaging in high-speed chases and visually fetishizing automobiles, *Thunderdome* foregrounds lonely desert vistas with no roads, images of pack animals like camels and horses, and men *and* women traveling afoot instead of in cars. Even in *Thunderdome*'s climactic car chase, Max and his compatriots are aboard a makeshift train—another key icon of the Western—traveling along a preset track. The image of the train, which stands for the civilizing and closing of the frontier, is an ideal conveyance to carry Savannah's group of lost children away from Bartertown toward safety. The train chase concludes with Max sending Savannah and her charges by airplane to Sydney, where they will permanently settle and (it is implied) lay the groundwork for a new (matriarchal?) civilization. Meanwhile, as the children fly away, Max's defensive action, driving a car back to meet Entity's onrushing vehicular assault, is the film's one bona fide—if extremely brief—car-on-car battle scene.

This stands in stark contrast to the first two movies, in which car culture is both narratively central and styled to suggest an exaggerated version of gay maleness. Rebecca Johinke notes that both the "bikies" in

Mad Max and Lord Humungus's gang in *The Road Warrior* are portrayed as "even more 'bent' than the usual reactionary and stereotypical representations" of such figures, though she does give these films credit for showing their queer villains to be "worthy opponents" whose "masculinity is never questioned."[26] She also notes, as numerous critics of the road movie have noted, that the open road is a masculine homosocial space that always carries homoerotic connotations due to its disconnection from the presumed-heterosexual space of "home."[27] The first two Mad Max films depict homosocial groups of men in the wasteland fighting over scraps of fuel and other scant resources, activities ultimately shown to be decadent, reactionary, and suicidal.[28] This reinforces Tranter's claim that the internal combustion engine and the car culture it engenders is incapable of supporting a sustainable civilization.

It is no surprise that with the introduction of towns, of stable spaces where civilization (in some form) can develop, the two latter entries in the Mad Max franchise also introduce more prevalent women characters. Instead of straightforward battles over one's individual family (*Mad Max*) or a solitary oil well (*The Road Warrior*), now the course of future civilization is at stake. In *Thunderdome*, "Max has moved beyond the intermediate world of petroleum-driven vehicles to an emergent world of new civilization."[29] The contest is now over basic resources in a much broader sense. Indeed, as *Thunderdome*'s Master insists when discussing pig excrement with Max: "Not shit, energy! No energy, no town!" What counts here is not the fluid itself (as in *Road Warrior*) but who regulates and controls it. Significantly, Aunty Entity, a woman, plays a key role in this struggle. This same dynamic applies to guzzoline, water, and women's bodies in *Fury Road*, with Imperator Furiosa arguably *the* key player in that film's central conflict.

The main liquids of interest to *Fury Road* are mother's milk and water. *Fury Road* includes the first images of *cultivated* growing green plants in the franchise, as in the greenery atop Immortan Joe's Citadel and the plant nursery in its depths. The most important thing Furiosa and Max (Tom Hardy) bring back to the Citadel and the undernourished people gathered there is the case of seeds provided by Keeper of the Seeds (Melissa Jaffer). While all the vehicles depicted are dependent upon gas—if the film carried the premise of the third film to its next logical step, the cars in *Fury Road* would all run on pig shit or some other alternative energy source—the acquisition and/or production of refined petroleum is not of any concern.

No, the main subject of *Fury Road* is a struggle over water resources. A montage of voice-overs during the opening credits refers to "water wars," and Immortan Joe presides over a water reclamation and distribution facility—he even bottles it. The Green Place to which Imperator Furiosa takes Joe's liberated wives is destroyed because its water supply went bad, became poisoned. As one of the sound bites in the opening credits montage says, "The Earth is sour." In foregrounding the problems of water and soil, the film depicts a milieu that wants to have it both ways: its focus on other issues, especially water, suggests a move away from the centrality of oil in favor of a meditation upon other themes, yet the very ubiquity of gas-powered vehicles and the ease with which the characters obtain and discard it tells us that an oil economy clearly exists. That's what Furiosa plans to trade to the hill people. It also seems to connect Joe to his neighboring tribes: they are partners in a microcosmic version of the multinational oil business.

This sense of the global pertains to the film's production as well as its diegesis. Shot mainly in Namibia and casting a South African and an Englishman in its leads, *Fury Road* is even more deterritorialized, more a product of the globalized film industry, than its immediate predecessor. In line with its globalized production circumstances, *Fury Road* subtly and implicitly supports the deregulated international petroleum economy. This is represented in the text by the free trade that seems to exist between the Citadel, Gastown, and the Bullet Farm. Rather than fighting over a limited resource as Entity and Master do in *Thunderdome*, *Fury Road*'s villains cooperate via economic agreements already in place by the time the film begins. The tension between *Fury Road*'s overt environmentalist feminist messages and its implicit endorsement of a *laissez-faire* petroleum-based economy brings to mind Andrew Hageman's discussion of the paradox of ecologically themed mainstream action blockbusters, which create "negative space" via their contradictions, showing the difficulty of genuine ecological action under global capitalism.[30] *Fury Road* surely fits Hageman's description of a film that "points out uncomfortably the narrowness of our own desires for positive environmental solutions that do not envision a break with capital."[31] Hageman finds a radical potential in the negative space created by such contradictions, but here it is rendered so subtly and is so overwhelmed by the film's tight plotting and nonstop vehicular action that I am not sure. Critical and fan discourse around the film usually centers upon its presumed environmentalist feminism, its foregrounding of Furiosa, and its use of the tropes of water and seeds.[32] The ubiquitous car chases are praised for their technical execution and the thrills they produce but have not been widely critiqued for implicitly endorsing an unsustainable petroleum-based global economy.

For example, Michelle Yates argues that *Fury Road* "links capitalism with patriarchy as the root causes of environmental exploitation, women's oppression and mass poverty" and that in the film "women's liberation from patriarchal power is predicated upon the liberation of nature from this same system of power and oppression."[33] I agree that *Fury Road* offers a critique of capitalist patriarchy, and I take seriously Yates's claim that Furiosa's return to the Citadel "represents the possibility of making the means of production communal."[34] Nevertheless, I see little evidence in the film that even under its new matriarchal leadership the Citadel will be completely free of exploitative, petroleum-based (or perhaps seed- and water-based) capitalism. Indeed, the last shot of the film shows Furiosa ascending to the higher levels of the Citadel while her subjects cheer her on from below; the camera, suggesting Max's point of view, watches as she rises slowly out of frame. While I agree that there is a possibility of a more communal society emerging at the Citadel and I am sure Furiosa will eliminate the more egregious systemic abuses perpetrated by Immortan Joe, it is harder to see her abandoning trade relations with Gastown and the Bullet Farm or completely forsaking the use of internal combustion technology.

That said, both *Beyond Thunderdome* and *Fury Road* are to be praised for foregrounding narratively potent female characters. Both films center on female-led communities rather than the male-dominated wilderness frontier and, as a result, they are more interested in parenthood, maternity, paternity, and future generations than the first two Mad Max films. *Thunderdome*'s Savannah Nix and Aunty Entity are female leaders intent on forging (relatively) more stable futures for their respective people, even though they both rely heavily upon white men—Entity on Master, Savannah on Max—to accomplish their goals. *Fury Road* is all about mothers and control of maternal lines. Immortan Joe tries to control women's bodies and exert patriarchal authority over the resources of the water-rich Citadel, but he fails. He is beaten by a coalition of women led by Imperator Furiosa, a female cyborg with one mechanical arm whom Max assists but does not dominate or lead. Her plans predate Max's arrival at the Citadel, and she would do what she does regardless of his participation. He is ultimately crucial to her success—he gives her a blood transfusion that saves her life—but not essential to her plans. While neither film truly unseats Max as the protagonist whose point of view the viewer shares, *Beyond Thunderdome* and *Fury Road* place women in charge of key narrative developments, casting Max in the role of a partner helping Savannah Nix and Imperator Furiosa achieve their goals.

Interestingly, *Mad Max: Fury Road* marks the franchise's return to the car culture focus of its first two entries, possibly indicating nostalgia for a conservative past: the 2010s look back to Reagan's and Kennedy-Miller's 1980s, just as Reagan's 1980s looked back to Eisenhower's 1950s and its car culture. While the latter two Mad Max films move away from blacktop roads, heading into the deep desert, *Thunderdome* does so mainly to de-emphasize car culture and to focus instead on the more human-scale, "primitive" stakes of the Western. Conversely, *Fury Road* fuses the car chase plots and vehicular aesthetics of *The Road Warrior* with off-road, desert locales, unfortunately reproducing the "acceptance of environmental degradation in the form of both a transformation of natural and man-made landscapes, and a reliance on nonrenewable fuels that contribute to global warming."[35] *Fury Road* also implicitly endorses—on and off screen—the destruction of fragile desert ecosystems: "A leaked environmental report claims film crew damaged sensitive areas [in the Dorob national park in Namibia] meant to be protected, endangering reptiles and rare cacti."[36] Like the recent *Fast and Furious* films, the similarly titled *Fury Road* "[demonstrates] that the environmental impact of cars and the car culture in America and elsewhere has been treated as natural and desirable, as a given."[37] This runs counter to the film's otherwise ecofeminist themes. Furthermore, in *Fury Road* gas is called "guzzoline," suggesting its abundance (the Citadel's vehicles guzzle it) in a way that echoes Reagan's myopic views on energy conservation.

All that said, *Fury Road* improves upon the gender politics of *Thunderdome* by distancing itself from Western genre conventions and instead centering its car chase narrative around Imperator Furiosa, a gender-bending female protagonist. Furiosa exhibits gender fluidity, exhibiting a combination of masculine (short hair, a tendency toward action over words, a steely resolve) and feminine (biological femaleness, a maternal attitude toward the escaped wives) traits. Beyond this, she is a "mulatto cyborg," a cinematic figure that Leilani Nishime claims "dismantles the boundaries between the organic and the inorganic" in order to highlight that "neither human nor machine is the true origin of selfhood."[38] Thus the term "mulatto," which points to anxieties over multiracial identity, is here displaced onto other categories of admixture, especially the human and the machine. As a mulatto cyborg, Furiosa does not hate humanity nor lionize it but rather accepts her hybrid, cyborg identity without expressing nostalgia for her human, pre-cyborg past. Like *Robocop*'s Murphy, she exhibits curiosity about her past: her memories of the Green Space, where she grew up before being kidnapped and enslaved by Immortan Joe, obviously undergird her escape plan for herself and the rescued wives.[39] Yet she reports her mother's death matter-of-factly and when she grieves for the loss of the Green Space in a dramatic sequence late in the film, one feels that she grieves not for the loss of her childhood or former family, which are long-gone in any case, but for the pragmatic gains the intact Green Space would have provided to her and the wives as a place to settle and live. Her plan is foiled, and she is temporarily enraged and lost—but not nostalgic. Despite momentary grief, she immediately makes plans to cross the salt flats, revealing that her goal is to find *a* home for herself and her cohorts, not to reclaim her former home of the Green Space.[40] She even accepts Max's proposal to return to the Citadel and settle there, the clearest repudiation of the notion that she longs for a lost past or her former childhood home. She will instead adapt to her changed circumstances, a flexibility mirrored in her cyborg body. Although she temporarily removes her mechanical arm during her grief moment, "Instead of suppressing hybridity or retreating from it" as so many cinematic cyborgs do, Furiosa ultimately "unflinchingly confronts and exposes hybridity," embodying fluidity with respect to the human/machine continuum and to gender.⁴¹

Of course, as a woman, Furiosa also taps into the liberatory potential of cyborg imagery and identity for feminism. As Donna Haraway writes, the figure of the cyborg "changes what counts as women's experience" in the late twentieth century and beyond.⁴² As "a creature in a post-gender world," the cyborg "skips the step of original unity" that underlies patriarchal subject formation, instead functioning as the "illegitimate" and potentially rebellious "offspring of militarism and patriarchal capitalism."⁴³ Indeed, non-objectifying images of androgynous, hybrid female protagonists such as Imperator Furiosa are rare in global blockbusters of *Fury Road*'s budget and genre and should be celebrated, as Furiosa has rightfully been.

Further emphasizing her potential to critique white patriarchy, Furiosa provides an interesting variant on the black male messiah figure who serves as the protagonist in several key post-apocalyptic zombie action movies. As Elizabeth McAlister writes, this figure "is called upon to destroy" the "hyperwhite apocalypse" that threatens human civilization in films like *I Am Legend* (2007).⁴⁴ Obviously Furiosa is not black or male but she is differentiated from the usual white male protagonist through her biological femaleness and her status as a cyborg. In fact, as a "mulatto" cyborg she analogously stands in for racial and other forms of hybridity, functioning as a "displaced [representation] of mixed-race people."⁴⁵ And there is no doubt that the pale, deathly white Immortan Joe and his fanatical mutant followers, the Half-Life War Boys, count as a horde of hyper-white antagonists who "not only embody death, they also bring it," as their prevalently displayed skull emblems and propensity for violence make clear.⁴⁶ The War Boys' very name suggests a half-living or undead state, and their obsession with suicide and reaching Valhalla through vehicular violence further emphasizes their intrinsic connection to death and to the suicidal dimension of masculine car culture. As McAlister claims, coded-non-white protagonists like Furiosa must primarily "save humanity from the affliction of *whiteness*" that villains like Joe and his War Boys represent.⁴⁷ Indeed, *Fury Road* seems centrally concerned with Furiosa's and Keeper of the Seeds's attempts to destroy the patriarchal, death-obsessed, hyper-white society of Immortan Joe and to replace it with a racially hybridized, gender-fluid, non-violent matriarchy.

However, Furiosa's potential as an ecofeminist heroine is possibly mitigated by *Fury Road*'s framing of the narrative around Max's redemption as a human being. He starts the film as a psychologically broken man suffering from traumatic flashbacks, and, via his experiences with Furiosa, he comes to appreciate life again (much like Gibson's Max does by meeting the lost children in *Thunderdome*). Thus Furiosa's agency is potentially compromised by her return to a civilizing, maternal role as the presumed new matriarch of the Citadel and the film's concluding focus on the nobility of a restored Max as he disappears back out into the wasteland: he has mastered his demons and is celebrated as the film's ultimate hero.[48] Furiosa's actions have saved the Citadel and saved Max, yet the film's last shot is from Max's point of view as he watches her ascend to Immortan Joe's previous station. She is the heroic instigator of the events of this film yet she is dependent upon Max, and he is our identification figure. We see her through his eyes.

Furthermore, Furiosa's cyborg status aligns her with the War Rig itself—"This rig goes nowhere without me," she tells Max, and she is almost never seen without it in *Fury Road*—and hence with the film's ubiquitous reliance upon abundant petroleum resources. It is noteworthy that her usual job, the one she sabotages on the day of her escape with the wives, is to pick up the regular shipment of guzzoline from Gastown in the War Rig. Meanwhile, Max himself, established early in the film as a "universal donor," is primarily associated with life-giving blood. While in horror films, blood is typically evocative of menstrual blood and gaping wounds that represent phallic lack, here, Max's blood is the ultimate natural resource, a potent, coded-masculine substance that Max injects into Furiosa in order to save her life in the film's denouement.

So while I mainly agree with Sarah Mirk's ecofeminist claim that "the toughest people you'll meet in this dystopia are a collective of old women who are diligent heirloom seed savers" and would like to believe that she is right to conclude that "nothing is more powerful in the desert than the simple forces of soil, seeds, water, and tender care," I also see a lot of contradictory impulses at play in *Fury Road*.[49] Its emphasis on spectacular car stunts and brutal violence, while appropriate for a great piece of action cinema, undermines or at least complicates its bid to be read as an ecofeminist text. Its real-life destruction of desert ecosystems during production in Namibia is demoralizing. And while Furiosa is an inspiring, gender-bending female cyborg unlike any other I've seen, her deep involvement in the film's petroleum-fueled car culture—she is Immortan Joe's best driver and road warrior—suggests that while she will obviously rule the Citadel much more magnanimously than the hyperbolically villainous Joe, she is unlikely to curtail the shipments of guzzoline arriving regularly from Gastown.

Significantly, *Fury Road*'s repeal of the possibly progressive depiction of an alternative energy source in *Beyond Thunderdome* is prefigured in the 1985 film itself: *Thunderdome* ends with Max destroying Bartertown's methane works and leading Aunty Entity's troops on a massive car chase. We might assume that those vehicles are running on methane-fueled motors, but the visual iconography of the car chase sequence is clear: though it displays a post-apocalyptic town temporarily thriving on an alternative, organic energy source, *Beyond Thunderdome* ultimately concludes that only the petrol-fueled automobile is finally viable. It suggests but never actualizes a matriarchal society beyond petroleum.

Mad Max: Fury Road is even less focused on oil culture, depicting instead a struggle over women's bodies, blood, milk, water, and seeds. *Fury Road*'s move away from the centrality of oil in favor of a meditation upon ecofeminist themes is encouraging, yet the very ubiquity of gas-powered vehicles and the ease with which the characters obtain and discard "guzzoline" suggests an inexplicably thriving oil economy. Aunty Entity's dream of an alternative fuel source is dead, replaced with an exuberant, catastrophic, and ultimately unsustainable dependence upon fossil fuel.

NOTES

1. Stephanie LeMenager, *Living Oil: Petroleum Culture in the American Century* (New York: Oxford University Press, 2014), 4.
2. Frederick Buell, "A Short History of Oil Cultures: Or, the Marriage of Catastrophe and Exuberance," *Journal of American Studies* 46, no. 2 (May 2012): 290.
3. Karen R. Merrill, *The Oil Crisis of 1973–1974: A Brief History with Documents* (Boston: Bedford/St. Martin's, 2007), 132.
4. Merrill, *The Oil Crisis of 1973–1974*, 132.
5. Merrill, *The Oil Crisis of 1973–1974*, 114.
6. Buell, "A Short History of Oil Cultures," 291.
7. Buell, "A Short History of Oil Cultures," 291.
8. Delia Falconer, "'We Don't Need to Know the Way Home': The Disappearance of the Road in the *Mad Max* Trilogy," in *The Road Movie Book*, ed. Steven Cohan and Ina Rae Hark (London: Routledge, 1997), 252–53.
9. Falconer, "'We Don't Need to Know the Way Home,'" 253.
10. Falconer, "'We Don't Need to Know the Way Home,'" 266.
11. Falconer, "'We Don't Need to Know the Way Home,'" 249.
12. Kieran Tranter, "Mad Max: The Car and Australian Governance," *National Identities* 5, no. 1 (2003): 69.
13. Merrill, *The Oil Crisis of 1973–1974*, 20, 22.
14. Jane Tompkins, *West of Everything: The Inner Life of Westerns* (New York: Oxford University Press, 1992), 33, 61.
15. Tompkins, *West of Everything*, 61.
16. Anne Billson, "George Miller Talks about Mad Max, Heroes & Tina Turner: The 1985 Interview," *Multiglom: The Anne Billson blog*, posted May12, 2015, https://multiglom.com/2015/05/12/george-miller-the-1985-interview/.
17. Tompkins, *West of Everything*, 7, 52, 31.
18. Tompkins, *West of Everything*, 32–33.
19. The lost kids call Max "Walker," and indeed *Beyond Thunderdome* mainly portrays people afoot. Yet they also call him this because many story elements and character names for *Thunderdome* are taken from Russell Hoban's 1980 novel *Riddley Walker*, which is written in a made-up language that provides the basis for the pidgin the lost children use in the film. Also, the novel uses the phrase "Aunty" to refer to the spirit of death, and *Thunderdome*'s Aunty Entity fulfills that role in the Bartertown legal system, presiding over Thunderdome duels and making proclamations like this: "Death is listening and will take the first man that screams."
20. Tompkins, *West of Everything*, 32.
21. Buell, "A Short History of Oil Cultures," 292.

22. "Bartertown" is surely a reference to "Bartorstown" from Leigh Brackett's apocalyptic science fiction western *The Long Tomorrow* (1955), which features a similar focus on the nuclear. Brackett also wrote screenplays for Hollywood westerns, including *Rio Bravo* (1959) and *Rio Lobo* (1970).

23. Tompkins, *West of Everything*, 28.

24. Tompkins, *West of Everything*, 24, 31.

25. David Ingram, *Green Screen: Environmentalism and Hollywood Cinema* (Exeter: University of Exeter Press, 2000), 36.

26. Rebecca Johinke, "Manifestations of Masculinities: *Mad Max* and the Lure of the Forbidden Zone," *Journal of Australian Studies* 25, no. 67 (2001): 121, 125.

27. Johinke, "Manifestations of Masculinities," 122.

28. Christopher Sharrett, "The Hero as Pastiche: Myth, Male Fantasy, and Simulacra in *Mad Max* and *The Road Warrior*," *Journal of Popular Film and Television* 13, no. 2 (1985): 84.

29. Dennis H. Barbour, "Heroism and Redemption in the *Mad Max* Trilogy," *Journal of Popular Film and Television* 27, no. 3 (1999): 33.

30. Andrew Hageman, "Ecocinema and Ideology: Do Ecocritics Dream of a Clockwork Green?," in *Ecocinema Theory and Practice*, eds. Stephen Rust, Salma Monani, and Sean Cubitt (New York: Routledge 2013), 77, 79.

31. Hageman, "Ecocinema and Ideology," 78.

32. Sarah Mirk, "The Ecofeminism of Mad Max," *Bitch Media*, published May 22, 2015, https://bitchmedia.org/post/the-ecofeminism-of-mad-max.

33. Michelle Yates, "Re-casting Nature as Feminist Space in *Mad Max: Fury Road*," *Science Fiction Film and Television* 10, no. 3 (Autumn 2017): 365, 360.

34. Yates, "Re-casting Nature," 366.

35. Robin L. Murray and Joseph K. Heumann, "Fast, Furious, and Out of Control: The Erasure of Natural Landscapes in Car Culture Film," in *Framing the World: Explorations in Ecocriticism and Film*, ed. Paula Willoquet-Maricondi (Charlottesville: University of Virginia Press, 2010), 156.

36. Nastasya Tay, "*Mad Max: Fury Road* Sparks Real-Life Fury with Claims of Damage to Desert," *The Guardian*, March 5, 2013, https://www.theguardian.com/world/2013/mar/05/mad-max-fury-road-namibia.

37. Murray and Heumann, "Fast, Furious, and Out of Control," 155.

38. Leilani Nishime, "The Mulatto Cyborg: Imagining a Multiracial Future," *Cinema Journal* 44, no. 2 (2005): 37, 36.

39. Nishime, "The Mulatto Cyborg," 44–47.

40. Yates notes that Furiosa's return to the Citadel disrupts the usual Edenic recovery narrative prevalent in Hollywood cinema, instead forwarding an environmentalist ethics based upon seeking sustainability in the "home" spaces where we live and work (367).

41. Nishime, "The Mulatto Cyborg," 44–45.

42. Donna J. Haraway, *Simians, Cyborgs, and Women: The Reinvention of Nature* (New York: Routledge, 1991), 149.

43. Haraway, *Simians, Cyborgs, and Women*, 150, 151.

44. Elizabeth McAlister, "Slaves, Cannibals, and Infected Hyper-Whites: The Race and Religion of Zombies," *Anthropological Quarterly* 85, no. 2 (Spring 2012): 478, 480.

45. Nishime, "The Mulatto Cyborg," 34.

46. Richard Dyer, *White* (New York: Routledge, 1997), 209.

47. McAlister, "Slaves, Cannibals, and Infected Hyper-Whites," 480.

48. Ingram, *Green Screen*, 40.

49. Mirk, "The Ecofeminism of Mad Max."

BIBLIOGRAPHY

Barbour, Dennis H. "Heroism and Redemption in the *Mad Max* Trilogy." *Journal of Popular Film and Television* 27, no. 3 (1999): 28–34.

Billson, Anne. "George Miller Talks about Mad Max, Heroes & Tina Turner: The 1985 Interview." *Multiglom: The Anne Billson blog*. Posted May 12, 2015. https://multiglom.com/2015/05/12/george-miller-the-1985-interview/.

Buell, Frederick. "A Short History of Oil Cultures: Or, the Marriage of Catastrophe and Exuberance." *Journal of American Studies* 46, no. 2 (May 2012): 273–93.

Dyer, Richard. *White*. New York: Routledge, 1997.

Falconer, Delia. "'We Don't Need to Know the Way Home': The Disappearance of the Road in the *Mad Max* Trilogy." In *The Road Movie Book*, edited by Steven Cohan and Ina Rae Hark, 249–70. London: Routledge, 1997.

Hageman, Andrew. "Ecocinema and Ideology: Do Ecocritics Dream of a Clockwork Green?" In *Ecocinema Theory and Practice*, edited by Stephen Rust, Salma Monani, and Sean Cubitt, 63–86. New York: Routledge, 2013.

Haraway, Donna J. *Simians, Cyborgs, and Women: The Reinvention of Nature*. New York: Routledge, 1991.

Ingram, David. *Green Screen: Environmentalism and Hollywood Cinema*. Exeter: University of Exeter Press, 2000.

Johinke, Rebecca. "Manifestations of Masculinities: *Mad Max* and the Lure of the Forbidden Zone." *Journal of Australian Studies* 25, no. 67 (2001): 118–25.

LeMenager, Stephanie. *Living Oil: Petroleum Culture in the American Century*. New York: Oxford University Press, 2014.

McAlister, Elizabeth. "Slaves, Cannibals, and Infected Hyper-Whites: The Race and Religion of Zombies." *Anthropological Quarterly* 85, no. 2 (Spring 2012): 457–486.

Merrill, Karen R. *The Oil Crisis of 1973–1974: A Brief History with Documents*. Boston: Bedford/St. Martin's, 2007.

Mirk, Sarah. "The Ecofeminism of Mad Max." *Bitch Media*. Published May 22, 2015. https://bitchmedia.org/post/the-ecofeminism-of-mad-max.

Murray, Robin L., and Joseph K. Heumann. "Fast, Furious, and Out of Control: The Erasure of Natural Landscapes in Car Culture Films." In *Framing the World: Explorations in Ecocriticism and Film*, edited by Paula Willoquet-Maricondi, 154–69. Charlottesville: University of Virginia Press, 2010.

Nishime, Leilani. "The Mulatto Cyborg: Imagining a Multiracial Future." *Cinema Journal* 44, no. 2 (2005): 34–49.

Sharrett, Christopher. "The Hero as Pastiche: Myth, Male Fantasy, and Simulacra in *Mad Max* and *The Road Warrior*." *Journal of Popular Film and Television* 13, no. 2 (1985): 80–91.

Tay, Nastasya. "*Mad Max: Fury Road* Sparks Real-life Fury with Claims of Damage to Desert." *The Guardian*. Published March 5, 2013. https://www.theguardian.com/world/2013/mar/05/mad-max-fury-road-namibia.

Tompkins, Jane. *West of Everything: The Inner Life of Westerns*. New York: Oxford University Press, 1992.

Tranter, Kieran. "Mad Max: The Car and Australian Governance." *National Identities* 5, no. 1, (2003): 67–81.

Yates, Michelle, "Re-casting Nature as Feminist Space in *Mad Max: Fury Road*." *Science Fiction Film and Television* 10, no. 3 (Autumn 2017): 353–70.

Epilogue

Christy Tidwell

In their explorations of gender and environment in science fiction, the contributors to this volume repeatedly underscore the importance of the narratives we tell (in sf and elsewhere) about the world we live in and the world we are creating. Michelle Yates, Carter Soles, and I emphasize the problems with existing narratives and the need for new ones; Bridgitte Barclay, Fernando Gabriel Pagnoni Berns and Juan Juvé, Steve Asselin, and Jill E. Anderson provide audiences with ways to revisit old narratives in new ways; and Amelia Z. Greene, Tyler Harper, and Stina Attebery explore some of the possible narratives being presented within sf. These moves are all necessary and valuable. And sometimes, because these are complex problems, these moves are undertaken in combination (as in Carter Soles's chapter, for instance, in which he identifies the positive potential of one aspect of *Mad Max: Fury Road* while simultaneously noting its limitations on other fronts).

Despite the commonly held popular perception of science fiction as unrealistic or far-fetched, science fiction always maintains a relationship with the world it is born out of. Through the processes of extrapolation and cognitive estrangement, the stories told in science fiction both reflect our reality and open avenues by which we can change our reality. And we need these possibilities. We live in a moment when the things we believed to be safe and protected are so no longer, in which we must work to actively create a future worth living in. *Roe v. Wade* is threatened. *The Handmaid's Tale* is shockingly relevant again. The Secretary of the Interior, Ryan Zinke, has slashed the size of several national monuments, overturned the moratorium preventing new coal mines on public land, and moved to eliminate current protections for endangered species. And the Trump administration as a whole actively denies climate change.

Science fiction cannot single-handedly undo these actions, but it can provide language and narratives that work against them. The proliferation of memes and shirts featuring Princess Leia (later General Leia Organa) during the 2017 Women's March, perhaps most notably artist Hayley Gilmore's image of Leia with the slogan "A Woman's Place is in the Resistance," provides one instance of this.[1] The Hulu adaptation of Margaret Atwood's *Handmaid's Tale* has brought the phrase *Nolite te bastardes carborundorum* ("Don't let the bastards grind you down") to the forefront, too, and it is another widely used slogan on shirts and signs at recent protests. Similarly, the costume design for the Handmaids has been brought into the real world and worn by women to protest actions intended to remove women's rights. And the Wives' battle cry in *Mad Max: Fury Road*—"We are not things"—speaks to the position of women in this moment as well as to the treatment of the natural world. These instances illustrate how the language of science fiction—both critical and creative—can help spur action in those who embrace it.

These phrases and narratives are a far cry from the narrative represented in the cover art for this book. Its retro style and nostalgic content still resonate today—within the genre and across Western culture—and this vision still appeals to many. But it resonates as a past we are outgrowing. At least that is our hope. That image of the white heterosexual couple colonizing a new planet was the future of the past, the future that the 1950s could imagine—what new futures can science fiction help us imagine now?

As is so often the case, Octavia Butler provides relevant commentary. As is *not* always the case, this commentary is at least cautiously hopeful. In her personal notes about the planned *Parable of the Trickster*, a follow-up to *Parable of the Sower* and *Parable of the Talents*, Butler writes, "WE ARE CREATING THE CULTURE, THE TRADITIONS, THE RIGHTS AND RESPONSIBILITIES OF OUR WORLD."[2] Gerry Canavan writes of this passage,

> There is a fierce and undeniable utopian futurity implicit there, despite Butler's tendencies towards biological reductionism, and her famous distrust of utopia and of utopians—despite all that, she retains the fundamental utopian critical insight that the future is a social choice we make collectively, one of many possible futures, rather than the unfolding of some supposedly automatic, "natural" process we can't interrupt or control. The future doesn't just happen; it is something we choose, something we craft.[3]

According to Canavan's reading of Butler, there is an "Eden—but not the one you wanted, and you're going to have to *work* for it."[4] And one central part of this work lies in learning to tell new stories. *Nolite te bastardes carborundorum*.

NOTES

1. Additionally, the message "rebellions are built on hope," from *Rogue One: A Star Wars Story*, resonates.
2. OEB 2062. Quoted in Gerry Canavan, "Eden, Just Not Ours Yet: On *Parable of the Trickster* and Utopia," *Women's Studies*, forthcoming in a special issue edited by Ayana Jamieson and Moya Bailey.
3. Canavan, "Eden, Just Not Ours Yet."

4. Canavan, "Eden, Just Not Ours Yet."

BIBLIOGRAPHY

Canavan, Gerry. "Eden, Just Not Ours Yet: On *Parable of the Trickster* and Utopia," *Women's Studies* (forthcoming).

Index

Adams, Carol J., 77
AI, xvi, 21, 22–23, 24, 27, 28, 37, 176
Alaimo, Stacy, 56, 103; *Bodily Natures*, 48, 124, 134–135, 142, 152; *Exposed*, x, xii, 118, 134; *Material Feminisms*, ix, 117; *Undomesticated Ground*, 35, 168
Aldiss, Brian, 89
alien, xii, xiv, 49, 68
alternative energy, xviii, 186, 187–188, 189, 193, 195, 198–199
Anderson, Christopher Todd, 177
animacy hierarchy, 36–37, 41n44
animal, ix, xi, xii, xvi, 3–4, 6, 7–9, 10–11, 13, 14, 15, 16, 26, 33, 45, 48, 50, 53–54, 55, 58, 59, 68, 71, 78, 84, 96, 100–101, 122–123, 131, 135, 136, 155, 162; animal rights, 78, 83; animal studies, xii, xix; metaphors, 92; species transformation, xvi, 51, 52, 54–56, 57, 60
Anthropocene, 139, 151, 169, 173, 181n10
anthropocentrism, 4, 6, 9–10, 15–16, 84, 90, 92, 96, 102, 107, 109n45
anthropomorphism, 38, 92–93, 140, 150, 154, 156
apocalypse, xvii, 89, 92, 97, 108n17, 110n62, 186, 188, 191, 197, 198, 200n22
Aquaman, xviii, 161–162
Ater, Malcolm, 156
artificial intelligence. *See* AI
Atomic Age, 149–153, 157, 160–161, 162
Atwood, Margaret, ix
Australia, 186–187, 190–191

B movie, 3, 4, 5–6
Bederman, Gail, 168
Bennett, Jane, 135

binaries: human-nature, 72, 81, 107, 192; living-nonliving, 70; masculine-feminine, 72, 77, 83, 84, 102, 104–105, 176, 189, 196; nature-technology, 196–197; subject-object, 75, 79, 83, 176; within sexualities, 162
blood, 8, 14, 172, 195, 198, 199
Braidotti, Rosi, xi
Bristow, Tom, 47, 53
Bryld, Mette, 52–53
Buell, Frederick, 186
Buscema, John, 159
Butler, Octavia E., 204; *Dawn*, ix; *Fledgling*, 55, 61n16; Parable series, 204; *Patternmaster*, 51; *Wild Seed*, xvii, 45–61; Xenogenesis series, 46, 51

Cabot, Susan, 4, 5
camp, xvi, 3, 4, 5–6, 8, 12, 14, 15, 16–17, 18n9, 18n14, 154, 158, 164n35
Canavan, Gerry, 46, 49, 55, 58, 204
capitalism, 30, 40n28, 67, 70, 77, 79, 82, 83, 153, 169, 177–178, 194, 197
car culture, 187, 193, 195–196, 197
Carrington, André M., 178
Carruth, Shane, 131–146
Chen, Mel Y., 36–39, 41n44, 106, 135–136
cli-fi. *See* climate fiction
climate fiction, xviii
Cohen, Jeffrey Jerome, 13, 16
colonialism, 69, 70, 72–74, 75–76, 77, 82, 187, 190
colonization. *See* colonialism
comics, 149–166
the Comics Code Authority (CCA), 156–157, 160
Connell, Raewyn, 74–75

207

Corman, Roger, 3–6, 11–20. *See also The Wasp Woman*
creature features, xvi, xvii, 3–17, 69
Cronon, William, 167
Cubitt, Sean, 71, 72
Cvetkovich, Ann, 134, 138
cyborg, 21, 33, 36, 185, 195, 196–198

dance, 3, 5, 6–8, 27, 40n19, 55, 73
Deleuze, Gilles, 137, 139
disability, 38, 41n39, 99, 102–104, 134–135
disease. *See* disability

ecofeminism, 196, 197, 198–199
ecomedia, vii, 7, 71, 131, 142–143, 178
eco-memory, xviii, 168, 170–173, 173–174
ecophobia, 97, 150, 152–153, 154, 161, 162, 163n14
ecoqueer, xviii, 149–166
Edelman, Lee, 58, 94, 95, 138
Eden, ix, x, xviii, 167–183, 204
Edenic recovery narrative, 167–168, 169, 173, 174, 176, 179, 180, 200n40
embodiment, 11, 23, 25, 34, 49, 50, 53, 57, 128n7, 133
environmental nostalgia, xviii, 168, 170, 171, 173, 174, 176, 177, 178
Erickson, Bruce, 59
escape, 25–26, 29, 30, 32, 34, 35
Estok, Simon C., 97, 152
Evans, Mei Mei, 153–154
evolution, xv, xvii–xviii, 23, 28, 30, 125, 151, 189
Ex Machina, xvii, 21–24, 25–29, 32–33, 35–36, 37–39
extinction, x, 28, 78, 90, 91, 95, 96, 97, 104, 107, 121, 122, 173

Feil, Ken, 6
femininity, 15, 22, 23, 24, 27, 30, 68, 69, 70, 72, 76–77, 93, 104
feminist ecology, 168, 180n4, 181n9
femme fatale, 22–23, 24
Finney, Carolyn, 179, 179–180
Frankenstein, 22, 89, 94
freedom, 25, 30, 32, 35, 36, 48, 54

garden, 36, 79–81, 161, 167, 169, 173
The Gardener, xvii, 68–69, 78–83
Garrard, Greg, 71
gaze: imperialist or colonialist gaze, 76; male gaze, 7, 16, 76; medical gaze, 133
genetics, 46–47, 50, 52, 60
George, Susan A., xv, 12, 15
gender: as social construct, 13, 55, 70–71, 84, 90, 91, 98, 125, 126, 136; performance, 4, 17n2, 99; roles, ix, xvii, 13, 55, 104–105; studies, vii, ix–xii, xii–xiii, xv, xvi, xxin35, 39, 116–117, 118
Giffney, Noreen, 4–5, 92
Graham, Richard L., 156
Guattari, Felix, 137, 139

habitat, 33, 120–126
Hajdu, David, 157
Hageman, Andrew, 194
Hall, Matthew, 70, 77, 81
Hamner, Everett, 46, 51
The Handmaid's Tale, 203–204
Haraway, Donna J., 17, 51, 54, 59; *The Companion Species Manifesto*, 46, 57; *Primate Visions*, 115–116, 126; *Simians, Cyborgs, and Women*, 127; *Staying with the Trouble*, xi, 17, 46, 126, 138; sf, 115
Harman, Graham, 117–118
Hayles, N. Katherine, 120
Hekman, Susan, ix, 117
Her, xvii, 21–22, 24–25, 29, 31–32, 34–36, 37–39
heterosexism, 71, 151
Heumann, Joseph K., xviii, 168–169, 170–173, 174, 175–176, 177
Hird, Myra J., 4–5, 14–15, 92
Hollywood, 5–6, 164n34, 167, 168, 178, 179, 180, 182n33, 200n22, 200n40
horror, xii, xvii, xviii, 8, 16, 67, 69, 78, 83, 140, 156–157, 160, 163n14, 197, 198. *See also* plant horror
Howey, Ann F., 181n20
human-animal studies. *See* animal studies
hybridity, 7, 15, 59–61, 162, 196–197

illness. *See* disability
imperialism. *See* colonialism
individuation scale, 37
interspecies, xvi, xvii, 8, 110n62, 131, 136–137, 139–140, 142–144
Iovino, Serenella, x, 152, 180
Ivakhiv, Adrian, 7, 9

Johansson, Scarlett, 21, 22, 24, 25, 39n1

Kaplan, E. Ann, xv
Keetley, Dawn, 42n54, 68
Kelly, Casey Ryan, 16
Kim, Eunjung, 38–39
Kimmel, Michael, 175
kinship, 46–49, 51, 53, 54, 58, 60, 124, 138, 142
Krinsky, Hindi, 161

landscape, 9, 32, 59, 73, 79, 100, 140, 192, 195
language, x, 17, 39, 45, 49, 50, 52, 54, 58, 116, 199n19, 203–204; of the flesh, 47, 49, 50, 51
The Last Man, xvii, 89–108
Latinx, 82, 83
Latour, Bruno, 59, 115, 117–118
Le Guin, Ursula K., ix, xi, xv, xix, 48
LeMenager, Stephanie, 185
Lykke, Nina, 52–53

Mad Max, xviii, 185, 187; *Mad Max*, 187, 193; *Mad Max Beyond Thunderdome*, xviii, 185–193, 194, 195, 197–198; *Mad Max: Fury Road*, xviii, 185, 186, 189, 190, 193–199, 203, 204; *The Road Warrior*, 185, 187, 189, 193, 195
Man-Thing, xviii, 165n46
Marder, Michael, 42n54, 68, 83
masculinity, xviii, 90, 98–99, 104, 167–168, 190, 197, 198; hegemonic masculinity, xviii, 74–75, 168, 171, 176, 178, 180, 192; monstrous masculinity, 69, 74; stereotyped as active, 70, 72, 189; white masculinity, 168, 171, 172, 175–176, 178, 180

material ecocriticism, ix–xi, xvi, 181n9. *See also* new materialism; material gender studies
material gender studies, ix–xi, xvi. *See also* material ecocriticism
McNaughtan, Hugh, 177
Merchant, Carolyn, 167, 169, 180
Merril, Judith, xiii–xiv
Mesa of Lost Women, xvi, 3, 5, 6–10, 14, 15, 16
miasma theory, 102–103, 106
Miller, George, 185, 187
Monani, Salma, 71, 72
monsters, 5, 13, 16, 67, 69, 70, 74, 81, 140, 161
Moore, Alan, 162
Moore, Jason W., 123–124
Morris, Michael J., 151
Mortimer-Sandilands, Catriona, 59
Murphy, Michelle, 142
Murray, Robin L.,, xviii, 168–169, 170–173, 174, 175–176, 177

narrative, ix, x, xii–xiii, xv, xvii, 4–6, 9, 15, 16, 17, 21, 25, 28–29, 31, 36, 39, 41n39, 46, 49, 50–51, 52–53, 56, 58–59, 60, 72, 78, 83, 84, 89, 92, 96, 99, 101, 107, 185, 186, 190, 203–204; Edenic recovery narrative, 167–180, 200n40; Last Man narrative, 94, 97, 98, 109n45
nature: as background, 31, 32, 33, 38; as lover, 91, 100–102; as mother, 91, 94–97; as villain, 91, 97–100; conflation of women and, xvi–xvii, xvii, 37–38, 69, 70, 72, 84, 89, 90, 93, 98; manipulation of, xviii, 30–32, 151–152, 154, 158, 161; separated from human, 33, 48, 72, 73, 78, 91; simulacra of, 31, 32, 34, 101; versus unnatural, 3, 12–13, 15, 23, 32, 82, 92, 105, 117, 118, 121, 154; urban nature, 15, 31
Nature Boy, xviii, 157–160, 162. *See also* Siegel, Jerry; Buscema, John
new materialism, ix–xi. *See also* material ecocriticism
Nishime, Leilani, 196; nonhuman, xi, xii, xv, xvi–xvii, xviii, 14, 16, 22, 30,

32, 34–35, 36, 38, 52, 59, 71, 91, 101, 105, 106–107, 118, 123, 124, 131–134, 136, 144, 149–166, 180; human/nonhuman, 3, 4, 7–8, 9, 10–11, 13, 14, 15, 16, 17, 117
nostalgia, xviii, 31, 32, 34, 167–180, 182n25, 196, 204

objectification, 24, 25, 38, 80–81
Oppermann, Serpil, x–xi, xvi, 152, 180
Ormond, Ron, 3–10, 16–20
Otto, Eric C., xvi

parasite, 52, 131–146
performing objecthood, 6–8, 18n17
petroleum, xviii, 185–186, 187, 193, 194–195, 198–199
pipe, 6, 11, 12, 13, 15, 149
plague, 89–108
plants, xvii, 15, 67–68, 83–84, 159–161, 173–175, 177, 193; flowers, 79–80, 81–83; monstrous plants, xvii, 73–74, 76, 77, 81, 84, 160–161; plant horror, xvii, 68, 163n14; plant studies, 42n54, 68, 70
post-apocalypse. See apocalypse
posthuman, xi, 25, 36, 38, 48, 96, 99, 102, 119–120, 128n7

queer, xvi, 4, 6, 8–11, 75, 80, 91, 97, 100, 103–104, 109n60, 150–151, 154, 155, 193; queer ecocriticism, xvii, xviii, 90, 91, 151; queer ecology, 47, 55, 57–58, 59, 92, 162; queer inhumanism, 38–39; queer studies, xv, 4, 94; queering, 6, 14–16, 93, 152. *See also* ecoqueer
Quinn, Tandra, 6–7

race, ix, x–xi, xvii, xviii, 6–8, 9, 17, 68, 72, 74–75, 77, 78–79, 90, 109n60, 144, 168, 170, 173, 174–175, 178, 190, 192, 196–197; blackness, xiv, 171, 172, 174, 176, 178, 179; whiteness, xviii, 168, 171, 172, 175–176, 178, 180, 197, 204. *See also* Latinx
rape, 14, 16, 19n36, 69, 74, 76, 134
Reagan, Ronald, 186, 188, 195

reproduction, xviii, 47, 54, 57, 70, 91, 94–95, 98, 101, 103–104, 131–144, 151, 190
reproductive futurism, 49, 58, 94–95, 100, 105, 131, 136–137, 138, 144
resistance, xvi, 3, 10, 14, 16–17, 23, 28, 38, 40n19, 48, 55, 102, 179, 203
Richardson, Kathleen, 41n44
Robinson, Kim Stanley, ix; 2312, xvii, 115–129
robot, 21, 38, 39n1, 41n44, 173, 174, 176, 181n20
Russ, Joanna, xiii, xiv
Rust, Stephen, 71, 72

Sandilands, Catriona, 47, 151. *See also* Mortimer-Sandilands, Catriona
Sands, Peter, 51–52, 61n16
Sargent, Pamela, xiii–xiv
science, ix–x, xi, xii, xiv, xv, xix, 3, 5, 10, 12, 13, 15, 22, 28, 29, 33, 37, 52, 94, 115–116, 123–124, 125, 126–127, 135; feminist science studies, xii, 143
scientist, 3, 4, 10, 15, 21, 69, 119, 160–161, 165n46
science fiction: as escapist, 48, 203; *what if* element, xi, xii, 3; Haraway sf, xi, xxn9, 115
Siegel, Jerry, 157, 159
sex, ix, xii, xiii, xvii, 8, 23, 67–68, 70, 74
sexism, x–xi, 24, 71–72, 124, 152
sexuality, xiii, 5, 7, 23, 25, 39n4, 49, 55, 57–58, 68, 69, 70, 73, 77, 84, 90, 92, 94, 101–102, 103, 104, 117, 118, 120, 134, 136
Seymour, Nicole, 18n14, 47, 56, 57–59, 92, 107, 151
Sharp, Patrick B., 13
Sheldon, Rebekah, 138
Shelley, Mary, xvii, 89–90, 97
Shotwell, Alexis, 54, 55
Singer, Peter, 78
Slater, Candace, 167
Smokey the Bear, 150, 154–156, 158, 162
Soles, Carter, 8
Soper, Kate, 168
Sontag, Susan, 154
sound, xviii, 72, 74, 131–146, 190, 193

Soylent Green, xviii, 78, 167, 168–174, 174–175, 176, 177, 178, 179
Sparling, Jack, 156
speciesism, xvii, 69, 71–72, 74, 78–79, 83–84, 152
The Stepford Wives, ix, 21
Stern, Jonathan, 133
Sturgeon, Noël, 168, 179, 181n22
superheroes, 149, 150, 153, 157
Swamp Thing, xviii, 160–161, 162, 165n46

Tarantella, 3, 5, 6–8, 10–11, 14, 16
Tarrat, Margaret, 67–68
taxidermy, 26
technology, ix–x, xi, xvii, 21–39, 125, 134, 144, 170, 171, 176, 181n22; as gendered, 21, 23, 25, 30, 36, 37
terraforming, xvii, 119, 121–123
Tevos, Herbert, 3–10, 16–20; toxicity, 103, 106, 133–134
trans-corporeality, xviii, 56, 102–103, 107, 133–136, 142, 144, 152, 154, 161. *See also* Alaimo, Stacy
transcendence, 25, 29, 34, 41n39, 119–120, 124, 139–140, 143
trauma, xv–xvi, xviii, 78, 131–138, 141–144, 156, 197
trophies: AI masks in *Ex Machina*, 26, 27, 28; trophy heads, 26, 33; trophy wives, 79, 81
Tsing, Anna, 131

uncanny, 68, 73, 74, 82
Upstream Color, xviii, 131–146. *See also* Carruth, Shane
utopia, xiv, 32, 36, 46, 204

Vint, Sherryl, xii, xix, 38
voice, 24, 29
Vold, Veronica, 150

Wagar, Warren, 89
WALL-E, xviii, 167, 168, 173–178
The Wasp Woman, xvi, 3, 4, 5, 11–16
water, 149, 161–162, 191, 193–195, 198–199
Weaver, Tom, 5
Weik von Mossner, Alexa, xv
Wein, Len, 161
Wendelein, Rudy, 156
Wertham, Frederic, 157, 164n35
westerns, 185, 188–192, 195–196, 200n22
Whatmore, Sarah, 48, 59
Whittington, William, 139
Wild Seed. *See* Butler, Octavia
wilderness, 32, 36, 153, 167–168, 169, 179, 190, 192, 195
Wom-animal, 3, 6, 7–8, 10–11, 16
Womaneater, xvii, 68–69, 72–77
Wood, Robin, 67–68

Yates, Michelle, 194

zoo, 33, 122, 155

About the Authors

Jill E. Anderson earned her PhD from the University of Mississippi and is associate professor of English and Women's Studies at Tennessee State University. She's published articles in *The Journal of Ecocriticism, ecozon@,* and *The European Journal of Ecopsychology.* She is currently at work on a book on domestic horror narratives from the Atomic Age.

Steve Asselin is a lecturer at Queen's University in Kingston, Ont., where he also received his PhD He has previously taught at the University of Alberta–Augustana. His research interests include ecocriticism, travel literature, speculative fiction, and utopianism. He has received funding from the Social Sciences and Humanities Research Council to pursue research projects into polar fiction in the nineteenth century and ecological catastrophism at the fin-de-siècle. He is also the published author of over a dozen SF short stories in a number of small press venues.

Stina Attebery is a PhD candidate in English at UC Riverside. Her dissertation explores representations of waste and pollution within Indigenous futurism. She has published articles in *Medical Humanities, Humanimalia, Extrapolation,* and *Trace* and contributed a chapter on cyberpunk fashion to the collection *Cyberpunk and Visual Culture.*

Bridgitte Barclay is associate professor of English and co-director of the Gender Studies Minor at Aurora University. She also serves as co-leader of the Association for the Study of Literature and Environment's (ASLE) Ecomedia Special Interest Group and serves on the Executive Council for A Clockwork Green: Ecomedia in the Anthropocene (ASLE's first Nearly Carbon Neutral virtual symposium). Bridgitte researches and teaches about intersections of gender, science fiction, and the environment, most recently presenting on camp in 1950s creature features at ASLE and satire and fourth-wave gender rhetoric in the sf comic *Bitch Planet* at RMMLA. Recent publications include work on gender and environment in museum habitat dioramas for *The Atlantic Online* Object Lessons series; humor and material feminist discourses in the satirical dystopian novel *Beauty Queens*; and a piece in *The Pocket Instructor* about teaching graphic literature.

Amelia Z. Greene is a doctoral candidate in English at The Graduate Center, CUNY, and teaches in the English Department at Brooklyn College and the New York City College of Technology. She co-organizes the Ecocriticism Working Group through the Center for the Humanities and approaches her research on British and American Romanticism, Speculative and Science Fiction, and Children's and Young Adult Literature through an Ecocritical lens. Her work has been published in *Essays in Romanticism, Modern Language Studies,* and *William James Studies*, and has been supported by fellowships from the New York Botanic Garden Humanities Institute (2017) and the Early Research Initiative (2014, 2016).

Tyler Harper is a PhD candidate in New York University's Comparative Literature department. His research interests include eco-criticism, contemporary philosophy, the history of science, romanticism and science fiction. Conceptually, his work focuses on questions concerning deep time, extinction, nihilism, and the non/in-human. He is currently working on his dissertation, provisionally titled "Amidst the Wreck of Worlds: On the Poetics of Environmental Nihilism."

Juan Juvé earned an MA in Social Sciences from the Universidad de Buenos Aires (UBA)—Facultad de Ciencias Sociales. He is a lecturer in sociology, horror cinema, and popular culture. He has published in journals such as *Lindes* and *Vita e Pensiero* and in books such as *Science Fiction and the Abolition of Man: Finding C. S. Lewis in Sci-Fi Film and Television* (edited by Mark J. Boone and Kevin C. Neece), *Bad Mothers: Regulations, Representations, and Resistance* (edited by Michelle Hughes, Tamar Hager, and Rebecca Jaremko Bromwich), *Requiem for a Nation: Religion, Politics and Visual Cultures in Post-war Italy (1945–1975)* (edited by Roberto Cavallini), and *The Rwandan Genocide on Film: Critical Essays and Interviews* (edited by Matthew Edwards).

Fernando Gabriel Pagnoni Berns (PhD student) works at Universidad de Buenos Aires (UBA)—Facultad de Filosofía y Letras (Argentina), as professor in "Literatura de las Artes Combinadas II." He teaches seminars on international horror film. He is director of the research group on horror cinema "Grite" and has published articles on Argentinian and international cinema and drama in the following publications: *Imagofagia, Vita e Pensiero: Comunicazioni Sociali, Anagnórisis, Lindes,* and *UpStage Journal,* among others. He has published chapters in the books *Divine Horror* (edited by Cynthia Miller), *To See the Saw Movies: Essays on Torture Porn and Post 9/11 Horror* (edited by John Wallis), *Critical Insights: Alfred Hitchcock* (edited by Douglas Cunningham), *Dreamscapes in Italian Cinema* (edited by Francesco Pascuzzi), *Reading Richard Matheson: A Critical Survey* (edited by Cheyenne Mathews), *Time-Travel Television* (edited by Sherry Ginn), *James Bond and Popular Culture* (edited by Michele Brittany), and

The Man in the High Castle and Philosophy (edited by Bruce Krajewski), among others. He is currently writing a book about Spanish horror TV series *Historias para no Dormir*.

Carter Soles is associate professor of Film Studies in the English Department at The College at Brockport (SUNY) and Director of the college's Interdisciplinary Film Studies Minor. His research interests include ecomedia studies, gender and sexuality studies, identity studies, and film genre studies. His ecocritical work includes chapters on the cannibalistic hillbilly in 1970s slasher films for *Ecocinema: Theory and Practice* (Routledge, 2012) and on animality, imperialism, and race in *I Am Legend* for *Screening the Non/Human* (Rowman & Littlefield, 2016). He has written on environmental apocalyptic themes in 1960s horror for *Interdisciplinary Studies in Literature and the Environment* and on the rise of geek culture for *Bright Lights Film Journal* and *Jump Cut* (with Kom Kunyosying), and he is working on a book-length project on cinematic ecohorror. He teaches film theory, film history, and film genre courses—including comedy, horror, film noir, and ecocinema—at The College at Brockport.

Christy Tidwell is associate professor of English and Humanities at the South Dakota School of Mines & Technology. She serves as co-leader of the Association for the Study of Literature and Environment's (ASLE) Ecomedia Special Interest Group and also served on the Executive Council for A Clockwork Green: Ecomedia in the Anthropocene (ASLE's first Nearly Carbon Neutral virtual symposium). She has published in *ISLE, Extrapolation, Americana: The Journal of American Popular Culture 1900 to Present*, and *Femspec*, as well as in multiple edited collections, including *Posthuman Glossary* (ed. Rosi Braidotti and Maria Hlavajova), *Gender: Matter* (ed. Stacy Alaimo), *Creatural Fictions: Human-Animal Relationships in Twentieth- and Twenty-First Century Literature* (ed. David Herman), and *Disability in Science Fiction: Representations of Technology as Cure* (ed. Kathryn Allan). She is currently co-editing a book on ecohorror (with Carter Soles).

Michelle Yates is assistant professor of Cultural Studies and Humanities in the Department of Humanities, History, and Social Sciences at Columbia College Chicago. Dr. Yates's work is situated in the environmental humanities at the intersection of film and media, critical theory, and gender and sexuality. She has published in journals such as *Science Fiction Film and Television, ISLE: Interdisciplinary Studies in Literature and Environment*, and *Antipode: A Journal of Radical Geography*. Dr. Yates is also co-founder and co-director of the Chicago Feminist Film Festival.

Made in United States
Orlando, FL
04 February 2023